NATIONAL IDENTITY AND ITS DEFENDERS
THAILAND, 1938-1989

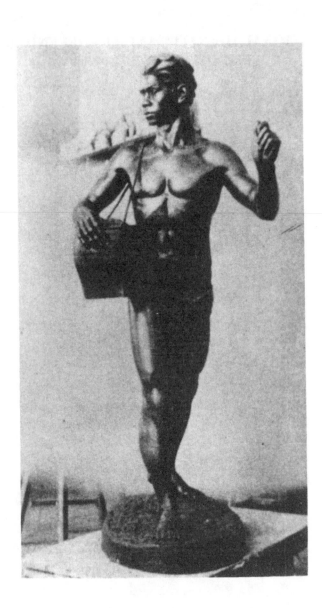

Farmer Sowing Rice, bronze, 1940
By Sitthidet Saenghiran (1916 - 1957)

NATIONAL IDENTITY AND ITS DEFENDERS
THAILAND, 1939 - 1989

EDITED BY
CRAIG J. REYNOLDS

SILKWORM BOOKS

ISBN 974-7047-20-9
National Identity and Its Defenders Thailand, 1939-1989
Edited by Craig J. Reynolds

Reprint in Thailand in 1993 by
Silkworm Books
54/1 Sridonchai Road, Chiang Mai 50100

This edition is for sale in Southeast Asia only

Typeset by Winnie Koh
Cover Design by T. Jittidejarak
Printed in Thailand

CONTENTS

ACKNOWLEDGEMENTS

On 8-9 September 1989 the Centre of Southeast Asian Studies at Monash University hosted a conference entitled 'Thailand: Aspects of Identity, 1939-1989' The theme of the conference emerged from conversations the Centre's Director, David P. Chandler, had with Sulak Sivaraksa, the keynote speaker, some twelve months earlier. All the contributors to the volume, with the exception of Annette Hamilton and Charles Keyes who were subsequently invited to contribute papers, attended the conference at the Centre's expense. We would like to express our gratitude to David Chandler, and his then assistant, Ondine Spitzer, for looking after the myriad details that such enterprises entail and for the hospitality that made our deliberations so enjoyable.

Cholthira Satyawadhna, John Girling, and Somsak Jeamteerasakul also gave papers at the conference, and we would like to thank them and the other participants, many of whom travelled from other states at their own expense, for their contributions to the discussion which was both lively and productive.

David Chandler, a lover of clean and efficient prose, applied himself to editorial tasks on the papers, all of which are much the better for his labours. Margaret M. Varghese professionally compiled the index, and Ian Faulkner offered valuable advice on the cover design. Finally, I would like to pay tribute to the patience and hard work of Julie Gordon and Jude Shanahan in the Research School of Pacific Studies, Australian National University, who completed the word processing, to Dorothy McIntosh, who looked after a number of details in the final stages, and to Winnie Koh who made the final preparations for printing.

CJR
Canberra
August 1991

ILLUSTRATIONS

Frontispiece   *Facing Title Page*
  Farmer Sowing Rice, bronze, 1940, by Sitthidet Saenghiran
  (1916-1957).
  Photo: courtesy of Helen Michaelsen.

Figure 1   *Page 86*
  Chinese hawker.
  Photo: *San sayam*, 26 August 1938.

Figure 2   *Page 156*
  Shrines on the Chiangmai-Chiangrai mountain road.
  Photo: Gehan Wijeyewardene.

Figure 3   *Page 177*
  Public notice in Mae Salong, Chiangrai Province, describing
  Kuomintang-Thai military friendship, 1989.
  Photo: Gehan Wijeyewardene.

Chapter 1

INTRODUCTION:
NATIONAL IDENTITY AND ITS
DEFENDERS[1]

Craig J. Reynolds

This volume of essays arose out of a conference held at the Centre of Southeast Asian Studies, Monash University in September 1989 to acknowledge the fiftieth year since Thailand became the name of the country then known as Siam. In Thailand itself the anniversary of the name-change was a non-event. The 1980s marked many important anniversaries in the history of Thai nationhood: the golden jubilee of the 'revolutionary coup' of 1932 and the Bangkok bicentennial in 1982; seven centuries of the Thai writing system in 1983; the fifth-cycle birthday of the Thai king in 1987; and commemoration of the longest reign in Thai history in July 1988. Yet while all of these were significant public events in the Thai calendar, the fiftieth anniversary of the country's name-change came and went in Thailand with little interest shown by the government, the media, or the public. Certainly the conference participants had no intention of celebrating the 1939 name-change, which has always been controversial because of the ethnic chauvinism it reflected and fostered.[2] Instead, at the instigation of the keynote speaker, Sulak Sivaraksa, who has long been critical of what he calls 'the Thailand concept', they saw the occasion as an opportunity to ask questions about Thai identity, a concept promoted by many Thai governments in this century as integral to Thai nation-building.

It must be said that Thailand is not the only country in the region to change its name either to capture and channel ethnic loyalties or to adjust to international realities. An extensive search was launched for a name for Taiwan, for example, when its position in the international community was radically altered in the early 1970s following the normalization of relations between The People's Republic of China and the United States of America. The new international alignment was an opportunity for China, which had claimed Taiwan as part of China since 1949, to assert its claim linguistically. In 1986 when Taiwan was joining the Asian Development Bank as many as sixteen names came under consideration, some of which were unacceptable either to China or Taiwan. Even the punctuation carried semiotic force and became a point of contention. The names with parentheses, such as 'China (Taiwan)', were favourable to the island's government, because the emphasis was on China, while the titles with commas, such as 'Taiwan, China', were not, because they suggested that the island belonged to 'the other' China, precisely the claim that China wished to assert (*AWSJ* 1986). The name of the island state would be an emblem of its sovereignty no less than of its relationship to China.

Elsewhere in Asia, Cambodia, Sri Lanka, and Myanmar have all changed their names in recent years. In the case of Cambodia, the country's name has changed four-times — in 1970, 1975, 1979, and 1990 — as different regimes have sought to signal particular leadership styles and international alignments or to disassociate themselves from deposed predecessors. Ironically, given the importance Cambodian governments have attached to the different terms, Cambodia and Kampuchea both derive from the same Sanskrit name of a tribe in northern India, the Kambuja, reputedly ruled by a monarch. The different transcriptions are for foreign as much as for domestic consumption. As with important toponyms in Thai history such as Ayudhya, Sukhodaya and many others, the Indic name Kambuja, incorporated into the Cambodian origin myth, had echoes in ancient Indian history. Word-play in the naming of principalities was a time-honoured way of conferring status and pedigree on Southeast Asian namesakes.

'Ceylon' and 'Burma' were legacies of the colonial period. They were favoured by the English-speaking, British-educated elites that came to power with independence essentially because Westerners were used to these names, and they were easy for foreigners, particularly English speakers, to pronounce. But, in fact, Ceylon was always called Lanka by its Sinhalese majority (Sri is a Sanskritic honorific), and 'Myanmar' is a closer rendering than 'Burma' of how Burmese speakers pronounce the name of their country. The decisions to adopt Sri Lanka and Myanmar represent a late phase in the continuing process of decolonization as former colonies of the Western imperial powers further authenticate their separation from colonial masters. Such decisions also signal internal power struggles as the dominant ethnic groups have laid claim to national symbols, the country's name being one such symbol with a high profile in the arena of international affairs and diplomacy.

Thus a country's name is relational not only to its past and the ethnicity of its inhabitants but also to the names of its neighbours, allies, and enemies. In an important way, names of countries, like the composition of national flags and anthems or the location of boundaries, are indicators of sovereignty. They denote a particular space on the earth's surface and the collectivity of peoples living in that space. National identity is a relational category brought into existence by comparison and contrast, and a country's name serves a vital differentiating function in that existential process.

However important a country's name is to itself, its neighbours, and the international community, a conference on the theme of identity seemed at first sight unpromising. Identity, now a catchword in pop psychology, is too amorphous a concept and too confused with self, essence, and uniqueness to sustain serious debate. Of all the disciplines, anthropology, sociology and developmental psychology are most confident of analytical procedures for studying identity. Bechstedt in this volume uses some of these procedures to illuminate how notions of authority develop in the Thai family. Personhood in his analysis takes shape against the backdrop of peoplehood in the national community but is a much more ambiguous and conflictual category than earlier culture and personality studies in Thailand had indicated.

Another reason for initial pessimism about the conference project is that official promotion of Thai identity within the country through the schools and the media has tied the notion of identity so closely to government policy and the marketing of the country domestically and abroad that its use as a category for analysis was questionable. Thai identity seemed at once too ubiquitous, too naive, and too vulnerable to official propagandizing to engage the conference participants productively. From the conference papers and the discussion it became clear, however, that articulation and communication of Thai identity by various regimes in the past fifty years raised a number of interesting issues. The notion of Thai identity could be interrogated for its history, its presumed content, and its deployment in fashioning cultural, ethnic and linguistic policy at the national level.

CULTURE POLICY AND IDENTITY

Siam had been a term used from ancient times by other countries such as Champa, China, and Cambodia to designate the kingdom dominated by the Thai-speaking peoples of the Chaophraya River valley.[3] The kings until the end of the absolute monarchy encouraged the use of Siam and prided themselves on being rulers of a diverse ethnic population. When the cabinet of the government under Field Marshal Plaek Phibun Songkhram decided in 1939 to change the name to Thailand, it was responding to nationalistic aspirations elsewhere in Asia and to concepts of nationhood that were, so to speak, in international circulation. By monopolizing the nation semantically for Thai speakers, the ruling elite sought to instil pride and equality with the West in the country's citizenry (Anderson 1978:212). *Thai* also had the advantage, significant in that era of high colonialism, of meaning 'free'. Through the decades Thai prose writers, poets, and orators, whether they be royalists or socialists, have delighted in the word-play of *thai / that* as it rolls off the tongue, the term 'free' being a near-homophone of the term 'slave'.

The name-change in 1939 was but one manifestation of culture policy during the first Phibun government from late 1938 until 1944. In a series of edicts that had a bearing on the national culture fostered by the government of the day and all governments since then, the Phibun regime sought to motivate the country's citizens to pursue national goals and to inculcate in them a sense of collective selfhood. As Mr. Sulak points out in his keynote address, 'The Crisis of Siamese Identity', the edicts, called *ratthaniyom* or Cultural Mandates, followed a practice under the absolute monarchy of issuing *phraratchaniyom* or 'royal prescriptions'.[4] In fact, the impulse of the ruling elite to prescribe cultural norms and to set guidelines if not fix the conventions for artistic creation was a deep-seated one during the absolute monarchy, especially during the four decades or so preceding 1932 when printing technology encouraged cultural production outside of the court's auspices, thus enabling commoners to challenge the court's prerogative to validate that production.[5] Moreover, as the power of the centre grew and expanded, the Thai state encountered regional and minority cultures different from its own. These encounters engendered reflection on what the dominant, national culture should be, and by the 1930s the government was undertaking strenuous efforts to codify and promote a national culture.

The name-change from Siam to Thailand was promulgated in the first Cultural Mandate issued on 24 June 1939, the seventh anniversary of the coup that overthrew the absolute monarchy. A second Mandate of ten days later set out in the most general terms what would constitute treasonous activity, for example revealing information to foreigners that might be damaging to the nation or acting against the national interest as agents or spokespersons for foreign governments. This edict helped to foster the belief in the ruling elite and the population at large, a belief later translated into legislation, that certain political groups or political activity — most notably communist — was 'un-Thai' or even 'anti-Thai' and thus dangerous, subversive, and destabilizing. By this Mandate Thai identity and national security were forever joined. The fourth Cultural Mandate of 2 August 1939 discouraged use of the terms northern Thais, northeastern Thais, southern Thais, and Islamic Thais in favour of 'the Thais'. The fourth, sixth, and eighth Mandates of 1939-1940 were designed to channel loyalties towards national symbols such as the flag, the national anthem, and the royal anthem and to encourage the prosperity and well-being of Thai as against Chinese or ethnic minorities. The words of the national anthem had to be approved by the army, another instance of the way identity was to be framed in terms of national security. With economic nationalism one of the hallmarks of the first Phibun regime, the fifth Mandate issued in December 1939 exhorted Thais to support the indigenous economy and to practise economic self-reliance. Others of the Mandates issued until early 1942 were aimed at building national growth and unity through hard work; encouraging people to use and respect the national language; prescribing proper dress, both Western and Thai; motivating people to engage in healthy, productive activities in their daily lives; and nurturing the protection and care of the young, the old, and the infirm.

The Cultural Mandates were foreshadowed in the House of Representatives under the previous government in 1937 and later realized in two royal decrees of 1940 and 1941 that gave legal force to the more detailed and specific measures affecting the country's citizens. The first decree, entitled the National Cultural Maintenance Act, defined culture as 'qualities which indicated and promoted social prosperity, orderliness, national unity and development, and morality of the people' (Thak 1978:256). The second decree, Prescribing Customs for the Thai People, defined improper dress and decorum. Certain kinds of clothing such as sarongs, sleeping garments, 'only underpants', or, for women, undershirts or wrap-arounds worn in public places, were deemed to be damaging to the prestige of the country (Thak 1978:257). So common was some of this clothing even in the capital, so appropriate was it in a tropical climate, and so long had it been worn, as one may see from Thai painting through the centuries, that it took more than a pronouncement by the state to prohibit people from wearing it. The much-ridiculed orders cited by Likkhit (1988:94) that husbands should kiss their wives before going to work and that women should wear hats and gloves in the Western manner were refinements of the Cultural Mandates. During the war years the wearing of hats became a particularly contentious issue, with those refusing to observe the custom subject to official investigation and reprimand. The old custom of chewing betel was also officially discouraged, along with spitting on roads and sidewalks (Thamsook 1977:33). Through such measures Old Siam was to be transformed into New Thailand.

In her accounts of the first Phibun period Thamsook Numnonda emphasizes how the Cultural Mandates sought to create in Thai citizens a sense that their country had entered a new epoch. In this new society the citizenry would cultivate the values of enterprise, propriety, decorum, self-reliance, valour, purity, and a sense of what the military regime deemed to be 'civilized'. The regime utilized print and broadcast media to promulgate these values, and thus the Cultural Mandates and the numerous supplementary orders, decrees, and acts that followed penetrated that part of Thai society exposed to such media in a way unprecedented in Thai history. Everyone who could read a newspaper or listen to a radio was aware of what the government wanted of its citizenry. The Department of Public Information (called the Department of Publicity in some English accounts) was the key bureau for disseminating the new culture policy, and its publications have left historians with a wealth of source material. The Great Communicator himself, Prime Minister Phibun, had a hand in producing some of the cultural programs. As Annette Hamilton shows in her essay, Thai adeptness at using new media technology — print, radio, film, and video — has given a particular and peculiar shape to national identity in Thailand by spawning lurid and violent images that defy what the national identity managers, beginning with King Vajiravudh, have sought to forbid and repress.

With the elite and the tiny urban bourgeoisie striving to align themselves with imagined international norms, the cultural pronouncements by the new military government finessed an ambiguity. While the intent of some pronouncements was to preserve a genuine and unique Thai culture, the intent of others was to override some cultural practices — so-called improper dress, for example, or betel-chewing — in order to save embarrassment in the eyes of Westerners who might regard such practices as uncivilized (Thamsook 1978:238). Parity with the West was a preoccupation of the Thai elite at this time, and parity applied to dress and deportment as well as to sovereignty. Being a pure and genuine Thai, however that was to be defined, had to be balanced against behaving in a way deemed acceptable to Westerners. In fact, this Western standard was as much a construction, an imagining in the minds of the ministers, officials, and bureaucrats who conceived and implemented the culture policy, as the 'Thai culture' being put forward as authentic and innate. Where, for example, did the culture managers acquire the idea that husbands should kiss their wives before going to work? From Western films and photographs? The pathways by which the ruling elite of the country that had never been a colony came to insist on Western — mostly British? — tastes, fashion, and deportment deserve serious investigation.

At this point a few comments are in order to provide perspective on the essays in this volume. For one thing, the edicts advanced the interests of the dominant ethnic group, the Thai-speaking people of the central plains, as against the interests of other Thai-speaking populations and the ethnic Chinese. The concept of Thai culture as the national culture masked cultural and ethnic heterogeneity in the name of national uniformity, but it was a contrived uniformity.

In matters of language policy, for example, Tony Diller's paper shows how promotion of Central Thai as the national language in the ninth edict involved a certain amount of artistry, since a large majority of people considered and still consider their domestic language to be other than Central Thai.[6] The ban on use of the region-based nomenclature for Thai groupings — northern, northeastern, and southern — in favour of 'Thai' assumed that language and ethnic differences could be eradicated or at least reduced merely by outlawing the common names for those groupings. Central Thai, especially in its written form, has been perhaps the preeminent component of identity for those seeking to define and promote a national culture. In any taxonomy of culture Thai language inevitably ranks first (e. g. Samnakngan khanakammakan 1988:38). Seminars are convened to discuss 'Thai linguistic culture', whose advocates understand that a national language is not naturally present but is something that the education system must nurture (e. g. Khana -anukammakan 1983:95). And keeping Central Thai in its preeminent place has involved considerations of national security, as we shall see shortly.

One dimension of cultural production in the new Thailand not covered in this volume was artistic expression as well as the populist drama, music, and literature fostered by the Office of the Prime Minister and the Department of Public Information (Charnvit 1974:39-40). Government patronage of the arts under the new post-1932 leadership began with the appointment of the Italian sculptor Corrado Feroci (Silpa Bhirasri) to the Department of Fine Arts. The appointment of a foreigner to such a position signalled a commitment to modern forms of expression, which, by and large, meant Western art forms (Michaelsen 1991:3). Phibun's eleventh Cultural Mandate was designed to encourage art appreciation by decreeing that Thai citizens should attend art exhibits (Michaelsen 1990:35). On the production side, the government sponsored art competitions, such as the one included in the annual Constitution Fair established in 1938 (Michaelsen 1991:7).

The robust bronze sculpture 'Farmer Sowing Rice' (ca. 1940), a work by Sitthidet Saenghiran that serves as the frontispiece for this volume, was a product of these pre-war years. As manifest in the numerous sculptures and painting of Feroci's students, government patronage of the arts during the first Phibun period put the stamp of heroic realism on art production that is still visible to drivers suffering through Bangkok traffic as they slowly circle the Democracy and Victory Monuments built in this period. Sculpture and monuments were particularly important not only because Feroci himself was a sculptor but also because their public exposure gave expressive force to the state ideology being fashioned.[7]

Another general point to make is that the claim inherent in the Cultural Mandates that they were shaping a national community is a debatable one. Chai-anan Samudavanija argues in his paper that the Mandates strengthened the state to the detriment of the nation by forging an ideology for the state. In giving that ideology a specifically Thai character, the ruling group was not only endeavouring to rationalize and legitimize its accession to power but also to undermine the influence of the Chinese bourgeoisie that had supported the change of government in 1932. Moreover, the Cultural Mandates had the effect of subordinating local or folk cultures, which had enjoyed more freedom of expression under the pluralistic name of 'Siam', by placing them in a hierarchy of importance with the state-defined 'national' culture at its apex. Thus what is at stake in the Mandates is the creation of a state identity separate from and in large part hostile to society, an identity that the ruling group could mobilize against those social forces that might undermine its power base. In Chai-anan's analysis, promotion of state identity stunted the growth of civil society and thus of Thai constitutionalism by placing severe constraints on cultural expression.

Finally, one may ask if the prescriptions initiated new culture policy or simply consolidated and codified notions of identity and ethnic Thai preeminence that had been aired in the Thai media during the previous two decades. Baas Terwiel's paper is an invitation to pursue this hypothesis, for his reading of historical tracts of the 1930s suggests that the Phibun government's Cultural Mandates embodied what popular writers had been saying for some time. These writers with a populist touch, the most famous of whom was Luang Wichit Watthakan, serve as a bridge between the royalist nationalism of King Vajiravudh (r. 1910-1925) and the nationalism of the military and civilian regime of the late 1930s. The focus of Terwiel's paper is Chamrat Sarawisut, who sought guidance from Luang Wichit on nationalism and took for granted that intrusions on personal behaviour, such as prescriptions in the eleventh Cultural Mandate on how Thai citizens should ration their working day and spend their spare time, are justified if they serve the well-being of the nation. Also manifest in this writing are totalitarian tendancies that shaped allegiances between the Thai people and their military rulers. Already in the early 1930s the Ministry of Defence was publishing in its magazine articles by Phibun himself on the world crisis that called forth a strong leader as much as 'an animal herd needs its leader' (Charnvit 1974:35, quoting a Thai source). Terwiel finds in the mass media certain predisposing sentiments and attitudes that help account for the ease with which the coup group translated ethnic Thai chauvinism into public policy.

Some of the measures that flowed from the Cultural Mandates were certainly popular, others were regarded as silly and laughable. But the nationalistic culture programs did not thrive simply because they were conceived and promoted in an ingenious, persuasive way. To the extent that it was successful, the cultural engineering struck a chord in the mentality of the day. It remains for other researchers to explore the question of the national culture programs in this crucial period as an instrument of rule by the Phibun regime, sometimes nurtured, more often imposed, by government ideologues.

At the same time, the national culture, as an elemental expression of individual and collective selfhood, was something that many citizens of Thailand recognized in their individual lives. Thai culture and its twin, Thai identity, cannot be explained away simply as concepts stage-managed by the state.

The National Cultural Maintenance Act of 1940 was followed by the National Culture Acts of 1942 and 1943 which established the National Culture Council, a body which enjoyed ministerial status and which was headed by the Prime Minister himself.[8] In the 1950s Phibun, by then Prime Minister for the second time, established a Ministry of Culture (Barme 1989:147), and there has been a stream of commissions, councils, boards and bureaux charged with national culture policy since then. Sometimes responsibility for the promotion of national culture has rested with the Office of the Prime Minister, an indication that the highest authorities in the land view Thai culture with grave concern, sometimes it has rested with the Ministry of Education, sometimes with both, and sometimes with other ministries such as Interior and Health. There is much bureaucratic competition for patronage of the national culture of Thailand, not least because the monarchy is one of Thai culture's most visible, most generous, and most grateful icons.

Thai Culture Magazine (*warasan watthanatham thai*) began publishing in the early 1960s under the auspices of the Ministry of Education. By the late 1970s the journal's advisory body was headed by the Director-General of the Department of Religious Affairs and his deputy, a sign of the role Buddhism plays in defining the national culture in Thailand. The journal's contents are typical of the several journals devoted to celebrating and promoting Thai national culture. Everything from food to folk culture, Thai martial arts, national holidays, and regional languages and rituals are presented in an unscholarly style for a popular readership. Very occasionally an article on Muslim culture in the south slips into the magazine.

Falling within the ambit of national culture policy, the term for Thai identity (*ekkalak thai*), with its connotations of uniqueness, is a comparatively recent coinage from English dating back only to the 1950s. The term does not appear in the 1950 edition of the *Dictionary of the Royal Institute* reprinted through 1968, but it does appear in a dictionary by Charoen Chaichana of 1958 with a gloss explaining its precise equivalence to English 'identity'.[9] This mid-century concept of Thai identity had a progenitor, however. Long before this time, in the twilight years of the absolute monarchy, the aristocracy had scanned the colonized horizons of its kingdom and effected a taxonomy of the 'national character of the Thai people' (*uppanisai khong chonchat thai*). In 1927, in a much-quoted speech about the Siamese political system and what Western social science now calls political culture, Prince Damrong Rajanubhab invoked history to aid in this enterprise, proposing that what distinguished the Thai people from Burmese, Vietnamese, Cambodians, and Malays was (in his English usage) 'love of national independence, toleration, and power of assimilation' (Damrong 1975:6).

What gave bureaucratic if not linguistic life to the concept of Thai identity was the violent coup of 6 October 1976 coup and the return to power of rightwing soldiers and politicians. In January 1977, the same month as the marriage of the Thai Crown Prince, an event that might have been timed to help restore some much-needed shine to the monarchy after the events of the previous months, the Office of the Prime Minister began issuing a monthly magazine, *Thai Identity* (*ekkalak thai*). In style and content *Thai Identity* articulated the now-familiar shibboleth that a strong national Thai culture was vital to the country's independence and sovereignty. Articles on Thai music, social values, maps, the writing system, kites, customs, popular Buddhist texts, and, in the manner of *Thai Culture Magazine*, a token piece on southern Thai Muslims found their way into its pages.

In the magazine's self-conception, *Thai Identity* was a kind of cultural soldier in the battle to maintain Thai culture as it tried to hold its own against the pressures of Western culture. But beneath the surface of this rhetoric another battle was underway. The prestige of state institutions had been badly damaged by the way the military had recently returned to power, and rightwing ideologues who backed the coup had portrayed elements of the Left during the 1973-76 period as un-Thai, even anti-Thai, and in some cases as less than human. Government patronage of Thai national culture could now serve the cause of social order and stability by demonstrating the state's commitment to what every Thai citizen was deemed to hold dear, namely, Thai identity. Thus the concept of Thai identity, with its disarming ring of transcendence and permanence, has a specific history and conditions of existence.

A royal decree of 25 February 1979 established the National Culture Commission, the body charged with coordinating the work of the numerous bureaucratic units responsible for national culture.[10] The Commission's charter laid down ten functions it was to perform in the preservation and promotion of Thai culture, stating that culture, 'a distinctive characteristic of nationhood', was essential in maintaining the stability and integrity of the nation (Khanakammakan 1982:721-24). It must have been about this time, but possibly as late as 1980 or 1981, that the government established the National Identity Board (*khanakammakan soemsang ekkalak khong chat*), responsible to the Office of the Prime Minister, to which several of the authors in this volume refer.[11] Many of the activities and programs involved with promoting national culture have since come within the Board's purview. Each year it publishes a long list of books and pamphlets in Thai and English on such topics as festivals, royal coronations, the ordination ceremony for Buddhist monks, and biographies of prominent figures in the royal family. Under the auspices of its Subcommittee for the Propagation of Thai Identity (*khana-anukammakan phoephrae ekkalak khong thai*), the Board has since 1977 also produced radio and TV programs. In the published transcripts, the programs are classified under the rubric of Nation, Religion, and Monarchy (*chat satsana mahakasat*), the three pillars of nation-state ideology in Thailand.

The publication of English books and pamphlets, the first of which, *Thai Life*, came out in October 1981, for the consumption of foreign visitors suggests something else about the government's promotion of Thai culture, namely, the connection between Thai culture and tourism. The marketing of Thai culture domestically and to foreign visitors subsidizes or underwrites the cost of efforts to preserve Thai culture seen to be under threat by Western ways. Like many developing countries with rich heritages, Thailand sells itself abroad by commodifying its culture and tradition.[12] In the historical moment in which this is taking place, the assimilation of non-Thai groups — as well as the exclusion or subordination that flows from a policy of assimilation — may be held in check, as it is disadvantageous to tourism to conceal ethnic differences. In the promotion of the country for foreigners it is important to go so far as to dramatize *some* ethnic differences, because they make the tourist adventure more diverse and attractive. Thus the packaged tourist jaunt to northern Thailand includes the villages of ethnic minorities in the hills, despite the fact that highland-lowland relations are no showcase of interethnic harmony. Some of the most bitter conflicts in the country over management of the ecosystem are occurring in the highlands.

In January 1981 the National Identity Board began to publish *Thai Magazine* (*warasan thai*), a glossy collection of essays distributed, at least initially, without cost. As with *Thai Identity*, respected academics are persuaded from time to time to write an article for *Thai Magazine*. The contents are decidedly royalist, with articles on past and present monarchical accomplishments, but the coverage also includes, at the opposite end of the socio-economic spectrum, 'The Peasant: Backbone of the Nation' (Oct.-Dec. 1981) . The current official formulations of what is quintessentially Thai never fail to include the peasant and the village. Philip Hirsch's essay in this volume itemizes the various ways the village is deployed in a discursive formation as the irreducible 'natural' community for governing the rural population and for managing rural development.

Culture has a very broad definition in the mission of *Thai Magazine*. More than customs, rituals, and traditions, culture encompasses Thai ingenuity and energy that is supposed to lead to economic progress and potential NICdom, Thailand's place among the New Industrialized Countries of the region. 'Technology and Thai Products' was the title of an article published in 1988 (April - June). It is thus not surprising to find 'the culture of work', a domain in which the social scientist prescribes the interrelations of human resources, Thai social values, and the requirements of the modern economy that will maximize productivity (Samnakngan khanakammakan 1988:89-102). In this vein the Ministry of Education in December 1989 sponsored a 'Festival of Arts, Crafts, and Vocational Studies' under the theme 'Education for NICdom' (*kansuksa su khwampennik*) and produced thousands of bumper stickers for the occasion, an example of the way the education bureaucracy can mobilize culture for national economic goals. NICdom itself, with its complex strands of bourgeois consumption, economic performance and global personhood, is thus being stamped onto Thai identity. At the same time, Thai identity has shown a great capacity to resist and modify the global products favoured by multinational enterprises.[13] The path from kingdom to NICdom is not without pain, however, as news from Thailand of lethal toxic spills and environmental degradation makes headlines in the international broadcast media.

In the fourth issue of *Thai Magazine* (October-December 1981) the editors, finding that the public was confused about the concept, addressed the question of the meaning of Thai identity by providing a brief etymology of *ekkalak* — an etymology notably inadequate for researching this introduction — and a concise schema of the concept's constituent parts. After due deliberation, the National Identity Board took the foundation for Thai identity to be nationalism (*chat*), whose six components include 1) territory, 2) people, 3) independence and sovereignty, 4) government and administration, 5) culture, and 6) pride. It is not clear whether the six components are listed in an order of priority, but there must be some rationale or sequence, for the arithmetic procedure of adding two more components — religion and monarchy — between numbers 4 and 5 yields a new result, the eight-fold schema labelled 'Thai identity'. Other taxonomies of Thai identity — or 'Thainess' — are even more elaborate after culture has been added to the nation-religion-monarchy trinity of Thai nationalism (e. g. Wira 1983:chap. 4).

ETHNICITY AND IDENTITY

Thailand is hardly unique in being a country where the boundaries of the nation-state do not coincide with the extent of an ethnic population or a single speech group. The first two components listed in the national identity construct are territory and people, and in virtually all discourses of nationhood there is a tension between ethnicity and territory. In trying to manage this difficult problem, Thai government policies of the late 1930s and many times since then have sought to favour ethnic Thai and to exclude or subordinate other ethnic groups. It could be argued that this favoured treatment of the dominant ethnic group creates barriers internally that mirror the boundaries or fences that demarcate the perimeter of the nation-state (Thongchai 1988:420).

It is no coincidence that the Phibun government was as active in dealing with the Chinese 'problem' as it was in making claims on territories of its former empire that now belonged to French Indochina. The Phibun regime's assertion of Thai-ness in the circumstances of the late 1930s was translated into efforts internally to give preferential treatment to ethnic Thai as against ethnic Chinese. The Chinese as an alien economic force, held responsible for backward conditions especially in the peasantry, was a historically-specific construct, reaching its apogee on the eve of the Pacific war (Seksan 1989: chaps. 4-5). This construction of 'Chineseness' had begun in the reign of King Vajiravudh and derived from the hardening of the nation-state's borders, events in China becoming politically important to the overseas Chinese as well as to the Thai ruling class, and the concept of citizenry that went hand-in-hand with the nation-state.

A 'pure' Thai-Buddhist society, uncontaminated by foreign elements, sat at the opposite end of this ethnic pole. Luang Wichit's historical works grounded this pure Thai-Buddhist society in the nation's life-history at Sukhodaya, thus demonstrating that an ethno-religious character specific to the Thai people had temporal priority (Reynolds 1991a). Recent debates over a text dating from the Sukhodaya period, surveyed by Peter Jackson in his essay, suggest that the pure Thai-Buddhist legacy of Sukhodaya is still contested terrain. And it is in this context of the modern, nationalistic meanings attributed to the early state of Sukhodaya that recent attacks on the authenticity of the putative first Thai inscription (e. g. Sujit 1988) have caused consternation among the official custodians of the nation's biography.

Just what does constitute the Thai historical heritage is problematic, however, as the chronicle of the purloined lintel by Charles Keyes indicates. Stolen from a Cambodian monument now located in Thai territory, the lintel has entered an existing history of Thai-Cambodian disputes over borders and ancient ruins. The controversy underscores how the historical record has become an emblem of national identity just as the country's name, its monarchy, its language, and its territorial sovereignty have become emblems of nationhood. The case of the purloined lintel became assimilated to the history of Thai-Cambodian disputes so easily because of the lengthy history of the Thai court's proprietary interest in Cambodian succession disputes from the late eighteenth century.

In the critical period of Thai national-identity formation the Phibun regime had laid claim to territory in Laos and Cambodia as Thailand's own. To make its case the military government issued a directive declaring that Vietnamese, Laotians, and Khmers who were Thai shared the same blood lines (*yat phinong ruam sai lohit*). In a revealing document of late 1940, just after the Thai invasion of disputed Lao territories and western Cambodia, the Department of Defence asserted that these Vietnamese, Laotians, and Khmers were of the 'same nationality' as the Thai, 'as if they were of the same blood', and should be referred to as 'our Thai brothers and sisters in Vietnam, Laos, and Cambodia'.[14]

In some circumstances this notion of 'the same blood' has been stretched even further, and by no means are the proponents of the notion always from the armed forces. Sujit Wongthes, a prominent Thai writer and intellectual who helped to champion the return of the purloined Cambodian lintel in his publications, argues that Siamese (a term which he prefers to Thai) ancestry includes the Mon-Khmer peoples who preceded the Thai in the lower mainland, an argument that anchors Thai claims to Khmer monuments in Thai territory and proves that 'the Thais were always here' (Sujit 1986).

Thai irredentism at the level of government policy thus has intriguing echoes in sentiments and yearnings for Tai affiliation among ordinary, if educated, Thai people. These yearnings quickly surfaced after diplomatic relations with China resumed in the 1970s, paving the way for visits to Tai 'brothers and sisters' in the Sipsongpanna area of Yunnan, but they were also prominent in the 1920s and 1930s. In July 1940 the famous Thai ethnographer and auto-didact Phya Anuman Rajadhon recalled how he had stood with a tour group at the confluence of the Mekhong and Ruak Rivers where the borders of Burma, Laos, and Thailand intersect. There he looked over to the opposite bank of the Mekhong and around him at the ancestral settlement areas of Thais now in the Central Plains, musing how the scattered Tai speech groups had come to be so different. In his epistolary account appended to the studies of Tai speech groups that resulted from this visit to the northern homeland, Phya Anuman remembers the moment with great affection and nostalgia, contributing with his words to the race memory that has entered the Thai discourse of nationhood (Anuman 1970).

On 7 September 1945 at the conclusion of the Pacific war the government of Pridi Phanomyong (1945-47) changed 'Thailand' back to 'Siam' in an effort to counter the semantic monopoly of Thai over other ethnic groups, thus asserting a more genuine national consciousness that would include all peoples within the country's borders, whatever their ethnicity (Anderson 1978:213). At a time when England was pressing the Thai for heavy war reparations, the name-change might have been intended to signal to the British that the new government, in contrast to its predecessor which had declared war on England under the name of 'Thailand', was non-expansionist and non-chauvinist (Preecha 1988:17). After Phibun returned to office 'Siam' again became 'Thailand' once and for all in 1948. On three occasions since then, however, the Thai vs. Siam issue has been debated during the drafting of new constitutions (1949, 1961, and 1974). As the extensive debates of 1961 indicate, what was at stake was the kind of national community the central government saw itself as fostering, with figures such as Luang Wichit defending the policies he embraced some twenty years previously (Suphot 1985). The persistence of the 'Thai' vs. 'Siam' issue also suggests that while alternative nationalisms have been marginalized, they are not dead and buried.

Just how and in what way military governments have been expansionist and chauvinist is open to question. Gehan Wijewardene contends in this volume and elsewhere that Thai governments have not pursued irredentist policies in the manner portrayed by many historians. The primary aim of border security has been to remove grounds of conflict rather than to extend the country's perimeters. Nevertheless, as he has pointed out (Wijeyewardene 1990:49), government strategies have sought to create 'Thai' out of other ethnicities, a consequence of policies which embrace 'the Thailand concept', to use Mr. Sulak's words.

Such strategies create resistance, as calls for ethnic autonomy by minority peoples vie with state demands for national integrity. Both the strategies and the resistance can take violent forms, as the case of the Lua in Cholthira Satyawadhna's pioneering study demonstrates (Cholthira 1991). The most populous highland group in Nan Province with a history of rebellion against lowland encroachments, the Lua was a showcase for the Communist Party of Thailand (CPT) before its demise in the early 1980s, thus confirming simultaneously the long-standing government prejudice that non-Thai populations were subversive and that communism was fundamentally non-Thai. Government policies in the 1980s to integrate the Lua into the nation-state have erected the kind of ethnic fences alluded to above and reversed the CPT policies that tolerated Lua cultural differences.

Anthony Smith has distinguished between two trajectories in the formation of nations, which he schematically associates with Western and Eastern nationalism (Smith 1986:chap. 6). His formulation builds on a dichotomy proposed several decades ago by Hans Kohn and holds that the Western concept of nation is territorial, whereas the Eastern concept tends to be ethnic. According to Smith's typology, ethnic nationalism is characterized by the successful transformation of ethnic into national ties. Smith thus sees the Western concept of nation as constructed, whereas the Eastern type is 'natural'. But the very notion of ethnicity is a modern, Western concept, a product of the territorially-bounded states in which elites have been obliged by the nature of the bounded unit to rule over diverse peoples. Smith's typology externalizes ethnicity, whereas it is in fact part and parcel of nationalist discourse everywhere. The modern national community, both Western and Eastern, was imagined as a new sense of ethnos, a kind of super-ethnicity (McVey 1984:12). This new sense of ethnicity was to be inclusive, but it perforce rendered some population groups anomalous and thus laid the foundations for separatist movements.

Though never forced to cede all its sovereign powers, the Thai ruling elite bears many scars of struggle over territory, in part because it had to 'learn' this kind of territorial nationalism during boundary disputes and conflicts over territory with the Western imperialist powers (Thongchai 1988). These disputes and conflicts have given it a sense of territorial selfhood, what Thongchai calls its geo-body. It is difficult to imagine how the ethnic nation could ever come into its own in Thailand, however significant Smith's criteria of 'genealogy, populism, customs and dialects, and nativism' may seem in the Thai case (Smith 1986:137). But the performance of classical and folk dances on the national stage, cherishing the supposed origins of the nation in the ancient kingdom of Nanchao in northern Southeast Asia, and the cultural populism sponsored by governments over the past half century have all reinforced the 'national imaginaire', as Chai-anan terms it, in which the Thai national community evolved 'according to its own inner rhythms' with 'self-expressions and destinies [that] are radically different, even unique' (Smith 1986:138).

The notion of a unique destiny for the dominant ethnic group enters into the nation's horoscope, as Nerida Cook says in her essay. Astrologers determined a horoscope for the new capital at Bangkok in the late eighteenth century, and it is this horoscope that through the years has become the national horoscope, conveniently binding together the destiny of Thailand's capital, its dominant ethnic group, the nation-state, and the present royal family whose ancestor founded the city and the present dynasty. But nation-building is a process far from over, and debates about the national horoscope betray the extent to which the nation is a unified entity especially in terms of its history. In spatial terms, moreover, such areas as the deep south of the country with its Malay Muslim population has a communal identity that continues to resist the guile and force employed by the Thai state to integrate it (Surin 1988).

Thus there are still rifts and splits in *chat*, the Thai word for the shared linguistic and cultural traits that make up nationality. *Chat* derives from Sanskrit *jati*, whose root-meaning of 'birth' has come into the Thai language carrying powerful resonances of blood-ties and, most importantly of all, shared descent (Keyes 1976:206). A recent study by the Malaysian scholar Tan Liok Ee has focussed on corresponding terms in the Malaysian case in an effort to understand problems of legitimacy when the nation does not naturally coalesce with 'ineluctable' communities. Her case study offers comparative perspective that may suggest a line for future inquiry with regard to *chat*.

In Malaysian nationalist discourse two terms for nation / nationality vie with each other in dialectical conflict, underscoring the communal conflict between Chinese and Malays in modern Malaysian political life. Malay *bangsa* entered the Malay language early via Sanskrit and originally denoted legitimacy of royal descent. Later on it came to mean race or ethnic group. Thai language has the term *wong*, the same loanword from Sanskrit meaning lineage, but *wong* was not destined to experience the same evolution in nationalist discourse as *bangsa*. Chinese *minzu*, a modern word not to be found in Classical Chinese, was coined via Japanese to evoke the concept of community held together by ties of descent, language, and culture that nineteenth-century Japanese and Chinese thinkers were confronting in the works of Western writers. Both Malay and Chinese have alternative terms for nation in the sense of an autonomous and sovereign political unit. These are *negara* in Malay and *guojia* in Chinese. In the Malaysian nationalist discourse 'the rhetoric of *bangsa* and *minzu* was consciously developed to assert (in the case of *bangsa*) or resist (in the case of *minzu*) dominance in the process of defining the claims of *negara* / *guojia* on citizens and to claim a moral legitimacy for their respective positions' (Tan 1988:45).

In the Thai case there has been no overt contest for *chat*, which denotes the cultural community with its shared ties (*chat thai*). The nation-state ideology seeks to make this cultural community coterminous with the autonomous and sovereign political unit (*prathet thai* or *muang thai*), but the 'fit' is not exact and requires constant tinkering and coercion. As there is no explicit *bangsa - minzu* struggle in Thailand, we might then ask what the 'other' is against which *chat* is mobilized. Is it the various minorities who straddle borders on the periphery and make it difficult for the nation-state to maintain its territorial integrity? Is it enemy *chat* on the other side of the borders, particularly the Vietnamese? Is it the ethnic Chinese within the nation-state? But what is 'ethnic Chinese' when so many Thai citizens are Sino-Thai? Much has been written about the assimilation process in Thailand over the past two centuries, but little attention has been paid to assimilation's counterpart, namely, repression of Chinese identity and otherness, a psychic as much as a social and political repression. Some thoughtful research needs to be done on the psychological dynamics masked by the tiny hyphen in Sino-Thai.

Perhaps *chat* contains traces of all these 'others' as well as any conceivable 'other' that does not conform to the Thai-Buddhist-monarchical-territorial construct enshrined by the National Identity Board schema. In any case, *chat* is not a monolithic, self-evident entity that springs forth prefabricated to serve the cause of national unity and harmony. There would not be such a lively, well-funded, publicly patronized discourse about Thai identity if it were so self-evident, nor would the state security apparatus express such an abiding concern for Thai identity's well-being.

NATIONAL SECURITY AND IDENTITY

It is typical of the magazines devoted to culture discussed above that, apart from the traditional martial arts, topics even remotely associated with the military are absent. And the eight-fold schema that defines Thai national identity fails to mention the military explicitly. But it does not take much imagination to see why the military would see itself as the guarantor of the robust health of the eight components. The integrity of the territorial self needs to be maintained, the people require protection, independence and sovereignty need to be defended, administration and government must be stable for efficient rule, and national pride as well as respect for religion from time to time need policing. Thai culture and its subtext, 'the Thai way of life', has become as sacred an object as the monarchy. Armed force shields these objects, so vulnerable because so sacred, and ensures their survival. The preservation of Thainess (*kanraksa khwampenthai*) requires the defence of Thainess. Thus the Thai military is a trace, an absent presence, in each of the eight components.

The martial ethos infusing the eight components has a lengthy history, which would have to be told properly from the reign of Vajiravudh if not before. Already in the 1930s, prior to the Phibun regime's Cultural Mandates, popular patriotic literature was drawing on the Japanese martial code of *bushido*.[15] During that time when Phibun was Minister of Defence the military had staged dramas and films portraying the vital role soldiers were playing in the country's destiny. The irredentist movement, usually identified with Phibun's claims on French territories in the early 1940s, had also begun to emerge some years previously, thereby framing the military's ambitions for permanent rule with motive and rationale (Barme 1989:108-114). The pervasive militarist imagery was too heavy-handed for Corrado Feroci, under whose direction the Victory Monument was designed and built after the war with France in the early 1940s. When forced to comply with the addition of soldiers to the base of the monument, Feroci referred to it as 'the victory of embarrassment' (Michaelsen 1991:6).

Thai identity in this formative period was thus already laden with notions of military valour and the ultimate sacrifice of life itself in the national interest. Luang Wichit's writings took episodes of national liberation from the historical record. Ayutthayan history in particular provided shining examples of warrior heroism in the person of King Naresuan and, at the end of the era, Taksin, both of whom were victorious over Burmese aggressors (Reynolds 1991a). The proclamation on 12 May 1944 of a national code of valour must therefore be seen not so much as a strategic imitation of Japanese military values in order to ingratiate the Thai government with the Japanese Occupation command as yet another codification of the militarized political culture already underway at least two decades previously (Thamsook 1977:36-37).

Another side to the new Thailand of the 1930s that bears on the issue of national security is the way opposition groups and movements, and specifically the socialists and communists, were characterized as alien to Thai society and culture. Anti-communism was deeply embedded in the country's elite from the time of the absolute monarchy, so deeply that until recently studies of Thai Marxism, socialism and communism have typically been studies of anticommunism.[16] The communist label made it easy for government authorities to attribute the activities of radical opposition groups to foreign powers. By shifting the inspiration of radical movements to an external, alien source, military governments in particular were able to declare those movements to be non-Thai, 'unnatural' to the Thai social fabric, and thus qualified for exclusion from the national community. This meant incarceration, of course, or, at worse, death by execution. It helped such an enterprise to be able to define the content of 'Thai,' hence the codification of Thai identity by Field Marshal Phibun's Cultural Mandates and General Prem's National Identity Board.

One of the keywords in Thai military jargon as well as Thai nationalist discourse is stability (*mankhong*), as is evident in the semantic weight put on the term in the Thai name for the Internal Security Operations Command (ISOC) (*kong amnuaykan raksa khwammankhong phainai*). The term for national security is in fact *khwammankhong haeng chat*. Stability and security being near-synonyms in this discursive formation, the same term applies to the stability of the family as to the security of the monarchy (Wira 1983:108-109). One of the early Phibun regime's greatest successes was a popular radio program in the 1940s in which two male characters, Nai Man Chuchat and Nai Khong Rakthai, engaged in a dialogue about what we might call national security for the masses.[17] The clever banter of Nai Man and Nai Khong covered all the pet topics of the era, everything from Chinese dress to nutrition and the right of the nation-state to self-defence. It is by such means as these programs that the spit-and-polish of military discipline has been fused with common Thai notions of tidiness, propriety, and orderliness (*khwamriaproi*).

Military order and bourgeois orderliness are amiable companions, a hint that what makes military coups successful in Thailand is not merely control of the instruments of force and violence. When the coup group of 23 February 1991 named itself the National Peacekeeping Council it used *khwamsangopriaproi* to reassure the public, a term that loses something in translation as 'peacekeeping'. The term signalled a return to what the military regarded as the status quo (i.e. to military rule before the elected Chartchai government came to office 1988) and neutralized the force necessarily deployed in a military takeover.

Among the innumerable instances that illustrate the way the Thai military has nurtured national culture for reasons of national security I would cite the attendance of the Secretary-General of the National Security Council at a seminar in 1983 to celebrate the seventh-century anniversary of the putative invention of the Thai alphabet. Squadron Leader Prasong Sunsiri was present as an active participant, presenting a paper on 'Thai Language and National Security' (Prasong 1984). On that occasion he made a number of pronouncements about the necessity of controlling as well as facilitating the study of foreign languages in Thailand, the need to monitor language study because incorrect usage is damaging to the social order, the fractious consequences to the Thai body

politic of non-Thai language use, and the extent to which knowledge
of Thai language is instrumental to the smooth functioning of
government. Thus language, which falls under Culture in the
National Identity Board's schema, was a matter of vital concern
for the chief official of the National Security Council.

The inescapable conclusion to this account is that the Thai
military has been assiduous, aggressive even, in promoting Thai
national culture and national identity and in the process has
enshrouded itself with the trappings of authenticity and legitimacy.
The genius of the military and the state security organizations lies
in having nurtured a mentality in the bureaucracy and social
institutions that embraces the very values the military cherishes.
National security, it might be said, is the parasol that shades and
protects the National Identity Board's eight-fold schema. Many
of the values nourished by the culture bureaucracy through the
education system and the mass media are equally at home in army
camps and police barracks, in monasteries and schools.

This aspect of Thai identity — the way it has come to serve
military ambitions — is inadequately theorized in Thai studies
and thus deserves more thought, as is the political-economy of
Thai national culture programs, about which so little has been said
here. This is not to affirm that the way in which national security
and identity connect is permanent or inevitable but that it has been
produced over many decades in distinct historical moments of great
complexity. In an epoch when the middle class and the business
tycoons insist on democratic institutions and a laissez faire economy,
the national security-national identity formation from time to time
frustrates the institutions of parliamentary democracy, despite the
fact that it is the military itself, rather than the radical movements
portrayed as such, that is alien or 'unnatural' to the Thai body
politic. Was it not Bakunin who stressed how separate the military
is from the people, having been transformed into enemies of civilian
society by military education and set apart by the ridiculous
embellishments of regiments and ranks, making all soldiers seem

like clowns?[18] Though the agency and process of its complex creation are beyond discussion here, suffice it to say that a discursive formation of security has come into being that permeates social and public life and embraces culture as well as defence and public order.

Many of the nearly fifty-six million people living in Thailand have notions of Thai identity in their heads, and the last question we might raise here is how this notion came into consciousness. The essays in this volume make clear that the answers to this question can be reached in an interdisciplinary way, through behavioural, historical, linguistic, anthropological, political, religious, and discursive studies. One theme running through most of the essays is that there is something hegemonic about Thai identity in Thai consciousness. In other words, the meanings of Thai identity are given to consciousness by those in power, by ruling elites, and by state managers. While there is plenty of evidence to show how this might have been accomplished since 1939, we have not paid enough attention to the implications of the proposition. To attribute the construction of Thai identity entirely to cultural programs of the Thai state is to subscribe to the theory of false consciousness. In other words, what Thai nationals believe about Thai identity, what they feel in their heart-of-hearts about their food, their language, their kinfolk, their religion, their monarchy, and so on has been planted there by state institutions to cultivate a sense of belonging that will make governing those fifty-five million people easier and more peaceable.

To put the inquiry into another register and meet this criticism of false consciousness one would have to develop a concept of the speaking subject, while giving due regard to the institutional determinants of identity formation. Under what circumstances and at whose prompting do Thai speakers find Thai identity natural and meaningful in their personal experience? How does the Thai-speaking audience, however specified in terms of class, region, or gender, mediate Thai identity and its discursive practices?

Subjectivity that may be called 'Thai' is constituted by many discursive practices and not only the ones given sanction by the National Identity Board.

A related criticism of Thai identity as a hegemonic construct is that the instrumentalist intent assumed in such a construct is misleading. Society does not cohere simply because the nationalist ideology, fashioned by the ruling elite, strikes a responsive chord in the population. The concept of a dominant ideology assumes an over-integrated, overly systemic view of society. Dominant ideologies are not 'clear, coherent and effective' but are fractured and contradictory in most historical periods (Abercrombie et al. 1980:156-9). In the spaces between these fractures appears an anarchistic and disordered world, full of unscrupulous power-holders and unpredictable spiritual forces, to borrow the phrasing of Annette Hamilton's analysis of mass media in Thailand. The mass media in Thailand pictures this world as lurid and violent rather than reassuring and serene, as the colourful promotions of the culture bureaucracy would have it.

Finally, there is not enough in these pages about resistance to the way in which identity of either the ethnic or national kind is promoted and internalized. How do people, particularly at the regional and local level, contest and struggle against the process? Or is Thai identity simply not an issue for them? We might better understand Thai identity as primarily a negative force, the name for that which resists the pressures and intrusiveness of what is foreign and alien. The power of Thai identity lies in its imagined capacity to differentiate inside from outside and in the process of doing so to hold the subversive Other at arm's length.

Some research on this issue is in order along the lines of a recent study of the reception of Pancasila rhetoric in Bali. The five principles of Pancasila formulate a pan-Indonesian nationalist ideology whose intent is to integrate the multi-ethnic, multi-religious polity. But local interpretations of this ideology often 'belie the official image of an unenlightened floating mass'. Using the theoretical insights of Gramsci and Bakhtin, Carol Warren has shown that the dominant ideology thesis presumes that subordinate classes are much more affected by hegemonic cultural production than is in fact the case. Precisely because the rhetoric that surrounds hegemonic cultural production has heavy symbolic loading and seeks consensual response, it is 'particularly susceptible to subaltern reconstruction' (Warren 1990:201).

Subordinate classes can respond creatively and constructively to the most hierarchical, repressive and paternalistic dominant ideologies. In this volume we have dwelt rather too much on hegemonic notions of Thai identity and have thus given them too much agency, even as we have pointed out that these notions are often reformulations of folk and ethnic traditions that lie far from the centre of power.

ENDNOTES

1. This introduction was completed after the military coup of 23 February 1991.
   In writing it I have benefited from many helpful references and comments
   offered by Annette Hamilton, Baas Terwiel, Carol Warren, David Chandler,
   Dipesh Chakrabarty, Gehan Wijewardene, Helen Michaelsen, Jim Warren,
   Kasian Tejapira, Matthew Copeland, Patrick Jory, Tony Diller, Vacharin
   McFadden and Yoneo Ishii.

2. Preecha 1988 gives the most exhaustive account of 'Thailand' vs. 'Siam',
   including a history of usage and the way the two names serve as markers of
   different positions in contemporary Thai political debates.

3. It is commonly understood that *sayam* in Thai is a translation of 'Siam' in English
   (or its equivalent in other foreign languages), but this may not be so. If the
   three treaties made in 1855-56 with Great Britain, the U.S.A. and France are
   compared it is noticeable that *sayam* occurs only after the de Montigny treaty
   of 1856. In the two earlier treaties we find *krungthep* or *muang thai* rather
   than *sayam*. It is not unlikely that *sayam* was coined during Mongkut's reign
   and is thus as coloured by political considerations as the country's naming in
   1939 or 1948. I am grateful to Professor Yoneo Ishii of Sophia University
   for this suggestion (personal communication, 4 September 1991).

4. The edicts have been translated into English in Thak 1978:243-54. The most
   comprehensive discussion of them is in the thinly-disguised sardonic wit of
   Thamsook Numnonda (1977:chap. 3; 1978); see also Likhit 1988:94-99 and
   Barme 1989:chap 6. Likhit and the contributors to Thak 1978 translate
   ratthaniyom as 'state-ism', which is a literal rendering of the Thai term. In
   terming the edicts Cultural Mandates, I follow Charnvit 1974 and other historians
   (Thamsook 1977, 1978; Wyatt 1983), while recognizing that the Thai term
   makes no mention of culture.

5. Although the history of culture policy pursued by Thai ruling elites both during
   the absolute monarchy and after 1932 has yet to be researched comprehensively,
   many instances have already surfaced of how state norms and conventions were
   contested. See, for example, Reynolds 1987 and 1991b.

6. For additional examples of linguistic engineering during the first Phibun regime
   see Thamsook 1977:34 and 1978:240-41.

7. This period is currently being researched by the art historian Helen Michaelsen of the Free University, Berlin, who is preparing a doctoral dissertation on the development and consequences of Western influences on Thai art. I am indebted to her for providing the frontispiece and for making invaluable suggestions on an earlier draft of this introduction.

8. These acts are translated in Office of the National Culture Commission n. d. The 1942 Act is also in Thak 1978:258-60.

9. As explained in Charoen's *Standard Dictionary and Thai Coinages* (*Pathanukrom kham mattrathan lae banyat sap phasa thai*), Kasem Bannakit Bookstore, 1958, *ekkalak* entered the Thai language at the instigation of the Coinage Committee (*khana kammakan banyatsap*), chaired by Prince Wan Waithayakorn (Kasian 1991).

10. Translated in Office of the National Culture Colmmission n. d.:28-29. The Thai text is in Samnakngan khanakammakan 1988:123-125.

11. For references in this section on the National Identity Board I am indebted to Vacharin McFadden of the Australian National Library, Canberra. I have been unable to date the establishment of the Board more precisely, but I suspect that the change of government under General Prem Tinsulanonda in early 1980 brought the National Identity Board to prominence.

12. There are a host of ways in which Thai women have come to exemplify Thai tradition. For general perspectives in terms of the trade in female sexuality see Heyzer 1986:chap. 4.

13. For an example of how these enterprises 'think' about the internationalizing of local snack cultures see the Spring 1989 issue of *Impact*, the in-house magazine of Pepsico Foods International, in which a Thai marketing manager says, 'I believe in the concept of a global product, but our version may not be identical.' I am grateful to Mr. Tim Hessell for this material.

14. The document, dated 7 December 1940, was signed by the Deputy Minister of Defence (Kasian 1991). On the annexation see Wyatt 1984:255-6.

15. See Terwiel's essay in this volume and the works cited there by Batson.

16. This situation will soon be rectified with the completion of a Ph. D. dissertation by Kasian Tejapira at Cornell University, 'Commodifying Marxism: The Ethno-ideology, Politics, and Business of Modern Thai Radical Culture, 1927-1958'.

17. A good selection of the radio programs has been translated in Thak 1978:260-316. The Thai ear easily put Man and Khong together as *mankhong*. *Chuchat* means 'uphold the nation'; *rakthai* means 'love for Thailand / the Thai'.

18. I owe this observation to Dr. Gill Burke of the Australian National University.

REFERENCES

Abercrombie, Nicholas, Stephen Hill, Brian S. Turner. 1980. *The Dominant Ideology Thesis*. London and Sydney, George Allen & Unwin.

Anderson, Benedict R. O'G. 1978. 'Studies of the Thai State: The State of Thai Studies', pp. 193-247 in *The Study of Thailand: Analyses of Knowledge, Approaches, and Prospects in Anthropology, Art History, Economics, History and Political Science*, ed. Eliezer B. Ayal. Athens, Ohio, Center for International Studies.

Anuman Rajadhon, Phya. 1970. *Ruang khong chat thai [On Thai Nationality]*. Bangkok. Cremation volume for Chaliew Phumichit.

AWSJ. 1986. *Asian Wall Street Journal*. 21 January.

Barme, Scot. 1989. 'Luang Wichit Wathakan: Official Nationalism and Political Legitimacy Prior to World War II'. M. A. thesis, Australian National University.

Charnvit Kasetsiri. 1974. 'The First Phibun Government and Its Involvement in World War II', *Journal of the Siam Society*, 62.2 (July), 25-88.

Cholthira Satyawadhna. 1991. 'The Dispossessed: An Anthropological Reconstruction of Lawa Ethnohistory in the Light of their Relationship with the Tai'. Ph. D. dissertation (submitted for examination), Australian National University.

Damrong Rajanubhab, Prince. 1975. 'Laksana kanpokkhrong prathet sayam tae boran [The Nature of Rule in Siam from Ancient Times]', pp. 3-29 in Khukrit Pramote et al., *Prawattisat lae kanmuang nangsu an prakop wicha phunthan arayatham thai [History and Politics: A Reader on the Fundamentals of Thai*

Civilization]. Bangkok, Thammsat University.

De Silva, K. M. et al., ed. 1988. *Ethnic Conflicts in Buddhist Societies: Sri Lanka, Thailand, and Burma*. London, Pinter Publishers.

Heyzer, Noeleen. 1986. *Working Women in South-East Asia: Development, Subordination and Emancipation*. Philadelphia, Open University Press.

Kasian Tejapira. 1991. Personal communication, 22 April.

Keyes, Charles F. 1976. 'Towards a New Formulation of the Concept of Ethnic Group', *Ethnicity*, 3, pp. 202-13.

Khana-anukammakan phoephrae ekkalak khong thai [Subcommittee for the Propagation of Thai Identity]. 1983. *Raingan phon kansammana ruang watthanatham thang phasa khong thai [Thai Linguistic Culture: Seminar Proceedings]*. Bangkok, National Identity Board.

Khanakammakan chat ngan sompot krung rattanakosin 200 roi pi [Bangkok Bicentennial Celebration Committee]. 1982. *Prawattisat krung rattanakosin pho so 2475 - patchuban [History of Bangkok, 1932 - Present]*. Bangkok.

Likhit Dhiravegin. 1988. 'Nationalism and State in Thailand', pp. 92 - 106 in de Silva 1988.

McVey, Ruth. 1984. 'Separatism and the Paradoxes of the Nation-state in Perspective', pp. 3-29 in *Armed Separatism in Southeast Asia*, ed. Lim Joo-Jock and Vani S. Singapore, Institute of Southeast Asian Studies, Regional Strategic Studies Programme.

Michaelsen, Helen. 1990. 'Modern Art in Thailand: An Outline of its Development from 1932 - 1960', *SPAFA Digest* (SEAMEO Regional Centre for Archaeology and Fine Arts), 11.3, 32-38.

--------. 1991. 'State-building and Thai Painting and Sculpture, 1930s and 1940s'. Paper prepared for conference on Modernism and Postmodernism in Asian Art, Humanities Research Centre, Australian National University, Canberra, 22-25 March 1991.

Office of the National Culture Commission, Ministry of Education. n. d. *Organizational Structure*. Bangkok.

Prasong Sunsiri. 1984. 'Phasa thai kap khwammankhong haeng chat [Thai Language and National Security', pp. 245-51 in Samnakngan Soemsang Ekkalak Khong Chat [National Identity Board], *Phasa thai kap sangkhom thai* [Thai Language and Thai Society]. Bangkok, Office of the Prime Minister.

Preecha Juntanamalaga. 1988. 'Thai or Siam?' *Names, Journal of the American Name Society*, 36.1-2 (March-June), 69-84.

Reynolds, Craig J. 1987. *Thai Radical Discourse: The Real Face of Thai Feudalism Today*. Ithaca, Cornell University, Southeast Asia Program.

--------. 1991a. 'The Plot of Thai History: Theory and Practice', in *Patterns and Illusions: Papers on Thai Topics in Memory of Richard B. Davis*, ed. Gehan Wijeyewardene and E. C. Chapman. Bangkok, in press.

--------. 1991b. 'Sedition in Thai History: A Nineteenth-century Poem and Its Critics', in *Thai Constructions of Knowledge*, ed. Andrew Turton and Manas Chitakasem. London, in press.

Samnakngan khanakammakan watthanatham haengchat [Office of the National Culture Commission]. 1988. *Watthanatham prachamchat [The National Culture]*. Bangkok, Ministry of Education.

Seksan Prasoetkun. 1989. 'The Transformation of the Thai State and Economic Change, 1855-1945'. Ph. D. thesis, Cornell University.

Smith, Anthony D. 1986. *The Ethnic Origins of Nations*. Oxford and New York, Basil Blackwell.

Sujit Wongthes. 1986. *Khonthai yu thi ni prawattisat sanghkom lae watthanatham khong chao sayam nai muangthai [The Thais Were Always Here: A Social and Cultural History of the Siamese People in Thailand]*. Bangkok, Sinlapa watthanatham. Special Issue.

--------, ed. 1988. *Charuk phokhun ramkhamhaeng khrai taengkan nae [Who Really Wrote the King Ramkhamhaeng Inscription?]*. *Sinlapa watthanatham*, Special Issue. Bangkok.
Suphot Dantrakun. 1985. *Thai ru sayam [Thai or Siam?]*. Nonburi, Santitham Publishing.

Surin Phitsuwan. 1988. 'The Lotus and the Crescent: Clashes of Religious Symbolism in Southern Thailand', pp. 187-201 in de Silva 1988.

Tan Liok Ee. 1988. *The Rhetoric of Bangsa and Minzu: Community and Nation in Tension, the Malay Peninsula, 1900-1955*. Clayton, Victoria, Monash University, Centre of Southeast Asian Studies. Working Paper no. 52.

Thak Chaloemtiarana, ed. 1978. *Thai Politics: Extracts and Documents, 1932 - 1957.* Bangkok, Social Science Association of Thailand.

Thamsook Numnonda. 1977. *Thailand and the Japanese Presence, 1941-45.* Singapore, Insitute of Southeast Asian Studies. Research Notes and Discussions Series, no. 6.

--------. 1978. 'Pibulsongkram's Thai Nation-Building Programme during the Japanese Military Presence, 1941-1945', *Journal of Southeast Asian Studies*, 9.2 (Sept.), 234-47.

Thongchai Winichakul. 1988. 'Siam Mapped: A History of the Geo-body of Siam'. Ph. D. dissertation, University of Sydney. University of Hawaii Press, forthcoming.

Warren, Carol. 1990. 'Rhetoric and Resistance: Popular Political Culture in Bali', *Anthropological Forum*, 6.2, pp. 191-205.
Wijeyewardene, Gehan. 1990. 'Thailand and the Tai: Versions of Ethnic Identity', pp. 48-73 in Gehan Wijeyewardene, ed., *Ethnic Groups Across National Boundaries in Mainland SEA*. Singapore, Insitute of Southeast Asian Studies.

Wira Amphai. 1983. *Khwampenthai [Thainess]*. Bangkok, n. p.

Wyatt, David K. 1984. *Thailand: A Short History*. New Haven and London, Yale University Press.

Chapter 2

THE CRISIS OF SIAMESE IDENTITY[1]

Sulak Sivaraksa

I

The Siamese must have realized their own identity even before intercourse with the West. They compared themselves especially with their neighbours — the Mons, the Khmers, the Burmans and the Laotians — despite the fact that all these peoples belonged to the same Theravada school of Buddhism. They noticed the differences culturally, politically and religiously between themselves and the Malays, the Vietnamese and the Chinese. Although they acquired much of their spiritual tradition and advanced technology from India and Ceylon, they lumped these peoples together as *khaek* (visitors or foreigners). They did not want to share much of their identity with the *khaek* who later came to be regarded as those with Hindu or Islamic background. Hence the Malays and the Javanese were also *khaek*, as were the Persians from the Middle East. And through the Persians or the Indians the Siamese got to know the West, as we still use the Persian or Indian language in referring to Westerners collectively as *farang*.

The Siamese wanted to keep the *khaek* and the *farang* at arm's length. They did not want to know them or to learn from them as they did from their immediate neighbours, and to a lesser extent from the Chinese. If the *khaek* and the *farang* wanted to have a relationship with the Siamese, it had to be on Siamese terms, as one could see from the case of Phaulkon and Chaek Amud who was an ancestor of the Bunnag family.

Even Buddhism became so Siamese that the Buddha left his footprint and his shadow at Saraburi. He passed away at Kanjanaburi and he descended from Tavtimsa heaven at Uthaidani. Please note that his birth place and the place of his enlightenment as well as the place of the first sermon were not so important to popular Buddhism, as the Thai sacred Buddhist places seem to be connected more with magic or miraculous aspects of the religion. Indeed the most sacred book that shaped Siamese Buddhist identity and ideology was the *Trai Bhumi* or *The Three Worlds* according to King Ruang of the Sukhothai period.

It was not until King Mongkut of the Bangkok period that Siamese identity was threatened by the *farang*. Had we followed our neighbours' political philosophy, we would have been colonized by the West, as Burma and Vietnam had already been subjugated. Even India and Ceylon, the sources of our Buddhism, were already under the control of the British, and the great Chinese empire was also being seriously threatened.

For Mongkut, Siamese identity meant bending to Western demands in order to preserve our independence politically, culturally and spiritually. We even lost some of our economic and judicial independence in order to be the masters of our own country. We had to give up some aspects of our identity for a more universal aspect of civilization not only acceptable to the West, but also righteous, i.e. according to the Dhamma, the Buddhist Middle Path, the pristine teaching of the Buddha that predated *The Three Worlds* which mixed Buddhism with Hinduistic cosmology.

Mongkut's strength was not only his understanding of the West, which none of his predecessors had, but his return to the root of Siameseness which he claimed to be in accordance with the original teaching of the Buddha as recorded in the Pali Tripitaka, the most authentic record of Theravada Buddhism. Hence to refute the *Trai Bhumi* he had to go back to King Rama Kamhaeng's inscription. As Rama Kamhaeng was the grandfather of Li Thai, the author of *Trai Bhumi*, he was not only older, but what he wrote was, to Mongkut, very important for Siamese identity: the love of independence, equality, fraternity and liberty. There was not much difference between king and commoner. The King was only a *Sommotti Deva* and not a *Devarāja* as in the Khmer and Ayudhyan concept. Although Mongkut liked to retain the old ideas of Lord of Life and Lord of the Land, intellectually he argued that the king must be righteous, a *Dhammaraja*, taking the Law as supreme, as stated in the Sutta of the Pali canon.

At the same time, by using classical literature as well as foreign source material, Mongkut managed to create a new identity, namely, the concept of a state beyond *muang* (principality) and *baan* (village) which had been keys to Siamese identity before his reign. Indeed the word Siam itself was made official by him, and he also created a spiritual guardian of Siam, Phra Sayam Devadhirāja. Hitherto we only had spiritual guardians of each *baan* and each *muang*. Now we have a national spiritual guardian of the state. Even today most Siamese believe in the miraculous power of this spiritual entity.

Mongkut also modified the Siamese life style, our dress, our architecture and other exterior aspects of our identity. More important, however, was our education, i.e. we had to understand the West and to change our outward identity in order to preserve our inner strength to cope with the West. Hence missionaries were no longer allowed to teach the royal children. To learn English and Western technology was to preserve the essential core of Siamese identity which was part and parcel of the spirit of Buddhism. Unfortunately the democratic aspects of the Buddhist teaching were not taken into consideration seriously, not even by his three sons: King Chulalongkorn, Prince Patriarch Vajiranana and Prince Damrong. What these three great men did in shaping various aspects of Siamese identity is fascinating but beyond the scope of our deliberation. However, their failure in implementing the democratic aspects of Buddhism and indeed Siamese identity, especially at the *baan* level, was to bring the absolute monarchy to an end in 1932.

In fact, Mongkut's grandson, Rama VI, even reverted to the *Trai Bhumi*'s concept which he managed to link with the British trinity of Empire, God, King and Country, which became in Thai *Chat, Sasana, Phra Maha Kasat* or The Nation, the Buddhist religion and the Monarchy. Indeed it was Rama VI who developed his grandfather's concept of the Siamese state to an extreme ideology of nationalism, patriotism and ethnicity at the expense of the Chinese whom he regarded as the Jews of the East. He also wrote about *Uttara Kuru*, an ideal state in the *Trai Bhumi* and mocked it as a communist state and a democratic failure.

Although Rama VI contributed many negative aspects to Siamese identity, one positive thing was his love of classical Indian literature. Unlike his grandfather, he did not know Pali or Sanskrit. Nevertheless he employed Bhrahmin Pandits as well as ex-Buddhist monks at the Siamese court, paving the way for young scholars of his generation to associate Siamese culture and literature with ancient India, the source of our tradition. People like Phya Anuman Rajadhon was a by-product of the King's initiative in this sphere of knowledge. Later Phya Anuman would play a crucial role in preserving traditional Siamese culture during the Thailand period, which will be discussed below. Unlike Rama VI, Prince Damrong regarded Siamese identity as having three entirely different aspects: 1) the love of freedom or independence, nationally, socially and individually; 2) the dislike of violence, i.e. if they have a choice the Siamese would prefer peaceful means or a nonviolent way of settling disputes; 3) the Siamese are good at assimilation, or compromise. For this last aspect he used the word *prasarnprayod* in Thai. They know how to draw what is good and useful from various sources and to make these Siamese. Damrong's whole career was in fact to create a new awareness of Siamese identity, not only through administrative reform, but also out of his concern for education, research work, and the national museum and library.

Last but not least was his creation of the Royal Council, an imitation of Academie Française, to shape national language and literature and to encourage the conservation of traditional arts, archaeological sites and national treasures.

Again, nobody of the old elites did anything for democracy. Indeed commoners who aspired to have their share in shaping the nation's future or destiny, if they did not join the civil service, were ignored, and if their views were expressed too strongly they were put in gaol, as the case of Mr. Tienwan, the most prominent Siamese intellectual during the absolute regime.

II

Prince Damrong's 70th birthday was celebrated in a grand style on 21 June 1932, two months after the 150th anniversary of Bangkok and the Royal House of Chakkri. The celebration was to show his achievement in preserving Siamese identity from the reigns of his august father, Mongkut, to his brother, Chulalongkorn, and to two of his nephews, Rama VI and VII. Damrong was a Supreme Counsellor of State and President of the Royal Council, in charge of all the arts and cultures of the kingdom.

Three days after his birthday marked the end of the absolute monarchy, the price the princes paid for not taking the commoners' aspirations into serious consideration as part and parcel of Siamese identity. Prince Damrong went into exile in Penang for a decade. The king himself went into exile and died in England, where he had been educated. Indeed Western education on the whole did more harm than good to our Siamese identity. I said this a few years ago by quoting an Englishman, Mr Scott, who had been in the service of King Chulalongkorn and who admired the King very much but concluded that his greatest mistake was to send the Siamese to be educated abroad when they were too young. And these youngsters who later became the elites in their own country

did not understand enough of Siamese identity and did more harm
than good to Siam.

As a result of my remarks plus a few other statements I was
charged with lese majesty which could have landed me in gaol
for fifteen to forty-five years had the case not been withdrawn.
However, I feel that this statement is still true now. And not only
for Siam, but for almost all the so-called developing countries.

Indeed, the leading promoters of the 1932 *coup* against the
absolute regime were all educated in the West. They wanted
democracy and ended up with a military dictatorship. They wanted
to promote Thai identity at the expense of other ethnicities and
ended up in looking down on our own indigenous cultures and
despising our neighbours, the Lao, Khmer, Malay and Burmese.
Worst of all we blindly admired the West for the wrong reasons
without realizing the dangers, and the West now included Japan
and all material progress and advanced technology. A consumer
culture bringing coco cola, fast food and blue jeans has replaced
our local Siamese ways of life. The great department stores and
shopping complexes have now replaced our *wat* which used to
be our schools, museums, art galleries, recreation centres and cultural
centres as well as our hospitals and spiritual theatres. Neither the
rich nor the poor have any idea of our own identity. We just grope
and strive to be like a developed country. We try to be one of
the Newly Industrialized Countries (NIC), to look East as we used
to look West, as if these countries were so perfect or ideal, a
hallucination of the elites who are mostly half-educated or only
educated in the material aspects of the West without understanding
our own spiritual and cultural identity.

All these negative aspects started not in 1932 but in 1939,
although 1932 was a breeding ground for the crisis of our identity.
1939 was the seventh year after the successful *coup* which had
ended the ancient regime. However Rama VI's concept of *Chat,
Sasana, Phra Maha Kasat* was not abandoned. Rather,

rathadhammanun (the constitution) was added to the Siamese trinity, as the Law must be supreme. In a way it was going back to the *dhammarāja* concept of Buddhism, as envisaged by Mongkut but never implemented by him or any of his successors, i.e. the King must bow to the rule of law. The King could be a national symbol as a constitutional monarch according to the righteous will of the people.

Positively, 1939 was the end of Western extraterritorial rights and the economic inequality with the foreign powers. Hence it was the first time that 24 June — the day of the first successful *coup* — was regarded as the national day. The Democracy Monument was constructed and declared open on national day, obviously without consulting an astrologer. The balloons which were to carry pink silk that covered the symbolic constitution would not fly into the air but fell flat near by. To most Siamese, then, it was a bad omen for our democracy.

Indeed, the Prime Minister in 1939, Pibulsonggram, who had been in office for three years, felt strong enough to be a dictator rather than a president of the ministerial council. He expanded Rama VI's nationalism and encouraged suspicion of the Chinese in a grand scheme for the Thai race as well as the Thai empire in imitation of Nazi Germany. He made himself the leader, the Führer, and declared that henceforth the name of all our people must be Thai, whatever their national or ethnic origins, and the country's name would be Thailand instead of Siam. Our national anthem was changed to be very patriotic and even racist. Yet the name of the country and the national anthem remain unchanged until now, although after World War II Pridi Banomyong changed Thailand back to Siam. Even so he changed the English version only, and the official name Siam lasted only for four years. Indeed we were told, nay, we were ordered, to salute the national flag, accompanied by the comical and chauvinistic national anthem twice every day at 8 a.m. and 6 p.m. This is still going on today.

I feel that if the country is ruled democratically, with sensitivity to various nationalities and ethnicities, especially the Malays in the South and the hill peoples in the North as well as the Khmers in the Northeast, we would have done away with the name Thailand and the national anthem, not to mention the military custom of forcing everyone to salute the flag daily.

The Thailand concept not only fostered hatred against the Chinese but also bred the idea of irredentism. As a result we went to war against the French in 1940 - 1941 in order to get back our lost territories in Laos and Cambodia, without realizing that we were tools of the Japanese. Hence we soon had to join Japan in World War II, and Japan returned to us our Malayan territory lost to the British, despite the fact that the government had declared publicly our strict neutrality. Pridi Banomyong tried his best to remind us and the world of Prince Damrong's argument that the Siamese preferred peace and a nonviolent approach to conflict. Pridi even wrote and produced a film in English, *The King of the White Elephant*, to inform the world as well as the Siamese elites who preferred to listen to a foreign tongue rather than their own.

Pridi and Pibul were in a tug of war on the national and international levels to preserve our independence as Mongkut and Chulalongkorn had tried during the ancien regime. With his clandestinely organized Free Siamese movement, Pridi managed to preserve our independence; the Victory Monument built by the command of Pibul became a mockery, since we were lucky not to be defeated along with the Japanese. And the so-called victory over the French in Indochina meant that we had to hand back territories to Laos, Cambodia and British Malaya. Yet every statesman going to Bangkok still lays a wreath at the Victory Monument which should be renamed 'the Monument of Shame'.

Although Pridi and his colleagues in the Free Siamese movement briefly preserved our independence as well as our democracy, he could not preserve our national identity, nor could he pave the way for a positive future. His intellectual and ideological challenge to Pibul began even before 1939, but that year seemed to be the clear starting point for Pibul's supremacy and all the false values accompanying the Thailand concept seem to have lasted until now.

Pibul's intellectual mentor was of course Luang Vichit Vadakarn, a bright ex-monk who kowtowed to the princes during the absolutist regime and who was sent to the Siamese Legation in Paris, where he met Pridi and Pibul. But his mediocrity in Western education and his ambition at the expense of ethical standards made Pridi distrust him. But Pibul needed a half-baked intellectual who glorified him and gave him ideas. So Vichit became a key man in shaping Thai identity and nationalism during the Pibul era, which ended in 1944.

Pibul and Vichit not only admired Hitler and Mussolini, but also Ataturk. Hence the term 'Young Turk' is still popular in the Thai Army even now. Pibul followed Ataturk in giving up the old traditions and by embracing almost every aspect of outward Western culture. We were told, nay, we were ordered to dress in Western style; even our women were ordered to wear hats and gloves at one time. The chewing of betel nuts was prohibited. Our youngsters now go for chewing gum instead. Men were told, this time not ordered but strongly recommended, to kiss their wives before going to work. Men had to have male names, women female names as in Europe. Any names or surnames which denoted Chinese origin had to be changed. Titles bestowed by former kings were abolished. Those who wished to join a naval or military academy had to prove that their grandfathers were pure Thai and not of Chinese extraction. Certain trades in foreign (i.e. Chinese) hands had to be preserved for Thai people, especially those dealing with the sale of ecclesiastical objects for the monkhood. Later Thais were to trade everything, including pork and noodles. And we were told to hate all the Chinese except our fathers and grandfathers. Yet, the Chinese outsmarted the government in all aspects.

Pibul's enemies were 1) the Chinese and all the foreign powers outside the Axis camp, including the British and the French; 2) the princes and the old nobility, since Pibul himself was a commoner with no aristocratic lineage to boast about and he claimed no Chinese blood in him.

With the help of Luang Vichit, the creation of Thailand was meant to destroy everything the princes had created and preserved, starting with the word Siam, royal ceremonies, traditional music and dance drama, and the Royal Council, the last creation of Prince Damrong. Even the royal museum and the royal library became the national museum and national library. The old Royal Council became the Royal Institute. This time he allowed the word Royal to remain, but all academicians were appointed or recommended by him personally.

The old royal prescriptions (*phrarachaniyom*) which used to be decreed to recommend that people change their habits and customs were replaced by the Cultural Mandates (*ratthaniyom*). Indeed the proclamation that Thailand replace Siam was announced through the first *ratthaniyom*, literally meaning statism or following the state; later came the phrase 'follow the leader' (*chua phu nam*). When the language was simplified *rattaniyom* was spelled differently and it meant 'following a car or a vehicle (blindly)'.

The Thai word for culture was coined by Prince Wan, who felt that the Siamese would lose most of their traditional identity. As modern Siam became more progressive or civilized, she would have to be more like the West. The only identity to be exclusively Thai would be the Thai language. Hence he was personally very concerned about shaping modern Thai language to suit the changing situation either through his newspaper *Prachachart* (*The Nation*) or through the newly created Royal Institute.

Most of the royal family at that time regarded Prince Wan as a turn-coat. Unfortunately many of them were put in prison or sent into exile. Of Damrong, Pibul said that if the old prince set foot in Thailand he would be arrested immediately. The Royal Institute would have been dead from the beginning, had it not been for the perseverance and patience as well as tact of the two succeeding presidents, Prince Wan and Phya Anuman. Both helped in compiling dictionaries, encyclopedia, and coining new Thai words to satisfy the demands of the growing nation.

In addition, Phya Anuman was able to preserve royal barges, traditional music and dance drama, while Luang Vichit was creating his soap opera for patriotism, which, I would agree with Dr. Johnson, is the last refuge of scoundrels. Western music became *plaeng sakol* (universal songs). Indeed anything *sakol* (universal) meant Western. For instance *suit sakol* means Western dress with trousers, necktie and a jacket, which was to be admired. Anything Siamese was old fashioned, decadent and to be looked down upon. I am afraid this concept still prevails in most fashionable circles in all Siamese cities.

Phya Anuman served under Pibul. He went along with the Dictator's whims in order to preserve what was to him very vital for Siamese identity. He was eventually trusted by Pibul, and he was successful in reconciling Prince Damrong with Pibul also.

Pibul even abolished the royal vocabulary the (*rajasabda*) in order to encourage equality in the Thai language and do away with its feudal connotations in modern expression. He simplified the spelling without caring for the Pail or Sanskrit roots. This he did by creating a Cultural Council which eventually became a Ministry of Culture. After his period, Pibul's creation was reduced to a small national committee without any power or social recognition. Although the National Culture Council and the Royal Institute still exist, they were in fact replaced by the National Identity Board and the National Research Council, each of which is also a mockery to the nation and the world.

Regarding the Chinese, as I have said earlier, they outsmarted Pibul on every count. Indeed when Pibul wanted to create Thai state monopolies, he had to rely on the Chinese, who changed their names to be Thai. Hence Mr. Chulieng became Mr. Chulindra Lamsom and the Thai Niyom company was supposed to be the first Thai grand commercial enterprise, literally translated as Company of Thai Favours or Thai Favouritism. Similarly, the Khao Thai company was supposed to have a monopoly over all Chinese mills in Thailand. Indeed it was through the Thai Niyom Company that Pibul became corrupted financially. This created precedents for Chinese or Sino-Thai merchants to be involved with Siamese politics to the present day.

III

Up to 1947 the princes and the aristocrats seemed to have lost their role in preserving Siamese identity or destiny. During World War II Prince Bidyalongkorn, former Vice President of the old Royal Council and a gifted poet, wrote a poem in his famous book *Sam Krung (The Three Capitals)* wondering about the future of Siam. For him, under the princes' firm control, the kingdom had survived uniquely and preserved its own identity marvellously. Had he known what Pridi and his Free Siamese Movement were doing, his poem would perhaps be more hopeful. Indeed Pridi, known to be a republican, a socialist, and even a communist, was gentle and helpful to the princes. As Regent of Rama VII he helped to preserve the constitutional monarchy.

Yet Pibul, with his war crime record, on his return to power in a military *coup*, managed to get rid of Pridi on the false charge of regicide. The mystery of the king's death in 1946 and the false charge against Pridi have not yet been lifted politically and psychologically. To me, this also affected the crisis of Siamese identity. With his return to power in 1947, Pibul now learnt to play with the princes, whom he still despised. He kept the monarchy strictly under control, politically and economically.

He also claimed to imitate King Rama Kamhaeng of Sukhothai and to follow the Buddha's instruction in ruling as a *Dhammarāja*. In a way, Pibul tried to go back to Mongkut, who used Rama Kamhaeng's throne (Manangasila) for his and his successor's coronation. Their first proclamation was 'We shall rule righteously over Siam.' Pibul's political party was named after Rama Kamhaeng's throne (Managasila Party) and the party's newspaper was called *Dhammadhipataya*—the best form of Buddhist polity, and far superior to democracy which in Buddhist terminology is *Lokadhipataya*.

Pibul, like most military dictators, needed to have enemies and models for his development. Since the princes were no longer overtly his enemies, nor the Chinese, he chose the communists as his enemies. This was fashionable for the Americans, and the United States of America became his model of development just as Hitler's Germany had been before the war.

However, when he realized that he led his country too deeply into American influence, as he realized too late with the Japanese during World War II, he tried to get out of the American shadow by joining the Bandung Conference as well as sending secret missions to China, as he had also done during the war. Again it was too late, for he also lost control of the army. The Americans in collaboration with the new commander-in-chief, Sarit Thanarat and the palace, managed to oust Pibul from Thailand forever in 1957. 1957 marked the 25th Buddhist centenary, a very important date for Siamese Buddhist identity, since this landmark could signify the decline and fall or the progress and advancement for Buddhism. For us, the year marked the beginning of the end of democracy and freedom, although there was not much of either of these during Pibul's regime. Worse than that, it was the return of feudalism, not aristocracy, and military dictatorship at its worst. The Americans for the first time had complete control over Thailand that even the Japanese did not have.

The American period in Thailand was successful because of American advisers, civilian and military, their education of the Thai both in Thailand and the U. S. A. and their propaganda against the communists as well as for the so-called Free World. Yet those who had been educated in the U. S. A. never attacked the military regime in Thailand openly. Worst of all, the so-called development model began to destroy our villages and the *baan* culture. Roads, dams, and electricity, radio and television in the name of development negatively affected our identity in every village and temple.

Luang Vichit returned to be Sarit's mentor, and all the false values and hypocrisy came back to the Thai civil service and education system worse than before. After Sarit and Vichit, things seemed to be a little bit better democratically, but the crisis in our identity caused by them, especially by Vichit from the 1930s, remain with us permanently. Sarit was worse than Pibul on three counts: 1) he had no regard for democracy at all; 2) he did not realize the American danger; 3) worst of all he played politics with the monarchy. And he allowed all kinds of economic advantages to the palace while he himself was the most corrupted man economically and morally. He used the monarchy and the monkhood to legitimize his rule and he did away with the constitution entirely. There was no rule of law left.

To me, this was the beginning of our identity crisis on the gravest scale in terms of the two pillars of our nation: the religion and the monarchy. And the nation has come to mean the military, the state within a state. We the people are only onlookers. The independent intellectuals feel frustrated and do not know what to do. The majority of the people — the farmers — have to sell their land, their daughters and their children. Many country people have to migrate to Bangkok and to the Middle East to find any job whatsoever. Sixty percent of our youngsters are now malnutritious, and Siam is supposed to be the rice bowl of Asia.

The only good thing during the Sarit's era and its aftermath until 1973 was that some honest and capable technocrats were allowed to run the country as civil servants. Unfortunately, most of them cared only for their own department or ministry. The only one who obviously cared for social justice and democratic rights of the people was the Governor of the Bank of Thailand, Puey Ungphakorn. Although he kept his mouth shut, later he was instrumental in getting non-government organizations (NGOs) operating outside the civil service in order to achieve alternative models of development, with emphasis on peace and justice, caring for the dignity of the people and their participation in deciding their own destiny as well as that of the nation.

IV

I do not want to talk in detail about the two decades after Sarit, although the 1973-1976 events were also very important regarding our identity — politically, culturally and economically. Nor do I want to talk about the present government [1989] which has lasted only one year.[2] Yet the dilemmas created by Pibul and intensified by Sarit still remain with us. As long as our elites look to the West, which now include Japan and the NICs, only in terms of material and technological advancement, we are still in crisis.

To change Indochina from a war zone into a market place may sound good politically and economically, but if we do not care about our moral commitments, and do not understand our neighbours' cultures and aspirations, we shall end up shamefully in our homeland and in those countries, as well as in Burma.

I do not want to talk about ASEAN or China, nor about Australia and the Pacific, which we also need to understand seriously. We should not only have dialogues with politicians and commercial people in this region. But we should also learn from the indigenous peoples of the Pacific as well as from the Whites who may only be serious about us economically, as there seems to be no genuine effort on the part of the Australian elites to understand our culture or our identity.

At present the Siamese elites seem to care only for power and money, as well as the material aspects of life. Most of them care nothing about social justice except by lip service. Some do social welfare work seriously, which means that the poor should remain where they are. They may be slightly better off, but they will not have a chance to decide their own destiny. Those who think they are in control of the country, whether they be in the army, the government, the civil service or in business, only work from day to day, solving one crisis after another in order to maintain the status quo.

None of them dream of our national identity, which should rebel against Western domination intellectually, even though of course we should learn from the West, as from Japan and China while keeping them at arm's length. We should first of all learn to be ourselves from the success and failure of our ancestors and we must understand our indigenous culture critically. We should build up the *baan* concept to be self-reliant, and it should be strong enough to safeguard itself from the *muang*, which has become the agent of the multinational corporations as well as consumer culture.

Luckily we have people who are now taking our spiritual tradition seriously and these people try to build up peace within as well as try to understand our society, both with its positive and negative elements. Then these people try to awake those at the *baan* level and to link them to the *muang* levels in order to understand the unjust system which enslaves us all.

We need to liberate ourselves spiritually and culturally as well as environmentally. Only when we are strong enough with our own spiritual and cultural identity will we be able to liberate ourselves from those who enslave us politically and economically. In 1932 the people did not really participate in the change of regimes to democracy. That is why the negative aftermath was possible clearly culminating in the period since 1939, the Thailand era. In 1973 the people did participate in popular demonstrations to get rid of the top leaders in the military dictatorship, but there was no opportunity to develop peoples' identity and culture in the political arena.

From now on we have to do things differently and non-violently, using success and failure from the past to guide us. Luckily, we have enough people in the various religious sectors and the NGO movements, so that Siam may perhaps find her own identity, which should be pluralistic, but must be just, peaceful and really democratic, i.e. it should be a SANTI PRACHA DHAMMA as envisaged by people like Pridi Banomyong and Puey Ungphakorn. Indeed the concepts of peace (*santi*), democratic participation (*pracha*) and justice or righteousness (*dhamma*) have been a positive contribution to our identity, especially from the commoners' perspective, going back before Pridi in the 1930s to intellectuals like Tienwan in the reigns of Mongkut and Chulalongkorn.

I hope these key concepts can be applied to present-day Siam and shape our future peacefully and justly for our own people as well as for our neighbours and other citizens of the world.

ENDNOTES

1. This keynote address was published in Bangkok in 1989 by the Thai Inter-religious Commission for Development as Occasional Paper 17 of the Santi Pracha Dhamma Institute. [Ed.]

2. The government referred to here was overthrown in late February 1991 by military officers who installed a civilian prime minister. [Ed.]

Chapter 3

STATE-IDENTITY CREATION, STATE-BUILDING AND CIVIL SOCIETY 1939-1989[1]

Chai-anan Samudavanija

The concept of the nation-state assumes the existence of national identity. It also reinforces the state's claims over other sources of loyalty and power in civil society. This enables states to have considerable autonomy and at times to formulate and pursue goals that do not reflect the demands or interests of social groups, classes, or society (Evans et al. 1986:9).

The development of the nation-state in Europe was conditioned by the rise of capitalism which in turn created and reproduced liberal democracy. The modern nation-states which emerged in Europe were therefore essentially 'modern' in all aspects — political, economic, as well as cultural. There was a connection between the rise of civil society and the exchange economy and the flourishing of scientific investigation (Gamble 1987:6). In other words, forces which gave rise to, maintain, and reproduce modern nation-states in Europe have usually been liberal with a great emphasis upon the desirability of being independent of the state and of curbing and limiting the centralized power of the state.

The rise of a modern nation-state in late nineteenth-century Thailand is in sharp contrast to that of the West, although technical aspects of Western civilization were utilized to systematize and centralize state power and its bureaucracy. The development of the Thai nation-state as an independent state having a non-liberal regime and a closed society with a dependent ethnic bourgeoisie is, therefore, much more complex than the development of the nation-state in the West. In the West the idea of the nation-state and state power can be subsumed under the same liberal-democratic rubric, and it is always possible to relate the character of the regime to the identity of the state. In the case of Thailand, as Ruth McVey rightly pointed out, the ideological enthronement of the nation-state was basically a matter between the king and the bureaucratic elite. The administrators did not need to mobilize the populace to their cause, and the king could not rally them to his because he had no means of reaching them save through the bureaucratic apparatus (McVey 1984:5-6).

Although the modern nation-state in Thailand was created to centralize state power, the nation-state building process did not essentially change the character of the state (its regime) or the identity of the nation. There was a serious attempt led by Prince Pritsdang in 1885 to propose such a change to King Chulalongkorn, but the security and stability of the throne achieved after the death of the Regent was perhaps the main reason that prevented the King from appreciating the necessity of forging an institutional link between the regime and the nation.[2] The Chakri Reformation in the nineteenth century resulted in structural change in the bureaucracy but left unresolved many substantive problems such as the plight of the people and bureaucratic inefficiency and corruption (Brailey 1989:73-99).

Under the absolute monarchy the nation-state was only a technical and administrative instrument of the regime. There was no need to build either a national identity or a state-identity since the identity of the nation-state or 'Siam-*rat*' was inseparable from the reigning monarch. It is not surprising, therefore, that state-identity creation and nationalism in Thailand became a separate process from democratization. In fact, bureaucratic and military elites have always sought to establish, maintain and reproduce a state identity separate from that of society in order to escape being encompassed by social forces. The creation of state-identity is, therefore, an artificial process intended to augment the capacity of the bureaucratic and military elites to prevent the emergent forces in civil society from controlling the state. It involves using the idioms and symbols of the state to legitimize its domination and self-aggrandizement.

State-identity building is guided by a state-creating class which is the official class whose major and primary interests and livelihood depend on the capacity of the state to manage and maintain its relative autonomy vis-a-vis civil society. In the context of peripheral countries where both capitalist and proletariat classes are normally weak the official class becomes the dominant intermediate class which seeks to utilize state power for its own purposes (Gramsci: 1978:409). The overdevelopment of the Thai state can thus be explained by analyzing the process of state-building on the part of the official class which was created by the Chakri Reformation. It is this class that has been striving to maintain its hegemony over civil society by utilizing various ideological and coercive methods.

It is the thesis of this paper that after 1932 the official class which captured state power from the ancient regime was confronted with a dilemma. Its 'revolution' was supported by an emergent bourgeois force which was largely ethnic Chinese. In the early stages of the new regime the role of this emergent bourgeoisie was tacitly recognized by the appointment of a number of Sino-Thai businessmen and Muslim leaders in the appointed legislature. Under constitutional rule, the state assumed a new character, and this essentially changed the identity of the state which, at least in theory, became inextricably linked with constitutionalism. The bureaucratic and military elites also rationalized and legitimised their newly acquired position by means of this ideology.

The commitment to constitutionalism presupposes an adherence not only to the rule of law and civil rights, but also to pluralism both in economic and cultural terms. Conflict soon arose within the new ruling elite as to its relation to other groups in society. Since the capitalist class was weak and dependent on the official class and the peasantry was scattered and unorganized, the official class was insulated from effective control by civil society. The absence of this control made it possible for the new ruling elite to develop gradually its own version of constitutional rule. Such an ideological departure culminated in the late 1930s, less than a decade after the establishment of constitutional rule when the new ruling elite succeeded in creating a new state-identity. This new state-identity, it will be argued, negated the principles of constitutionalism. It promoted centralization of state power and authoritarianism, resulting in a modern variant of absolutism. More importantly, it drastically changed the identity of the nation which had been pluralistic in nature under the name of Siam. The identity of the nation and the state became one under the name of Thailand while the character of the nascent constitutional regime and state also changed.

On 8 May 1939 the cabinet spent a mere ten minutes making a historic decision which had a tremendous impact on the identity of Siam.[3] Six men discussed an agenda proposed by Luang Pibul Songgram, the Prime Minister, to change the name of Siam to Thailand.[4] The three ministers who were not in full support of this change were Luang Pradit, Luang Thamrong and Chao Phraya Srithammathibet, but it was clear that Luang Pibul and Luang Vichit had already decided to change the name of Siam to Thailand and the three cabinet ministers who disagreed with them simply could not resist Luang Pibul's power to impose his will on them. Luang Thamrong argued that there were many races in Siam, and they were all loyal to Siam. If the name of the country was changed from Siam to Thailand other races would feel discriminated against, especially the Pattani people who were not 'Thai'. Luang Pradit only commented that the word 'Thai' was known only by Eastern historians, while 'Siam' had been familiar to Europeans since King Narai's time during the Ayudhayan period. Mom Chao Wan suggested that the government should issue a *ratthaniyom* or Cultural Mandate along the same lines as the *phrarachaniyom* of monarchical times.

The cabinet consulted the Legislative Adviser, R. Guyon, and it is interesting to observe that in his note concerning the change of the name Prates Siam to Prates Thai, Guyon concluded that there was no need for legal revision since the word 'Siam' was a customary word, not a legal word. In his words,

....there is no provision of law which has ever enacted that this country has the name of 'Siam'. There is none in the old laws. There is nothing to that effect in the constitution where the words 'Kingdom of Siam' (Sect.1) are used as a matter of fact, following the old custom, but there is nowhere said that this country must be called the 'Kingdom of Siam'.[5]

The point Guyon made is the one which I am putting forward in this paper, that Luang Vichit and Luang Pibul were using state power to legalize or bureaucratize custom and tradition. Guyon rightly pointed out that rules established by custom stood only as long as there was no statutory law to supersede them, but custom did not have to be expressly reiterated when a statutory law abolishing or modifying it was promulgated. He continued:

The new law, by the very fact of its existence, abolishes the custom. The consequence of this is that there is no need in the new law of a provision to the effect that the names 'Siam' or 'Siamese' are abolished.

As a rule, it is rather rare that the law of a country specifies the name by which the country shall be known, the reason being just the same as for Siam up to now, that is to say that the name is generally created by custom, and then used since a long time as a matter of fact.

But when a new country comes to existence, and has no old name by custom or has an uncertain name, it has been necessary in some cases to give a name to that country by statutory enactment.[6]

Guyon added that the change should be made by an amendment to the constitution because 'Amendments to the Constitution are important things, and should not be made unless for important matters. But the change of the name of the country is an important matter. It is an historical event, which practically initiates a new period in the life of the nation'.[7]   Guyon presented two drafts of the Constitution Amendment Act B.E. 2482 (1939), the first amendment to the 1932 constitution.[8]   Guyon did not live long enough to witness other changes which came after the first amendment he drafted for Pibul's government.

In this paper I will analyze Pibul's nationalism in terms of state-identity creation and state-building, rather than nation-building. Pibul's state-identity creation and state-building replaced constitutionalism with military statism.   It was an extremely important project which dramatically changed the character of the nascent political order.   It will be recalled that the ideological basis of the state and regime emerging after the 1932 revolution was a constitutional one.   The state mechanism, the bureaucracy, both civilian and military, had been patterned after the Weberian ideal-type which was, in principle, legal-rational, non-ethnic and was supposed to be equally accessible to every group in society irrespective of race or socio-political status. It was crucial for the new regime to maintain and propagate this myth at the initial stage of political consolidation, because the newly-established constitutional state was a negation of the ancient regime.   Although, the urban bourgeoisie lent its support to the People's Party, it was a civilian and military bureaucratic group that overthrew the old regime by a coup d'etat.   The predominant social and political base of the new regime was, therefore, the bureaucracy which had been absorbing progressive elements in civil society through a modern educational system and open, expanding civil and military services. The bourgeois element, mainly ethnic Chinese, was still small and had been subservient to the aristocracy for a long time.

The bureaucracy is not merely officialdom and an instrument of the state but is also a specific social and political entity. It is social to the extent that its values and behaviour have had a great influence on societal values. The Thai bureaucracy has not only been a major avenue of social mobility. It also acts as an important source of the socialization process. Its social character is most evident when entry to the bureaucracy marks the beginning of a continuing process of ethnic assimilation. A son of a Chinese immigrant will remain Chinese if he chooses to be a businessman, but once he enters the bureaucracy his ethnic identity disappears and he becomes a *kharatchakan* or civil servant. The bureaucratic Weltanschauung and the civil servant's former cultural background are naturally in conflict, resulting in a decision to embrace bureaucratic values in order to survive and prosper in the new social entity.

The bureaucracy is a *political* entity because it has always been the main power base of the state through which the state exercises its power over society. The bureaucracy existed prior to the constitutional order, and owing to this fact, we have to distinguish between *state* power and *political* power. The military and the civilian bureaucracy represent the state (they are the state within the state), and state power has been vested in laws, regulations and orders. State power elites create constitutions, so it is not surprising to see that many laws in Thailand exist even when they are in conflict with the constitution.

While the Thai bureaucracy possesses social and political characteristics, it has not been an important economic force in society. Immediately after the 1932 'revolution', Pridi Phanomyong (Luang Pradit Manudham), one of the coup leaders, attempted to link economic activity of peasants to the state by making them state employees, but such a proposal was misinterpreted as a communist-inspired scheme. In the late 1930s economic nationalist policies also reflected the official class's attempt to build an economic base for state power. However, it turned out that state power was more successfully utilized to build personal economic bases as is evident in the business empires of such post-war figures as Field Marshal Sarit Thannarat and Police General Phao Siyanon (Thak 1979).

The most important factor which prevented the bureaucracy from becoming an economic-oriented entity was the creation of a professional civil service as early as 1928 by means of the Civil Service Act. The civil service was patterned after the Weberian ideal-type organization with a strong emphasis on the separation of self-interests and state or common interest. Although these values are not upheld in real bureaucratic life, they nevertheless prevent a total personalization of the state, and they force state power elites to find other avenues and means to amass their wealth.

It should be pointed out that under the absolute monarchy the aristocracy and the bourgeoisie were not in conflict. Unlike the European experience, there was no confrontation between the Thai aristocracy and the Chinese bourgeoisie. On the contrary, both groups cooperated in capital accumulation. Confrontation between the two groups did not arise because the small Chinese bourgeoisie was mainly compradorial in its economic operations and performed useful functions as entrepreneurs and middlemen without posing serious challenge to political authority.

After 1932, constitutional rule did not activate forces in civil society to compete for political power. It restricted and restrained these forces by closing the political arena and prohibiting freedom of political association by not allowing a political party system to emerge. The Chinese bourgeoisie, who were set free from the old patron-client ties with the aristocracy, had no institutional means to develop their political potential. Although they were left alone to carry out their businesses, they lacked the opportunity to become an independent bourgeoisie because the new ruling class had its base of support in the state power structure rather than in civil society.

The new ruling elites were salaried officials who had to seek wealth to support themselves, and, later on, to distribute benefits to their various factions. They could not immediately use state power for their own benefit however, owing to the universalization of state power expressed in the ideology of constitutionalism. State power after 1932 was supposed to be impersonal, as against the personalized power of the ancient regime. State power was also supposed to shape society in a non-partisan manner. This meant that most organized and well-endowed groups in society were bound to benefit from the newly-constituted state.

The first identity established immediately after the 1932 revolution was not national identity but a purely political identity divorced from any cultural identity. Constitutionalism, as a system of rule, can not possibly be modified to safeguard any particular interest group, let alone establish the cultural identity of that interest group. As an ideology, constitutionalism and democracy posed a number of issues for the new ruling group, the most crucial of which were its implication for the distribution of power and a long-term transformation of economic power into political power. If constitutional democracy was allowed to develop fully, the new rules of the game would have allowed economic forces in civil society to capture state power gradually. In this sense, the constitutional democracy that was adopted by the official class as an ideological weapon against the old regime became a potential threat and a direct negation of bureaucratic power.

It was, therefore, necessary for state power elites to prevent the development of an independent bourgeoisie and the possible transformation of economic forces into political influence and power. The easiest way was simply to deny access of this group to the political process. This was possible by applying the criterion of citizenship, and it was legitimate to do so. A more serious problem was how to deal with this potential threat in the long run, since Chinese born in Thailand would one day become Thai citizens.

Two related problems then emerged to confront the Thai ruling elite. To what extent should the new regime allow the Chinese to accumulate wealth, and what would be the long-term implications for the distribution of power in society? Second, once constitutional rule was adopted, and under such rule individual and group rights and freedom were guaranteed by the state, how could the state effectively curb the influence of economically powerful groups which were not fully integrated into the cultural and political milieu of the bureaucratic state?

Within this new political context, direct political coercion was not possible, and such a policy would have had adverse effects on the economy. The state power elites had to devise a set of strategies and policies to deal with these problems. National identity propagated by King Vajiravudh from 1910 to 1925 became a liability for the newly constituted regime, because the concept would enhance the development of a national bourgeoisie in the long run once the Chinese economic force could find a broader non-ethnic source of loyalty in the democratic political system. If such a natural process of democratization was allowed to occur political parties would have become a new source of loyalty transcending ethnic identity. Under a strong party system ethnicity would have become secondary to concrete economic interests. But this new form of loyalty and political identity was not allowed to take root in Thai society. Instead, bureaucratic power elites created a state identity which was elevated above the political values inherent in constitutionalism.

Under the absolute monarchy there was no pressing need for the kings to establish any state identity, because such a policy would not have been effective owing to the inability of the center to impose its control over distant territories. Regional identities were, therefore, tolerated as long as they did not challenge the supremacy of the center. There was, however, a need to create a nation, although the identity of the state was never expressed in any specific racial or ethnic form. On the contrary, there had always been conscious attempts by the kings to utilize Buddhism and kingship as a common framework for the coexistence of various races and ethnic groups.

The state was given a specific *Thai* character in Pibul's period as a result of a combination of factors ranging from the desire to claim jurisdiction over other Tai races beyond the existing territory of Siam to the suppression of emergent ethnic Chinese influence in politics and society. It is not an exaggeration to say that since that time state identity and national identity have become synonymous with the emphasis on the superiority of the former. Once state identity was established, the state assumed a special place in civil society in the sense that *raison d'état* became an overriding force and was regarded as having a higher value than constitutionalism. At this juncture, there was a movement from universalism to particularism resulting in the shrinkage of both social and political space. The state could issue orders like the Cultural Mandates which otherwise would have been unconstitutional had the state not elevated itself above society.

The Chinese bourgeoisie was stripped of its opportunity to develop into a potent political force, because there was no other form of political relations it could enter into apart from the old patron-client networks. New forms of political loyalty did not emerge to capture economic forces, while institutional arrangements such as trade associations had always been severely controlled by the state since the Association Act was promulgated in 1914. Even after 1932, these associations were not recognized by law as political entities.

It is not surprising, then, that the Chinese who were marginalized had to resort to underground or secret associations to protect themselves. Others developed political links with the Kuomintang or the communists. In all cases their political relationships were considered illegal, external, and subversive to the state and the regime. The state had succeeded in externalizing these political forces, in effect identifying them as alien and 'un-Thai'.

It was also during this period of state-identity creation that an official version of culture and cultural norms was superimposed on popular culture and sub-cultures. The establishment of a Ministry of Culture and a National Council on Culture, passage of a series of legislative acts, and executive orders such as the Cultural Mandates reflected the priority the leadership assigned to state-identity building. This new bureaucratic structure was very effective in shaping a new Thai consciousness through a combination of legal and socializing instruments. The cultural aspect of state-identity creation which authorized appropriate cultural values and recreated a series of new *national* dances, plays, and songs was reminiscent of the monarchy's standardization of the Mahachart, or Great Birth Story of the Buddha, in the Ayudhyan period. In the same manner that King Trilok had authorized the court version *(khamluang)* of the Mahachart, Luang Vichit and Pibul consciously created an official version of Thai culture as the national culture.

It should be pointed out that in this period the new elites greatly utilized new technology of mass communication. The Department of Public Relations was established with modern broadcasting equipment. The state completed its control cycle by adding the operation of the only radio station to inform the masses — especially in urban areas — of its policies and propaganda. The influence of this new technology of communication became so strong that nationalistic feelings were effectively aroused through the broadcasting of martial and nationalistic songs as well as a dialogue program in which Mr. Man and Mr. Kong discussed nationalist policies and gave guidance to people on desirable behaviour. It is during this period that the identity of a good person became inextricably linked with the identity of a good Thai citizen.

Unlike King Vajiravidh, whose literary contributions were essentially his personal concern oriented at times to arouse national consciousness, the plays, songs and prose of Luang Vichit Vadhakarn were specifically produced to create a new state identity and to direct the process of state-building (Pra-onrat 1985; Pisanu 1986; Barme 1987). While King Vajiravudh's plays were performed within limited court circles, Luang Vichit's plays, songs, novels and essays were produced for mass consumption, especially the educated elite and urban population. Most important of all, the new national culture was embraced as the culture of the bureaucrats, as reflected in the practice of popular *ramwong* dancing among officials and their families, and the use of *ramwong* as the basic mode of party entertainment during the 1940s and 1950s.

The official version of culture did more than socialize the bureaucrats. It also set state-identity apart from popular cultural identities especially at the local level. Many popular traditions and cultures became 'folk' or 'sub-cultures' during this period and thereafter. At state functions official versions of cultural dances were performed and presented as genuine traditions of the Thai state.

It is important to note that this project of state-identity creation was a subtle synthesis of historical imaginaire and cultural diversity presented through stage performances as bourgeois entertainment. In this sense, the stage performances of Luang Vichit's plays and songs became a major form of cultural entertainment of the official and the small urban classes, replacing such traditional performances as *like* and *plengphuenban*. What Luang Vichit did was to create a cultural bridge between the official realm and the public realm. A Chinese who frequented Luang Vichit's plays, sang his songs, and read his novels and articles was, in effect, undergoing a transformation in cultural identity as important as the adoption of alms-giving. Thai state-identity and state-building were, therefore, both political and cultural. The state during this period took up new functions of depoliticization, bureaucratization and socialization simultaneously. Such functions have been inextricably linked with the state to the present day.

The official versions of national culture and national identity were constructs based on the creation of an historical imaginaire. It was during this period that the people were told of the origin of the Thai race. An official historical version of the Thai state was also created, and plays, songs and novels relating to the ancient kingdom of Nanchao, the putative homeland of the Thai, were produced. This historical imaginaire of the Thai state established a distinct and concrete community driven southwards by the Chinese. In the process, the Chinese became the enemy of the Thai state both in historical and contemporary perspectives. The idealized kingdom of Nanchao and the forced migration of the Thai races aroused nationalistic feelings of positive and negative effects at the same time: positive because it reinforced the pride of the Thai race as a people with a long cultural as well as political tradition; negative because it identified the crumbling of that kingdom with Chinese hegemony and militarism.

The identity of the state propagated by Luang Vichit and supported by Pibul transcended the old regime's historical imaginaire. It was asserted that there was already a kingdom before Sukhothai, the capacity to survive successive threats being symbolized by the ability of the leadership and the unity of the people. The decline and destruction of kingdoms were associated with corruption and the weaknesses of leadership or overpowering attacks and invasions from other races, or a combination of both. It is interesting to recall that during the period of political polarization in the 1970s messages in the songs played by state and military radio stations were very clear, namely, 'we can no longer retreat', and the present Thai territory is the last remaining on which the Thais must unite themselves to defend in order to ensure their own survival against the Chinese and the un-Thai activities of the communists.

The identity of the Thai state was enhanced by the nature of the threat which its elites defined for civil society. The threat to the security of the Thai state and nation was, therefore, linked not only to the *political* aspect of an ideology, but also to the *ethnic* aspect of that ideology. Communists in the 1940s and 1950s were either Vietnamese, Chinese, or Northeastern Lao, but never 'Thai'. Communism as an ideology has been regarded as a totally un-Thai enterprise, a negation of the livelihood, history and civilization of the Thai race.[9]

The Chinese were, of course, the most affected group in this process of adjustment. They were forced to abandon their identity at two levels. At the cultural level, they had to prove that they recognized, accepted and were willing to socialize under dictates of the state which established a set of criteria for its citizenry. More importantly, at the political level, they had no political option open to them. Many of them who were born in Thailand were not allowed to vote unless they possessed additional qualifications. They could not look for any other political identity within the constitutional framework apart from that offered by the state. The state ideology had no relevance for the enhancement of democratic values which the bourgeoisie could embrace as its political doctrine and capitalize on in order to capture state power. The new identity of the Thai state after 1932 was proclaimed by the constitution as a constituted state, distinguishing it from the old monarchical state, but constitutionalism was soon replaced by militarism and a cult of personality in Pibul's period. With the advent of communist and socialist ideas and parties, the identity of the Thai state became a staunchly anti-communist ideology with emphasis on the triad Nation, Religion, and King. In such a context, state ideology succeeded in removing politics from civil society and relocating it in the bureaucracy which became the main theatre of politics (McVey 1982). This process of relocating politics has resulted in different interpretations of politics and 'democracy' between the bureaucratic elites and other forces outside officialdom.

Owing to the lack of an alternative political source of loyalty and the absence of democracy, the problem of political identity in Thai society intensified in the late 1960s and early 1970s resulting in the 1973 student revolution. Because of this lack of institutionalization of the democratic system, activist political forces in Thai society found an alternative in socialism of the Maoist brand as evident in the 1973-1976 period. During that period, there were a series of identity crises especially among the younger generation, ranging from family relationships to the cultural, political and economic spheres (Morell and Chai-anan 1981).

The identity of the Thai state was challenged by these new forces on all fronts. The state power elites responded by making a series of attempts to revive the spirit of 1940s nationalism, which included the establishment of a National Identity Board. But in the 1970s, Thai society was buffeted by many pressures. It was beyond the ability of the state to arrest the forces of change as it had done in the 1940s by simply issuing Cultural Mandates or resorting to military statism a la Pibul or Sarit.

The communist challenge forced state power elites to embrace and propagate capitalism which resulted in a continuous rise in the power of the bourgeoisie. The communist threat also forced the state power elites to relax their bureaucratic control and seek an alliance with capitalist and middle classes. The media which had been under tight control by the Sarit regime was given more freedom after his death in the early 1960s and became an important source of social and political diversity in the late 1960s. The Chinese in Thailand in the 1970s became a 'positive factor' for development, and a Public-Private Consultative Committee was set up to promote economic development. Chambers of commerce were encouraged in all provinces. However, the rise of the bourgeoisie and its wider and more active participation in politics created grave concern among state power elites, especially the military, over the long-term implications of these changes. The stabilization of the semi-democratic system in the 1980s and the rapid democratization process which has taken place since 1988 made it possible for new forms of loyalty outside the state to emerge in civil society. The bourgeoisie have a new source of political loyalty which they can use to further their economic interests. Political parties thus became political institutions in which Chinese businessmen could identify themselves without having to show their ethnic identity. Political parties, elections and the legislative process therefore provide for new institutional frameworks in which ethnicity is not a factor. In this new political context, the names of political parties which are purely Thai (such as Chart Thai, Prachakorn Thai, Ruam Thai) and have no ethnic connotations serve as a legitimating instrument, transforming an otherwise Chinese bourgeoisie economic force into a non-ethnic political entity.

Since the 1970s the capitalist aspect of the economy has become a dominant factor in the Thai state. In this context of Thailand's becoming a Newly Industrialized Country, the identity of the Thai state has been dramatically changed. Civil society has become more heterogeneous where middle class forces continue to put pressure upon the bureaucratic state to respond to their demands. The contested terrain has been shifted from the attempt on the part of state power elites to dominate the political arena to the dynamic formation of alliances among strategic groups of which state power elites are but one element. In this context, it is not possible for state power elites to resort to the same old strategy of creating a separate state identity and using it to impose its will upon society. The only way state power elites can prevent the capturing of state power by non-state forces is to limit the growth of the capitalist economy, but this is impossible. The identity of the Thai state at present coincides with the identity of the extra-bureaucratic forces in civil society, and they will continue to reinforce each other as long as the democratization process is not disrupted. In other words, the democratic constitutional order makes it possible for the emerging middle class to develop its separate identity based on liberal democratic values which are basically different from the old state ideology.

Looking back at the early 1940s, we can conclude that it was during this period when the identity of the Thai state was created and served a number of functions for state-building.

(1)   It established hegemony of state power over civil society, especially vis-a-vis economic forces.

(2)   It strengthened and legitimized institutional power of the military in general, and the position of the army commander in particular.

(3)   It was the main instrument of state capital accumulation, resulting in the creation of a strong bureaucratic intermediate class (Ahmad 1985:43-46).

(4)   It established a clear and concrete historical imaginaire and a state ideology separate from the constitutional order to which citizens were obliged to sacrifice their freedom and liberty, both as individuals and as a group, to serve that imaginary identity.

(5)   It made possible a simultaneous application of social and political coercion to suppress and coopt potential challenges emanating from an economically powerful ethnic community by dispersing its cultural identity and solidarity which otherwise would have been politically consolidated.

(6)   It regulated state-society relations through specific codes of conduct and legal measures which clearly defined political and economic boundaries.

(7)   It made possible integration of the state, the nation, the regime, and leadership into one imaginary entity above constitutionalism.

The effects of state-identity creation under Pibul were pervasive and long-lasting. The Thai state had become an entrenched bureaucratic state with a specific identity imposed on civil society. It has taken more than four decades for civil society to gradually withdraw from this relationship and to question the bureaucratic *raison d'etre*, although it has yet to challenge and take control of state power. This lack of will to challenge and capture state power is a direct result of the socio-historical development of state-society relations in Thailand. Economic forces and local influences, although very strong and theoretically capable of becoming potent political forces at the national level, have in practice been restricted and denied access to the normal political process which has been authoritarian rather than democratic in character. Prior to 1978, when there was discontinuity in the participatory political system, economic forces at every level were channelled into the bureaucratic system if they wanted to be relevant actors in the state decision-making process. And because of the elaborate legal system pervasive in the Weberian organizational structure, extra-bureaucratic arrangements in processing surplus exchanges are not articulated through formal political institutions, but through mafia-like or patron-client networks.

It should be noted that, owing to the lack of democratization and political institutionization, certain sections of the economic forces gradually gained effective political power at local government levels, but there existed no democratic channel for their expression. Mafia-type power finally emerged as a modern variant of the secret societies that Thailand had known earlier in its history. The *chaopor* phenomenon has recently found its best ally in the democratic process where local influences and money are of vital support for party candidates (FEER 1991). The existence and pervasiveness of these 'dark influences' have posed a direct challenge to the state.

In most cases, dark influences are merely non-institutional marriages of state power and non-state power in the common pursuit of extracting economic rent from civil society. In some cases, these mafia-type influences develop to a point beyond the control of state power, and state violence has to be applied to suppress them, although not in a legal manner.

The legacy of Pibul's state-identity creation had, therefore, adverse effects upon the democratization process. The Pibul period lasted long enough and the application of state-identity over society was intense enough that they left a lasting memory on the 1940s generation of the military and civilian elite who became political leaders later on. It should not be forgotten that Thai politics between 1950 and 1980 was dominated by leaders who were influenced by the process of state-identity creation in the Pibul period.

What state-identity creation and state-building in the Pibul period did to civil society was to eliminate a potential link between the social-economic base and the state. To be more exact, the most advanced social and economic base in society was the Chinese entrepreneurial class which was demobilized and depoliticized during this process of state-building. The peasantry, which comprised the Thai and non-Chinese ethnic groups in the 1940s, was not the target of depoliticization, but it suffered the same fate because the military regime had become so personalized. Political mobilization in this period was essentially a pro-state enterprise aimed simultaneously at the propagation of the Thai identity of the state and at the cult of personality. This state-building project resulted in the elimination of an intermediate political class, or, to put it in more specific terms, the elimination of intermediate political institutions. The state had, therefore, a regime but no political system. The state fused its political power with bureaucratic power and used that power to discriminate against the bourgeoisie. It succeeded in preventing a natural emergence of a larger and stronger middle class and in delaying the development of a progressive and independent bourgeoisie. What the state had created, although unintentionally, was a peculiar extra-political, extra-bureaucratic class of 'influential people' against whom Sarit had to use extra-legal, extra-constitutional measures in order to control.

The mafia-type influence of *chaopor-nakleng* reemerged after the Sarit period when the state relaxed its authoritarian control but still blocked the development of bourgeois-democratic forces from entering the political system. It is not surprising, therefore, to observe that instead of the institutionalization of intermediate political organizations such as political parties, there has been an institutionalization of these extra-political, extra-bureaucratic influences. Because of their donations to various state-sponsored projects, these *chaopor* received royal dispensations, symbolically linking them with state power. Many of them were awarded and are wearing emblems of the royal guards. The *chaopor* and the *sia* have become local party bosses who sponsor electoral candidates or support party candidates. In recent years many of them have run in local elections. People like 'Sia Yae' of Angthong (Chat Thai Party), 'Sia Jew' and Kamnan Por of Chonburi (Social Action Party), and Sia Leng of Khonkaen (Ekaphab Party) are products of this peculiar socio-economic and political development. The dilemma of Thai-style democracy is how to transform these undesirable influences into legitimate political authority.

State identity-creation in the Pibul period was, therefore, not a mere imaginary exercise. It became so real and so 'natural' that the leadership of these emergent forces in civil society became mere power-brokers instead of daring to capture state power itself. By this I mean that one of the most important anti-political values invented by Pibul has been the identification of civil servants *(ratchakan)* with the sole and legitimate source of state-society management relations. The ethnic Chinese have been socialized to prevent their involvement in politics. Since they constituted the most important group in society with great potential to develop into a distinct political class, state-identity creation in the Pibul period naturally devised both an ideology and policy measures to exclude them from participation in the political process. The public sector in Thailand has, until recently, been identified with the *ratchakan* domain rather than a larger entity comprising both the bureaucracy and participant political institutions. Such a process had a similar impact on the general populace, although it offered a broader choice to Thais and ethnic Chinese who became Thais (through naturalization, adoption of Thai names and surnames, education in Thai schools and, most importantly entrance into the *ratchakan* system, both civilian and military).

While the political arena shrank as a result of this process, what has been continuously expanded and sustained to the present day is the extra-political, extra-bureaucratic domain, which exists independently of both bureaucratic and democratic frameworks, yet actively interacts with these entities. Forces in this extra-political, extra-bureaucratic domain have partially moved into the formal political process as democratic rule has gradually become more institutionalized. The outcry against 'capitalist influences', and attacks on *thanathippatai* (plutocracy), as well as a yearning for 'genuine democracy', 'power to the people' and so on, are all reactions of the state power elites (intellectuals and technocrats included) to the rapid merging of the extra-political, extra-bureaucratic influences with formal democratic institutions and processes both at the national and local levels.

The Thai-*ratchakan* identity of the state is thus undergoing a drastic and rapid transformation. Democratic ideology is essentially a bourgeois ideology, and the power base of this ideology is basically economic in nature. The *ratchakan* domain has shrunk in recent years while the private sector has greatly expanded. Traditional social identity such as religion and love for the monarchy are perhaps the only sources of power which can be utilized to counter the excessive and undesirable influences of capitalism. But it is doubtful whether these traditional loyalties can continue to be dominant values in a modern capitalist state. The bureaucracy is becoming more and more irrelevant, at least to those who produce goods for export. In this context of increasing globalization Thai state-identity will weaken unless state power elites are successful in regressing to the old concept of Thai-style democracy cloaked in the language of popular sovereignty or pure and absolute power of the masses. It is not unlikely that as Thailand moves towards a more export-oriented economy, there will be a revival of neo-Pibulism to counter this runaway internationalism.[10] Although it is not possible to recreate the same type of state-identity as that of Pibul and Luang Vichit, Thailand in the 1990s will surely face a serious national identity crisis which accumulated wealth and sustained economic growth can not sufficiently accommodate.

ENDNOTES

1. This paper is the first part of a larger study on the Development of Modern Entrepreneurs in Thailand's Regional Context, a research project of the Social Science Association of Thailand supported by the Asia Foundation.

2. See Pritsdang's Notes on Siamese Administration, Relations with Foreign Powers, and Life in the King's Palace in Brailey 1989:70.

3. Secretariat of the Cabinet. Minutes of the Cabinet Meeting No. 4/2482 Monday, 8 May 1939.

4. They were Major General Luang Pibulsonggram, Luang Pradit Manudham (Minister of Finance) Mom Chao Wan Waithayakorn (Adviser of the Prime Minister), Group Captain Thamrongnawaswasdi (Minister of Justice), Luang Vichit Vadhakarn (Minister without Portfolio) and Chao Phraya Srithammathibet (Minister of Foreign Affairs). The first Pibul cabinet (December 16, 1938 - March 5, 1942) was the ninth cabinet, and was composed of twenty-six ministers. Pibul also held the portfolios of Defence and Interior.

5. Minutes of the Cabinet Meeting, op. cit. The first Cultural Mandate was issued on 24 June, 1939 (Ratthaniyom No. 1, 'Name of the Country, Peoples and Nationality to be called Thai'). For discussion of the culture policy implemented by the Cultural Mandates see the introduction to this volume.

6. R. Guyon, 'Note concerning the change of the name Prates Siam to be Prates Thai' (June 18, 1939), pp. 1-2.

7. Ibid, p. 4.

8. The amendment to the constitution was passed by the Parliament on September 28, 1939.

9. It is significant to note that Luang Vichit's 'Research on the Tai races' was reprinted in 1961 by the Central Intelligence Department 'to be used in the official functions of the Department'. Luang Vichit at that time was serving as the chief adviser to Field Marshal Sarit, and it was during Sarit's rule that the Chinese Communist menace was 'recognised' by the ruling elite. Luang

Vichit's above-mentioned work became the 'bible' once again for Thai intelligence officers.

10. The tensions implied in this analysis surfaced in the military coup of late February 1991. [Ed.]

REFERENCES

Ahmad, Aijaz. 1985. 'Class, Nation, and State: Intermediate Classes in Periphery Societies' in Dale L. Johnson, ed., *Middle Classes in Dependent Countries*. Beverly Hills, Sage Publications.

Barme, Scott. 1989. 'Luang Wichit Wathakan: Official Nationalism and Political Legitimacy Prior to World War II.' M. A. thesis, Australian National University.

Brailey, Nigel, ed. 1989. *Two Views of Siam on the Eve of the Chakri Reformation*. Arran, Scotland, Kiscadale Publications.

Evans, Peter B. et al. 1986. *Bringing the State Back In*. Cambridge, Cambridge University Press.

FEER. 1991. 'Time for a Cosy Chat,' 'Shady Connections,' 'Chonburi Chieftain,' *Far Eastern Economic Review*, 18 April, pp. 25-30.

Gamble, Andrew. 1987. *An Introduction to Modern Social and Political Thought*. London, Macmillan.

Gramsci, Antonio. 1978. *Selections from Political Writings, 1921-1926*. New York, International Publishers.

McVey, Ruth T. 1982. 'The Beamtenstaat in Indonesia' in Benedict Anderson and Audrey Kahin, eds., *Interpreting Indonesian Politics: Thirteen Contributions to the Debate*. Ithaca, Cornell University, Modern Indonesia Project.

--------. 1984. 'Separatism and the Paradoxes of the Nation-state in Perspective' in Lim Joo-Jock and Vani S., eds, *Armed Separatism in Southeast Asia*. Singapore, Institute of Southeast Asian Studies.

Morell, David and Chai-anan Samudavanija. 1981. *Political Conflict in Thailand: Reform, Reaction, Revolution.* Cambridge, Mass., Oelgeschlager, Gunn & Hain.

Pisanu Sunthraraks. 1986. 'Luang Wichit Watakan: Hegemony and Literature.' Ph. D. thesis, University of Wisconsin-Madison.

Pra-onrat Buranamat. 1985. *Luang wichit wathakan kap bot lakhon prawatisat* [*The Historical Plays of Luang Vichit Vadhakarn*]. Bangkok, Thammasat University Press.

Thak Chaleomtiarana. 1979. *Thailand: The Politics of Despotic Paternalism.* Bangkok, Social Science Association of Thailand and Thai Khadi Institute, Thammasat University.

Figure 1:　Chinese hawker, newspaper cartoon, 1938.

Chapter 4

WHAT MAKES CENTRAL THAI
A NATIONAL LANGUAGE?

Anthony Diller

'Thailand' — a half-century-old linguistic construction — is an important instance of how shifting state policies and attitudes are signalled through a shift in language. But the new name 'Thailand' and its internal Thai equivalent *prathet thai* have not been mere signals useful to the state in advertising a particular political fabric; rather these names are 'in the cloth' as well. They work as parts of a larger pattern of meaning that interweaves language, mentality, political ideology, cartoons and even, on occasion, tanks and guns.[1]

INTRODUCTION: THAILAND, THAI AND THE TRACE OF SIAM

In 1939 when 'Thailand' (*prathet thai*) was to replace Siam (*sayam*) as the official name for the nation, intertwined projects included a press campaign of rather crude anti-Chinese propaganda. Ten months before the renaming of 'Thailand', the cartoon shown in Figure 1 had appeared in a Bangkok Thai-language paper, San Sayam. Visually, we are given a Chinese banana hawker. He is calling out the approximate Thai equivalent of: 'Nations for sale, nice and hot'. However, in Thai, the expression contains a near-transparent 'hypogram'.[2] The hypogram turns on a rather poignant play-on-words, because a standard way to say 'traitor' in Thai is *khon khai chat*, literally 'person - sell - nation'. Syntactically, the pattern is structurally the same as that used to refer to street pedlars, e.g. to a banana hawker: *khon khai kluai*.

The hawker then, through his stylized calling (confirmed by a formulaic phrase *mae oei*, the stereotypic 'pedlar's-call' closure) is both re-identifying himself as an economic type and proclaiming himself to be a traitor.[3] Perhaps additional interpretations can be allowed. In spite of the hawker's ungainly stride and crude appearance, he is no ignorant or harmless coolie. He is rather a more dangerous and clever traitor who shoulders the nation's economy (controlling its food supply) and who can pun with the language of those whose country he is trading in.

This particular cartoon, through its not-so-subtle hypogram, is helping to weave the pattern of Thai-centered mentality (or perhaps of Thai ethnic chauvinism, if one prefers). It is a portent for the name change in ten months' time: 'Siam' to 'Thailand'. The cartoon with its visual stereotyping and linguistic hypogram helps to bring out certain oppositions: non-Thai/Thai; traitor/patriot. 'Thailand' and *prathet thai* are to follow shortly as signifiers, adding more linguistic substance to these oppositions.

The oppositions established by the cartoon and similar texts are, in the case of the name 'Thailand', to be linked to an absent opposite: 'Siam'. 'Siam' is thus a crucial trace operating in the name 'Thailand'.[4] The name 'Siam', in one common reading, was to denote a tolerant and even pluralistic national polity. 'Siam' in this reading was a nation with a potential role for the Chinese and others, a role that could even include management of capital and resources.[5]

In the Thai Constitution of December, 1932, and in associated official documents, the nation's name was given variously in four forms (several of which had been in use earlier): (1) *ratchanacak sayam* (the 'Kingdom of Siam'), (2) *prathet sayam* (the 'nation of Siam') and, subjecting the above phrases to reversal of word-order following Indic compounding rules, (3) *sayamratchanacak,* and (4) *sayamprathet.* In the Constitution, the nation's citizens were referred to as *prachachon chao sayam* ('the Siamese citizenry'), not officially as 'Thai'. The name of the nation on postage stamps, coins and in similar contexts was simply *sayam* ('Siam'). As though to underscore the Siam/Thai contrast, the first national anthem played explicitly and repeatedly on the difference between *sayam* (the political/territorial unit) and *khon thai* (the Thais, signifying the dominant ethnic group).[6]

State control of names, along with media campaigns employing hypograms, metaphors and other tropes, would be cardinal examples of the political use of language to shape a particular frame of mind, a mentality that construes ethnicity along particular political lines. However, as suggested above, propaganda is but one side of the coin. Language itself — in this case, the Thai language — is an important (or perhaps the preeminent) *component* in the type of mentality under construction.

This means that language is here not seen merely as an arbitrary or neutral signalling device. It is not merely an efficient tool useful to those in power in putting forward political positions or in selectively transmitting information to mold the mentality of the citizenry. The name Thailand and the Thai language are interwoven even more tightly than this. Along with the Thailand name change, Thai as a language, and Central Thai in particular, must be seen as caught up in the system of Thailand/Siam traces and oppositions mentioned above. The Thai language cannot escape being an important part of what being Thai means in the sense specified by 'Thailand'.

How is it that these nuances have gone into the constitution of Central Thai as the dominant language of Thailand? To what extent in fact has Central Thai come to function as a national language, following the usual criteria associated with this term? The sections below examine the background of these questions and conclude that, for the linguistic variety called Central Thai, different senses of the term 'central' can be discerned. How these meanings are interacting at present both affects how Central Thai functions as the national language of Thailand and also sheds light on some wider aspects of current Thai social change.

THAILAND AND THAI AS A NATIONAL LANGUAGE

Especially during the period since 'Thailand' has been the nation's name, typical modern national-language functions of Thai have become ingrained and obvious; so much so, that to claim that 'Thai is the national language of Thailand' now sounds like a tautology, in fact. However, examining the claim more closely reveals important issues concealed by the seemingly redundant repetition of 'Thai'. As Smalley (1988a:246) observes, 'Thailand is a case study in linguistic diversity and national unity'.

It seems obvious that by comparison with India, the Philippines or even Malaysia and Burma, Thailand has had virtually no 'language problem'. There have not been language riots and linguistic policy issues seem largely academic; they are seldom treated as controversial by the local Thai press or debated by politicians. The single qualification to this statement might involve the Malay-speaking Islamic communities in Southern Thailand, but even here language issues are seldom isolated from more general cultural differences. The more parochial issue of foreign influence on Thai does receive some attention. Written Standard Thai lacks apparent competition in the sense, say, that Hindi, Tagalog (/Pilipino) or even Indonesian/Malay must confront competitor codes and must be defended by proponents from time to time.

THAI AND TAI

'The Thai language' as commonly used seems unproblematic in referring to some assumed, well-formed and cohesive linguistic entity. For many speakers, this entity might be reified in the distinctive symbols of the Thai writing system. However in practice

'Thai' (*phasa thai*) is not confined to the written medium. 'Thai' as a language name remains (usefully) vague and underdetermined.

By a Western academic convention now widely accepted, the spelling 'Thai' is used to refer to language varieties restricted to Thailand proper, i.e. to varieties located inside of the present national boundaries (rather arbitrary, as far as dialect criteria called 'isoglosses' are concerned). Regional dialects are differentiated by qualifiers: 'Central Thai' and 'Southern Thai'.

'Tai', on the one hand, generally refers to the greater family of which 'Thai', Lao, Shan, Ahom, etc., are members.[7] There is some quandary as to whether this term should be restricted to languages in which a term like Thai/Tai occurs as an ethnonym, or whether all languages related to the Thai language of Thailand should be considered in the 'Tai' family. A case in point would be the Zhuang and Bui languages of Guangxi and Guizhou. They are firmly related to Thai, but speakers do not use a word like Thai/Tai to refer to themselves. Yet these speakers have been classified in a 'Northern Tai' subgroup of the Tai family by Li (1977), and many linguists have adopted this nomenclature. On the other hand, it seems an imposition on these speakers, who number over 15 million, to call them 'Tai'. Even 'Lao' presents some problems of this sort, as Lao nationals do not normally call themselves Tai/Thai (unqualified).[8]

Recognition of the extent of the Tai language family, however named, outside of Siam/Thailand proper was an underpinning of a 'Pan-Tai' consciousness that was strong at the time of the 'Thailand' name-change and during World War II. In 1943 (Tai-speaking) Shan areas of Burma, Kengtung and Mu'ang Pan, were incorporated into Thailand with Japanese sponsorship. The name change, as Wyatt (1984:253) has pointed out, 'suggested a more than linguistic kinship with Thai- (or Tai-) speaking peoples outside the borders of old Siam.'

CENTRAL THAI, STANDARD THAI, BANGKOK THAI, AND SIAMESE

More specific terms like 'Central Thai' (*phasa thai klang*, or more often simply *phasa klang* - the 'Central Language') evoke their own particular tropes, traces and patterns of usage. For our purposes, it is sufficient to note that both 'Thai' and 'Central Thai' commonly refer to what speakers would typically identify as the dominant linguistic variety of Thailand. Thus *inter alia* these terms refer to Thai as a national language, as distinct from other languages or dialects that one might consider when analyzing the language situation in Thailand.

Certain national-language functions pertain to the highly normative version of Central Thai, which is closely linked to the codified written form of the language. This normative variety has recently been referred to as 'Standard Thai' (*phasa thai matrathan*) by academic authorities such as Nidhi Aeosriwongse (1984; the term is probably a calque based on English). Nidhi sees Standard Thai as deeply rooted in an earlier high form of Central Thai associated with class-based social divisions, but as having undergone a degree of egalitarian leveling over the past century due to print technology, mass education and changing political attitudes.

Mastering Standard Thai, which has a multitude of sub-styles - including *rachasap*, special royal-vocabulary substitutions — is one of the main tasks of formal education. At least in theory this codified linguistic variety is the language of bureaucratic administration and also of academia and of upper-strata print media. Commonly, and even in technical academic writing, *phasa (thai) matrathan* and *phasa (thai) klang* are used more or less interchangeably.

I propose to use these terms as follows. 'Standard Thai' (which in fact has sub-registers like 'bureaucratic Thai' or *phasa ratchakan*) is in a proper subset relationship with 'Central Thai'. The latter in turn is actually a class name referring to a set of phonologically- and lexically-determined dialects spoken mainly in the Chao Phraya River basin. 'Central Thai' is in a looser relationship with the more vaguely-determined 'Thai' (used as a language name). 'Thai' then can be used to mean either 'Central Thai', 'Standard Thai' or, very loosely indeed, to include other Tai varieties in Thailand.[9]

In fact, relationships involving Standard Thai are more complex, since the traditional Thai writing system (which Standard Thai is closely associated with) is to a large extent 'dialect neutral'. That is, it allows for different local phonological realizations.[10] This opens the possibility of non-Central-Thai oral readings of Standard-Thai written texts.

Standard Thai, taken somewhat narrowly, falls short of being the actual code used in much mass media and commerce. In fact, the extent to which 'pure' Standard Thai could function as a spontaneous conversational register at all is perhaps debatable, but issues of this sort tend to arise wherever standardized languages are discussed, especially when written/spoken registers are considered. For this reason it is useful to distinguish a register of colloquial spoken (Central) Thai. Brown (1967:xii) has referred to a type of such Central Thai speech as 'Bangkok Thai' and has taken the following initial consonants and clusters to be particular indicators:

Standard Thai	r	kr/l	kw	khw	khr/l	pr/l	phr/l	tr
Bangkok Thai	l	k	f	f	kh	p	ph	k

In fact Brown's 'Bangkok Thai' is a usefully extreme statement. It defines the end of a continuum characterized by different degrees of *r-* > *l-* substitution, cluster simplification and phonetic intermediates. This loosely correlates with sociolinguistic contextual variables, as Beebe (1975) and others have established. Other phonological criteria relating to the continuum are contractions (*yang-ray* > *yang-ngai* > *yangai* 'how') and similar sandhi-like tone- and vowel-length shifts.

Phonological simplification is but one feature of colloquial Central Thai. Lexical, syntactic and discourse-level features are also relevant in establishing the continuum. Another way to refer to it would be through a height metaphor sometimes used by Thai authorities. Thus one could refer to 'Low' or 'Lower Thai', following authorities who use 'high' (*sung*) / 'low' (*tam*) in their language-use characterizations. For example, many lexical pairs like *sunak* / *ma* 'dog' occur, where speakers regard one form as 'high' and the other as 'low' and treat usage of the forms in an associated manner.

In Thai, the more colloquial registers are referred to by a number of names: *phasa phut* or *phasa pak* ('spoken language'), *phasa talat* ('market language'), and so forth. These terms are not technical and do not even seem restricted to varieties of Central Thai. Also, some have used the term 'Standard Thai' in a generous sense (e.g. Smalley 1988a) as a relatively more educated or prestigious form of colloquial Central Thai. In this sense, Standard Thai could be naturally acquired by children as a first language (and in fact by Smalley's count, some 11 million speakers have done so; see Table 1). On the other hand the use of the term (or rather of its Thai equivalent *phasa thai matrathan*) by Nidhi Aeosriwongse (1984) and by other Thai educational authorities seems to apply to acquisition through formal learning and to preclude entirely non-formal acquisition.

TABLE 1.   SPEAKERS OF TAI VARIETIES IN THAILAND

Regional population (1983) (Theraphan 1985)		Estimates of Tai-variety native speakers (Smalley 1988a)	(after Keyes 1987)
North	**9,833,727** **20.1%**		
Kam mu'ang		3,500,000	20%
Northeast	**16,720,201** **34.3%**		
Lao (=Isan)		11,000,000	31%
Central	**16,246,796** **33.2%**		
Thai klang		12,000,000	25%
Standard Thai		11,000,000	
South	**6,046,203** **12.4%**		
Southern Thai (=Pak tai)		4,000,000	5%
(other) -			2%
Phu Thai			100,000
Lue		50,000	
Lao Song			25,000
TOTALS	**48,846,927** **(100%)**		
		41,675,000	83%

'Siamese' as a language name has a long history of use in Western-language writing as loosely equivalent to 'Thai', which has been widely used as well. Equivalency of the two names is explicitly indicated through the Latin word *sive* 'or' appearing in the title of the 1854 edition of the Pallegoix dictionary: *Dictionarium Linguae Thai Sive Siamensis.* More recently the term has gained some currency in linguistic work published in English. Tai comparative-historical linguists have used the term in a technical sense (especially with reference to comparative phonological systems) to specify Central Thai as opposed to other varieties, e.g. Southern Thai, Shan, etc. (Li 1977; Gedney 1980). Used in this sense it is a convenient way to minimize potential 'Thai'/'Tai' confusion.

'Siamese' as a linguistic term is now rare in Thai-language sources. In 1932 Prince Wan Waithayakorn gave a lecture in which he created the term *sayam-phak* 'Siamese speech' and also used the expression *phasa sayam* 'the Siamese language'. Both of these 'Siamese' terms were to specify a register similar to what above was called Standard Thai. His *phasa sayam* was especially characterized by much use of Pali-Sanskrit and Khmer loan vocabulary, which distanced it from *phasa thai doem* 'Ancient Thai' (cp. Proto-Tai of the comparative linguists). In the lecture he expressed the view that the name *phasa thai* 'the Thai language' could be confused with *phasa thai doem* 'the ancient Thai language'; therefore it was preferable to use 'Siamese' *phasa sayam* in referring to the modern national language of Siam (Wan Waithayakorn 1932). However, few followed this usage and at least by the time of the 'Thailand' name change, Prince Wan himself had abandoned it.

LAO (ISAN) AND OTHER TAI VARIETIES IN THAILAND

In broad terms, Central Thai is characterized by all of the main features usually ascribed to a 'national language' but one. In phonological organization, at least, it is not the first dialect actively learned by the majority of language learners of the nation. It is rather their second. Keyes (1987:15), using 'Thai' in the sense of 'Central Thai', says of native residents in Thailand that 'the large majority of those who speak Tai languages consider their domestic language to be other than Thai.' What Keyes has in mind by 'other than Thai' are regional dialects such as Lao (the 'Isan Language').

It is an ironic consequence of early nineteenth-century war-captive resettlement policies pursued by the Bangkok court that at present, by a number of good linguistic criteria at least, the first-learned language of Thailand with the most speakers could well be considered Lao. This language variety - or rather group of Lao-related dialects - is usually referred to as 'Isan', an Indic loan for 'Northeastern', by Thai authorities and increasingly by the population concerned themselves.[11]

In Thai non-technical discourse, local varieties of the Tai language family spoken in Thailand are usually identified by region. This is done by adding qualifiers (cp. 'Central', 'Northern', 'Southern', 'Northeastern') after the word *phasa* language / dialect. There is also more technical linguistic rationale for the resulting four-way general classification, including a good proportion of shared lexicon and certain distinctive vowel and consonant features. But this may be an oversimplification. Brown (1965) and others have identified over 50 local dialects which are distinct in terms of tonal phonemic system, so the four-way regional classification is at best rather rough. Determining discrete dialect boundaries for island-like Southern Thai is not difficult; for the other regional dialects, such boundaries are more problematic or even arbitrary.

Depending a good deal on particular linguistic features used in classification, one could estimate that just over one-third of local residents in Thailand speak Lao as their native or first linguistic variety. Slightly under that figure could claim varieties of Central Thai as theirs.[12] If it were one's purpose to dispute this claim, then one could easily juggle dialect-boundary criteria and come up with a different picture. For example, issues like how to treat the divergent Korat dialect (is it a Lao variety?) and just where to draw the Central/Northern-Thai line are subject to considerable interpretation. In this way, Lao (Isan) and Central Thai speaker numbers might either be made to coincide approximately, or else be made to diverge even more, depending on one's purpose.

Theraphan L. Thongkum (1985:31) gives an accurate break-down of regional population data for 1983, as shown in Table 1. These figures from the Chulalongkorn University Institute of Population Studies appear to include both native speakers of Tai varieties and also first-speakers of non-Tai minority languages. Many, but not all, of the latter eventually become partially bilingual in local Tai varieties as well. It is useful to compare these figures with somewhat different estimates of native Tai-variety speakers of Smalley (1988a:249) and of Keyes (1987:16). Differences in figures in Table 1 reflect both divergent criteria and time frames, and also point to a degree of more basic uncertainty which should be assumed in all current statistical estimates such as these. Note that by Keyes's estimates - and indirectly by Theraphan L. Tongkum - Lao should be considered Thailand's largest first-language variety. On the other hand, in Smalley's figures, the total for Central Thai (i.e what he refers to as *Thai-klang* plus his 'Standard Thai') would exceed the figures given for Lao.

Statistics for regional dialects and other Tai minority varieties are given extra complexity by widespread bi- (or tri-)lingualism in some border regions, particularly in Khmer-speaking areas of the Northeast (Smalley 1988a, b). Also, in Central Thailand, a number of transported Lao (and Black Tai or Lao Song) communities are still to be found speaking modified forms of original language varieties; for linguistic purposes, some groups perhaps should be removed from the 'Central' statistics and added to 'Northeast' ones.

NATIONAL LANGUAGE FUNCTIONS: A CHECKLIST

Apart from lacking universal first-language status, Central Thai (or where relevant, Standard Thai) has the main national-language credentials as normally recognized. In the following list, criteria are those expounded at length by Omar et al. (1987); application to the Thai case follows Prapart Brudhiprapha (1979), Nidhi Aeosriwongse (1984) and field observations of the writer.

(1) Aurally, census data and most other reports confirm that Central Thai is at least moderately-well understood by the great majority of native residents. The 1960 census (the last to include language questions) reported that 97% of the over-five-year-old population could "speak Central Thai". However there is clearly a great (but largely undocumented) variation in how well this 97% would speak Central-Thai.

(2) By most reports, somewhat over 90% of the population can read basic messages written in the Standard-Thai form of Central Thai.

(3) Central Thai is the official prescribed medium of instruction at all levels of public education.[13]

(4) With only minor exceptions, Standard Thai is the sole language of law and of official internal government business. Significantly, Standard Thai is the language of all internal legal codes and of the dozen or so constitutions which have been promulgated since 1932.[14]

(5) For most residents in Thailand who are native speakers of different non-Central-Thai dialects, but needing to communicate to one another, Central Thai would be the natural choice for interaction.

(6) It is the leading prestige dialect favored by professionals and other high-status individuals. It is thus the variety that most parents would like to have their children learn to speak well for reasons of social mobility and occupational security.

(7) Central Thai is the norm for 'impersonal' public announcements, especially when electronically amplified, even in localities where it is not the majority dialect spoken.

(8)   Central Thai is similarly the norm for many religious and other ritual purposes, even where it is not the majority dialect spoken. Up-country Buddhist sermons are routinely preached in Central Thai.

(9)   Central Thai accounts for the majority of print- and electronic-media communication, although in this case it is not exclusive.

(10) There exist institutionalized controls and bureaucratic means for enforcing Central Thai (i.e. Standard Thai) linguistic norms, although measures are rather benign and indirect when it comes to actual enforcement.

More importantly, the standardized form of Central Thai is widely conceived of as a crucial national symbol, particularly in its written form (Nidhi 1984:18).   It is an often-mentioned component of the Thai 'national identity' (*ekalak thai*) discussed in the other papers of this book.   The fact that Thai has its own distinctive written script should not be underestimated when assessing local attitudes towards national-language forms and functions.[15]

A good measure of this significance can be seen in the 'Ramkhamhaeng controversy'. The Ramkhamhaeng Inscription is traditionally taken as the first example of Thai writing, but this view has recently been challenged. What started out as a rather academic debate on philological detail relating to this inscription has aroused an astonishing degree of public concern and comment. Even the popular press has reported parts of the debate. One key allegation is that King Mongkut faked this inscription and is responsible for its writing system, which diverges in some respects from later Thai. It is noteworthy that Princess Galayani Vadhana, the elder sister of the King, has followed the debate closely and has arranged several well-publicised debates and discussions on the topic.[16]

THE DEVELOPMENT OF LANGUAGE STANDARDIZATION

Since 1939 various official organs and committees have been responsible for setting and maintaining norms relating to Standard Thai. However Thai language standardization has a prior development that could be seen as rooted in traditional Buddhist practice relating to Pali texts. The gradual deterioration (or 'entropy') of Buddhist knowledge and texts through time has been a widely-held teaching. To slow this natural attrition, Buddhist scholars have assembled from time to time to compare versions and issue purified recensions the Pali Tripitaka. These councils have typically been associated with the legitimation of royal power and have been sponsored by Buddhist kings; King Rama I called together such a council in 1788.[17]

As for the Thai language, in the Ayuthaya and early Bangkok periods most attention to language norms focused on correct poetic composition. Expertise in the various traditional meters and forms of traditional Thai poetry was the purpose of the first (extant, at least) Thai-language manual *cindamani*, probably written in the late seventeenth century. For the aristocracy, poetry was undoubtedly the most important expressive form that language could take. Attention was thus not turned to normalizing prose. In particular, spelling variation abounds in older prose texts: in inscriptions, legal codes, letters and diaries.[18]

Thus variation must have been tolerated in earlier Thai writing practice. However, as the printing of Thai gained momentum in the nineteenth century, King Rama IV (1851-68) became concerned in his writing over a new linguistic 'entropy', perhaps reminiscent of that of the Buddhist texts mentioned above. Missionaries sometimes published texts in 'lower Thai' — reflecting the speech of commoners - that offended the king.[19] He took direct personal interest both in printing and in establishing norms of the 'higher Thai' written language. At this time, then, Thai language reform and standardization became a royal interest as well as prerogative. The King issued explicit language edicts concerned with spelling, usage of prepositions, proper classifiers and other matters; certain words were proscribed, at least in the royal presence. This prescriptive activity set precedents for future language policy or even for linguistic engineering by later central governments.

Specifying norms in language might be viewed as among various standardizing symbols instituted to impart to the realm a nation-like central cohesion. The great clock tower the King had constructed in Bangkok to signal a nation-wide Thai counterpart of Greenwich Mean Time shows something in common with his norm-setting interests in the Thai language.

NORMATIVE GRAMMAR

Formal Thai language textbooks were introduced during the 1870s, and by 1905 a prescriptive 'Thai grammar' was prepared by educational authorities.[20] This specifyed rules for 'correct' Thai and was much revised and expanded during the next reign (King Rama VI, 1910-25), culminating in the three-decade masterwork *Principles of the Thai Language* (*lak phasa thai* 1919-37) of Phaya Upakit-silapasan (Nim Kanchanachiwa, 1879-1941).

If a sobriquet such as 'Champion of Thai Formal Grammar' were ever awarded, Phaya Upakit would be an obvious candidate. He was a commoner of modest background, who through a local monastic education, first in Dhonburi and later at Wat Suthat in Bangkok, showed great aptitude for language studies and skill in teaching. As a teacher at the prestigious Suan Kulap School, he was able to rise and join the ranks of the mainly princely educational hierarchy. In 1912 he was appointed to the *krom ratchabandit*, the department which was precursor to the Royal Institute mentioned below. In 1930 he become head of the Textbook Division (later *krom wichakan*) of the Ministry of Education, lectured at

Chulalongkorn University and was recognized as one of the leading academic authorities on the Thai language of his day. His impact on written norms is thus significant; also the colloquial spoken language has been affected by his work. For a start, according to one authority, he was responsible in the 1930's for the propagation of the polite forms *sawatdi* 'hello/goodbye', *kho'-thot* 'pardon me' and *kho'p-khun* 'thank you.'[21]

Principles of the Thai Language, which has been the model for succeeding Thai language textbooks, combined the normative tone and even many substantive categories of English traditional school grammar, but expounded categories and rules using Indic terminology. Very little overt English appears in the entire work, but every page reflects the style of contemporary Western school grammars. It relies quite heavily on a conception of a standard language as formulated through explicit but complex rules that need to be mastered. A context of institutionalized education is presupposed. For style of presentation, authorial tone, complexity, and occasionally explicit rules of grammar, *The King's English*, a standard school text in wide use in England by 1905, offers some close parallels.

Prospective teachers were the main readership of *Principles*. It figured crucially in their qualifying examinations. Extracts from it and related discussion by Phaya Upakit were regularly broadcast on radio in 1932-37.[22] Although some of its more cumbersome terminology and awkward constructions are no longer taught in schools, the notions of formal grammar as a school subject and centrally-controlled language norms are still crucial to understanding the current status of Standard Thai.

It is important to add that the rules in *Principles* and similar texts have a certain ornamental quality that are not always functional in a direct sense. Thus when Thai authorities characterize a linguistic expression as correct or, especially, brand it as incorrect, there may not be any specific, previously formulated rule that relates to the example at hand. Even when an error is identified by using an expression such as *phit lak phasa* ('wrong according to language principles'), often there is not in fact any relevant, explicily-stated rule in Phaya Upakit's *lak phasa* or in similar works covering the case in point.

The 'correctness' of Standard Thai then may actually be more a tacit or presupposed set of stylistic habits, probably mastered inductively through imitation of 'good examples'. Note that briskly-selling handbooks are available with sample Standard-Thai essays, letters, etc., to be memorized as exemplars for use in taking examinations. Rules of grammar, at least in earlier times, were learned in their own right to pass 'grammar' sections of examinations. They have seldom been seen as practical tools to arrive at acceptable sentences in compositions. Nor have such rules even been useful in establishing grammaticality through deductive principles. Perhaps for these reasons sections dealing overtly with grammatical analysis have been reduced or omitted in a number of recent examinations.

OFFICIAL DICTIONARIES AND THE ROYAL INSTITUTE

Probably the most tangible marker of language standardization is an official or authoritative dictionary. In the Thai case, dictionary compilation was started by missionaries in last century, with the Thai-Latin dictionary of Bishop Pallegoix (1854) being the first major work. The first dictionaries were to be tools for translation, not standardization. In 1927, Phaya Upakit and colleagues in the Textbook Department of the Ministry of Education issued a monolingual dictionary for school students. As its introduction warned, it was rather limited in scope and not intended to serve as a comprehensive or authoritative dictionary.

After the 1932 revolution, a number of language and cultural institutions were reformed into the Royal Institute (*ratchabanditayasathan*). In the official charter, proclaimed in

1934, European standard-language institutions were explicitly mentioned as prototypes, especially the French Academy and its related bodies set up in Hanoi and Pnom Penh. Interestingly, the charter also distanced the Royal Institute from the royal family, many of whom were in exile and disgrace in 1934.

Since its founding, the Royal Institute has had a variety of functions and affiliations with different ministries, leading to a degree of plurality in its objectives.[23]   In terms of language standardization, its main impact has been through the 1950 official Royal-Institute *Dictionary*, compiled under the leadership of one of the foremost scholars of Thai language and culture, Phaya Anuman Rajadhon, a commoner of Chinese background. A new, moderately revised edition was issued in 1982. The latter volume is considered authoritative by most Thai educators as far as lexical matters are concerned. On the other hand, it is hardly thought of as sacrosanct; academics often challenge specific entries and some authorities, such as Sulak Sivaraksa, have heaped scorn on the entire volume.[24]

LANGUAGE REFORM AT THE TIME OF THE 'THAILAND' NAME-CHANGE

The beginning of the 'Thailand' period is noteworthy for a remarkable series of projects of state-controlled linguistic engineering in some ways reminiscent of the language decrees of King Rama IV. Although both programs sought to control language norms by legal decree, the series of reforms during World War II were more sweeping in scope and effect, although short-lived. Also, the rationale of Phibunsongkhram in the 1940s was arguably opposite that of King Rama IV. In the interpretation of Nidhi Aeosriwongse (1984:31) the earlier royal concerns were designed to defend the threatened usage of the elite, while those of the 'Thailand' era were, in design at least, to be popular simplifications which would result in a uniform national language more accessible to the less-educated masses. Objectionable linguistic coding of status distinctions was to be discontinued. Central Thai was to be learned and used by all.[25] The resulting simplified national language would therefore foster general literacy and the government's rather Fascist conception of cultural uniformity and economic progress. Phibunsongkhram later claimed the reforms were undertaken at the instigation of Japanese advisers.

In practice these goals involved some contradictions. As Nidhi (1984:31) observed, the policy of rigorous enforcement of Central Thai during this period as the national medium of instruction did not take account of the fact that numerically the majority of the nation's school-aged speakers would speak non-Central dialects (e.g. Lao) natively. The policy naturally led to increased difficulty in schooling on the part of upcountry students. The burning of materials written in Northern Thai script, including Buddhist texts, did nothing to win local popularity for the language reforms. (Singkha Wannasai 1975:8).

As mentioned above, central control of naming (such as 'Thailand' and the Chinese name decrees) was an important manifestation of the new policies. Similarly, bestowed titles were banned and given names had to be gender-specific. Following on the 'Thailand' change was a decree of 2 August 1939 discontinuing expressions such as 'Northern Thai' and 'Southern Thai' that might have been seen as having decentralizing or fragmenting tendencies, as though one could eradicate a dialect by eradicating its name.

Astonishingly, as part of the Phibunsongkhram linguistic engineering program, pronouns were also legislated in the same context of centralized uniformity, as were final particles. The pronominal paradigm was to conform to an Indo-European-like model distinguishing 1st, 2nd, 3rd, singular/plural pronouns. Thus the traditional Thai personal reference system in which other distinctions were important, e.g., sex of the speaker or deference toward the addressee, was overturned.

The particular forms selected for 1st and 2nd persons - *chan* and *than* respectively - had potentially incompatible nuances, *chan* normally indicating informality and lack of deference toward addressee, but *than* indicating just the opposite. According to contemporary reports, speakers felt awkward about using the forms as prescribed and few did so in private. In the controlled press, novelists would cease writing serialized stories rather than submit to government censors who would change their pronouns thereby changing personal relationships and characterizations.[26]

The greeting *sawatdi*, originally conceived in the 1930s by Phaya Upakit, was ordered to be used by all civil servants when they met one another each morning. It was intended that usage would spread to the general population in this way.[27] Another means of spreading language reform in the spoken medium was through the state-controlled radio.

Spelling was also 'simplified' in that the number of consonant letters of the alphabet was reduced from 44 (including 2 obsolete) to 31; vowel signs were reduced as well. The intended effect was for Indic-provenance (especially Sanskrit-derived) vocabulary to be spelled in a way somewhat more in accordance with how native Tai-provenance vocabulary was written. Even the Thai spelling of the nation's new name, *prathet thai*, was slightly affected, with the final consonant in *prathet* modified. However, since the simplification did not go all the way to a one-to-one sound-writing phonemic representation (as Lao had experienced under the French), there was uncertainty as to how the spelling reform was to be put into practice, although all newspapers and other printed media were expected to conform. One confusing result of the simplified spelling - one which dogs phonetic spelling reforms generally - was the falling together of words that formerly had been spelled differently.

Phibunsongkhram's language reforms were drawn up in May 1942 by a committee of nine, including (Luang) Wichit Watthakan, (Phaya) Anuman Rajadhon, (Prince) Wan Waithayakorn and the Prime Minister and his wife. The spelling and pronoun reforms came to an end with the downfall of Phibunsongkhram's first government two years later.[28] Most reforms were not reinstated when his second government was formed in April, 1948. 'Thailand', of course, was reintroduced. Also, Central Thai remains dominant in the school system and *sawatdi* has become a widespread, although rather urban, greeting.

CENTRAL THAI AND SHIFTING SENSES OF 'CENTRAL'

The preceding sections raise a question as to the key senses of 'central' in the linguistic label 'Central Thai'. In this final section I argue for a polysemous approach to interpreting the term 'Central Thai'. The polysemy is an index of changing conceptions of what Thailand and being Thai may be coming to mean.

It is useful first to review some points relating to Central Thai recently raised by Nidhi (1984), Sulak (1987), William A. Smalley (1988a) and others. Smalley presents an elegant analysis of 'Thailand's hierarchy of multilingualism' through a Venn-diagram-like arrangement of overlapping linguistic varieties. He also uses 'Standard Thai' in a superordinate sense as the 'internal language of Thailand'; here we use the same term to refer to a more normatively-defined linguistic variety.

A somewhat different way to proceed, but one that arrives at similar conclusions, is to consider the richness of meaning that the term 'Central Thai' can have when it appears in writing on Thai language matters. A hint of polysemy in the term *phasa klang* (Central Thai, or more literally, the 'Central Language') can be seen in the definition for *klang* in the 1982 official *Dictionary*:

the part which is not inclined toward (*kho'n*) any particular side; by extension, an intermediate place or interval, e.g. *klang-fon* 'amidst the rain'; central nexus (*thi-ruam*), as for an operation that has branches,e.g. central office, central post office.

According to this definition, *klang* admits semantic values associated with English notions like 'centre, core, nexus' and also like 'intermediate, in-between, neutral'. Note that English words 'mid, middle' admit a similar sort of range. Compare the different senses of: 'middle of a target' versus 'middle *ring* of a target'.

In Thai, lexical compounds with *klang* are a useful tool in elucidating polysemy. To begin, the expression *phak-klang* ('region' + 'middle') is virtually a proper toponym referring the the 'Central Region' of Thailand. Next, compound expressions such as *sun-klang* (Sanskrit 'centre' + Thai 'central') or *cai-klang* ('heart' + 'central') are used to refer to a central core or nexus, perhaps to a 'nerve-centre' of controlling power. In this semantic value for *klang*, the focal centre is contrasted with a receding arrangement of layers, sub-levels or branches, often terminating in a periphery with attenuated power. *Klang* in this sense is frequently encountered in Thai discussions of government, bureaucracy or of large commercial operations. As in the dictionary example, the *samnak klang* of an organization is the 'central headquarters' where leadership and responsibility reside and from which power in the form of norms and rules emanates. This *klang* is hierarchical and seems to have a nuance of absolutist power.

A third contrasting set of compounds emphasizes neutrality and commonality or sharing. A *khon-klang* ('person' + 'middle') is an intermediary; *pen-klang* ('be' + middle') means not to take sides in an argument; *kha-niyom-klang* refers to 'common or shared social values'. This *klang* seems inherently more 'egalitarian' and less normative than the preceding one, a 'lowest common denominator' in other words.

Smalley (1988a:258) has observed that *phasa klang* "means both 'language of the (geographic) center' and 'central' in the sense of 'normative'." To this can be added the third sense of 'intermediate' or 'common'. Thus three semantic contributions of *klang* can be distinguished that give rise to three readings of *phasa klang* :

1. 'Central$_1$ Thai' in the geographical sense of the dialect(s) of the central region of Thailand - the lower Chao Phraya basin and surrounding areas;
2. 'Central$_2$ Thai' in a sense of normative language (Standard Thai) imposed and controlled from the centre of authority;
3. 'Central$_3$ Thai' in the sense of the intermediate or shared variety, similar to a *lingua franca* or *koine*.

Phasa klang in the Central$_2$ reading of *klang* conceives of Thai as a prescribed code emanating from the centre of Thai administative power. This is the linguistic entity that King Rama IV attempted to hone and polish through his language edicts. It was 'the King's Thai' enforced through decrees with a focal centrality. In times prior to 'Thailand', Nidhi (1984) sees this type of language as based in traditional class divisions. It would have been associated with aristocrats and other elite members of society. The language associated with traditional literacy and with the older elites (but probably not what they actually spoke in informal circumstances) gave rise to the code that Phaya Upakit codified in his grammar to what Prince Wan called *sayam-phak,* and to what we have referred to as Standard Thai in a restricted normative sense. The strong connection with writing and with the Royal Institute official *Dictionary* should be kept in mind.   •

Phasa klang in the Central$_3$ reading of *klang* would account for a more colloquial or common range of speech, perhaps even closer to what was called 'Bangkok Thai' or 'Lower Thai' above. *Inter alia,* this would be the natural functional medium of spoken communication for educated Thai speakers from different dialect regions. In many cases, even educated speakers sharing the same non-Central dialect communicate with each other most easily in Central Thai.[29]

Returning to the 'national tapestry' view of language, we are now in a position to discern three of the 'hues' or semantic threads in the linguistic strand referred to as 'Central Thai.' I argue that these have intertwined in ways that have rendered the hues sometimes more blended-together, sometimes more discrete. In the language policies of Phibunsongkhram at the beginning of the 'Thailand' period the three semantic threads are tightly braided together. The language of the Bangkok area (Central$_1$ Thai), through the regime's Cultural Mandates, is to be the standard (Central$_2$ Thai) imposed on the entire nation from the centre nexus of political power. The imposition involves the suppression both of non-Tai languages and of non-Central dialects through state censorship, compulsory education, mass media, the burning of objectionable texts, etc. The relevant laws and strictures issue from the central authority or *phu-nam*, the (uncomfortably autocratic) 'leader'.

On the other hand, in substance, the language ordered for nation-wide use has been subjected to a series of 'simplifications' such as spelling reforms, pronominal compressions, and so forth. In a provocative interpretation of these changes by Nidhi (1984), the reforms are seen as a sincere attempt at creating a less elitist and easier-to-learn Thai variety. In the terms above, this would be the engineering of a form of Central$_2$ Thai (a simplified norm) more appropriate to serve as Central$_3$ Thai (a common language for all citizens). If this view is correct, then language policy of the Phibunsongkhram era was in effect a tight braiding together of all three of the potential 'centrals' of Central Thai. The more common view is to dismiss the 'outlandish' language reforms as yet one more unmotivated episode along with silly laws about hats and gloves for which Phibunsongkhram is often derided.

What of subsequent developments? To trace the convolutions of Central$_2$ Thai first, with the issuing of the official *Dictionary* in 1950, the lexicon of our current version of Standard Thai became codified. This fixing of the orthographic form of the language undid the Phibunsongkhram reforms with a vengeance that restored, and even created anew, etymologically learned spellings. These were replete with Indic silent letters and enforced an extra distinction, only vague in earlier practice, between Pali-based and Sanskrit-based orthographic patterns. Forms were to be 'correct' (i.e. etymologically motivated) often at the cost of being difficult for non-experts to spell. Based on formal writing norms and *Dictionary* spelling, the 'correct' top end of a stylistic continuum has become firmly established as Central$_2$ Thai. By and large, in spirit, if not always in letter, the *Dictionary* represents a return to the standards of 'the King's Thai'[30].

Institutionally, the older guardians of language norms, the Royal Institute and the schools, have recently been joined by the influential Radio and Television Administrative Committee or *ko' bo' wo*[31] The latter committee oversees spoken, and also written, language broadcast over public airways and has been known to legislate down to quite detailed areas of linguistic usage.[32] Occasionally higher government units take direct linguistic action. On 12 January 1988 the Prime Minister's office issued a proclamation warning the bureaucracy to pronounce /r-/ and /l-/ distinctly and also to give full articulation to the clusters of Standard Thai, as distinct from the simplifications of Colloquial Thai or 'Bangkok Thai'.

The Prime minister insists that his suggestions concerning pronunciation are to be strictly observed by all government officials. Government officials must be careful in their pronunciation and their use of Thai which is the national language... Superiors at all levels should advise and warn their subordinates in this matter.[33]

It is clear from the Prime Ministerial concerns that even senior civil servants are subject to lapses from pure Standard Thai or what is referred to as 'the national language' (i.e. Central$_2$ Thai). It is undoubtedly 'Central Thai' in the sense of Central$_3$ Thai that they are 'guilty' of using instead. In this they are joined -if we follow the 1960 census - by the 97% of the nation that 'speaks Central Thai'. The spread of Thai elementary public education combined with the influence of film and especially of electronic media have to a large extent realized one facet of the language policy of the 1940's, but this has been through the spread of Central$_3$ as a medum of mass communication, with Central$_2$ in effect unattainable as a practical *spoken* code by all but a small linguistically self-conscious elite minority.

It is interesting that this Central$_3$ Thai is partly a matter of a set of phonological simplifications of Standard Thai / Central$_2$ Thai, but they are not the particular orthographic simplifications specified by the 1940's reforms. In a recent development, popular novels, commercials and other unofficial writing more and more are attempting to represent natural-speech forms - contractions, particles, tone-shifted pronouns, non-*Dictionary* lexemes, etc. These are common in substandard Central$_3$ Thai speech. The Thai writing system is especially conducive to indicating phonetic detail of this type through manipulated spelling.[34]

Thus the written form of the language no longer seems to be the exclusive domain of Central$_2$ Thai. Observers such as Sulak Sivaraksa (1987:87) and conservatively-inclined educational authorities may decry this trend and, using terms like *phasa-wibat* and *phasa-an-wipharit* 'corrupt/contorted language', express opposition to some or all of these new usages.[35] Debate sometimes employs the phraseology of 'linguistic entropy' introduced above, perhaps to be linked to Buddhist predictions of doctrinal and textual dissolution. A set of tropes or comparisons is often encountered. Some expressions involve notions of impending deterioration (*su'am*) on the one hand and the need for cherishing and caring for (*thanu bamrung raksa*) on the other. Similarly to be found are expressions of purity (*khwam-bo'risut*) and defilement; also of defence (*po'ng-kan*) and incursion. In these tropes, Central$_2$ Thai becomes, for purposes of discourse, either a virgin about to be defiled (viz by Central$_3$ styles of Thai or by 'English influence') or a country whose territory is about to be breached and overrun.

However, these innovative applications of the traditional writing system to represent non-Standard features of Central$_3$ Thai speech, as well as the associated debates and reactions, have close parallels elsewhere. They follow a path not uncommon in the shifting mores of written language generally, that of increasing 'vernacularization' or rather of greater tolerance for representing natural or unscripted spoken language as one particular type of writing. This type of writing may then gain status associated with new prose genres.[36] Probably electronic technology such as the cassette tape recorder, allowing convenient transcription of interviews as commonly printed in Thai periodicals, has had some effect on this general trend. A related debate in Thai academic circles would appear to malign the dignity of Central Thai somewhat by a bold hypothesis that phonological simplifications characteristic of Central$_3$ Thai, such as cluster simplification, are based on an eighteenth-century 'Chinese-accent' pronunciation of a then-current form of Central$_1$ Thai. Argument over this issue continues.[37] Whatever linguistic plausibility the proposal may be eventually shown to have, the possibility of the debate itself is of interest in showing that Thai academics are willing to see in 'Central Thai' some problems to be analyzed if not some assumptions to be 'deconstructed'.

Finally, even Central$_1$ Thai, the dialect(s) of Central Thailand, has also come in for attention and differentiation. In Thai university linguistics departments, local subdialects of Central-region Thai, such as those of Suphanburi, Ratburi, etc., have come under scrutiny and been described in detail. Several have been shown to differ considerably from the particular version of Central$_1$ Thai basic to the colloquial form of the national language - to what we have monolithically labeled Central$_3$. Along with this has come the suggestion that 'Bangkok Thai' is a 'dialect', i.e. that this version of Thai is merely one structural variety among others. Its special position is owing to the fact that it has achieved preeminence for external reasons: war, politics, television, etc.[38] It is not through its own internal structures or on its 'linguistic merits', such as through any inherently privileged relationship to Thai writing.[39]

This recognition has marked Thai university work in linguistics in the 1970s and 1980s. As a part of a more general movement called *tho'ng-thin-niyom,* perhaps to be translated 'localism' (with a touch of 'local pride'), academic interest has increasingly turned to serious study of other regional dialects. Regional and local 'cultural centres' have sprung up. Local academic institutions such as teacher-training colleges and up-country branches of universities have arranged seminars on local history and culture. Dialect dictionaries have been compiled and published. In a remarkable development, Lanna (Northern Thai) script shows signs of rehabilitation, albeit abetted by tourism, that might even result in its revival as a practical means of written communication.

Also, there appears to be underway a subtle shift in the functional range considered appropriate for local dialects. In some cases, public situations that a decade ago would have required Central$_3$ Thai (or even normatively-correct Central$_2$ Thai) now admit local varieties. A number of recent novels have made extended and consistent efforts to represent local non-Central dialects in print. Radio and television broadcasts in local dialects are common and acceptable. On the other hand, some Central-oriented authorities such as the soldier-scholar Prasong Sunsiri (1983:150) have expressed reservations about *tho'ng-thin-niyom* :

In addition to Central Thai, there are local dialects of the Thai language. At present there is a movement to allow a greater role for local dialects. An example is fostering the use of Lanna (Northern Thai) script and the study of regional literature in local dialects. This may be beneficial in preserving local dialects as part of the national heritage, but it should not be to the point of allowing *tho 'ng-thin-niyom* or *phak-niyom* (feelings of local or regional pride), since our nation must have a high degree of unity at this time.

It is interesting that according to the Sixth Economic and Social Plan (1987-1991) a substantial degree of economic decentralization is projected. Twenty-four up-country cities and towns have been selected to become 'regional centres of progress' (*mu 'ang sun-klang khwam-caroen nai phumiphak*; Wirot Sararattana 1987). Those selected can look forward to a high level of infrastructure investment. Linguistically, this new use of the term *sun-klang* 'central/focal' for locales *other* than Bangkok, along with related economic policies, may be instructive: is there anything here in common with the movement of *tho 'ng-thin-niyom* 'localism' of concern above? In any case, one linguistic effect of the economic policies can be predicted: regional urban dialects, such as the Southern Thai 'urban hybrid'[40], will increase considerably in functional significance, with local *koine*-like attributes similar to those of Central$_3$ Thai nationally.

The history of Central Thai as a national language during the 'Thailand' period could be summarized as both an increased local discrimination of, and a partial innovative re-braiding of, these component threads in Central Thai. During the Cultural Mandate period, an attempt to propagate a 'simplified and progressive', but contrived and unpopular, national code was associated with a state-defined version of 'Thai culture'. This was unified and imposed from the centre, but the propagation was only partially effective. Since 1944, a heightened discreteness in the linguistic threads, the different centralities of Central Thai, can be progressively discerned. Thai educators, academics, authors, media journalists and even citizens with less interest in language *per se* have become aware of the linguistic richness and variability - that is to say non-uniformity - of the present-day Thai communicative context.

A climate of secular commercialism, where special language must be 'manufactured' to sell commodities on television, is contributing but one among many new speech genres. There are increasingly varied ways of speaking and printing Central Thai, as well as ways of head-lining, bill-boarding and pop-singing it. In non-Central areas, with or without economic decentralisation, the *tho'ng-thin-niyom* mentality is clearly on the ascendant, and with it, a somewhat new status for local dialects, local scripts or regional linguistic hybrids. But can they compete with Japanese cartoons dubbed into Central Thai on after-school T.V.?

Reactions to 'language pollution' caused by these developments, including censorship measures of official committees, must not be overlooked. Nor should one downplay a national education system surprisingly effective in spreading at least the rudiments of the standard written language. All of these linguistic threads still combine as the Thai language strand in what might be called the tapestry of Thai national identity (*ekalak haeng chat*), but the language strand seems more complex and variegated now than it did fifty years ago. This perceived complexity lies partly in the eyes of the observers. In particular, an increased interest in and awareness of linguistic variation is evident on the part of Thai language authorities. Increasing complexity also characterizes the observed linguistic data, as witnessed by new styles or genres of Thai taking shape or new attitudes and functions attanced to older forms.

At the same time, a degree of uncertainty and ignorance in how Central Thai (Central$_1$, Central$_2$, Central$_3$, ...) is actually acquired and how it functions in present-day Thailand must be frankly admitted. There are calls for more statistics, field research and analysis. Official census reports have not included language questions for several decades. Estimating numbers of native speakers of Thai regional varieties remains problematic.

In the near future, Central Thai will surely *not* be de-centered as Thailand's national language - quite the reverse - but the connotations of its centrality, what it means to be 'central' as well as 'Thai' in the national texture of the next decades, is already acquiring a new semantics of traces and oppositions. Although 'Siam' itself may be left behind as an outmoded trace, vernacularization, localism and and new language attitudes (some even reminiscent of the older 'Siam') can no longer be avoided in considering Central Thai as a national language.

ENDNOTES

1. The Thai National Research Council has kindly facilitated field research reported here. My particular thanks goes to Scot Barmé for making this cartoon and materials relating to its context available to me. This paper has also benefitted from discussions with other contributors to this volume, and from Wilaiwan Khanittanan, Preecha Juntanamalaga and Banyat Ruangsri. Craig Reynolds has kindly spent much time and effort in relevant discussion and in improving the text. Defects and questionable views undoubtedly remain in the paper and are my responsibility.

2. Riffaterre (1978) has used this term to refer to an idiom-like subtext that would be understood by a knowing reader.

3. For more on 'oei', see Diller and Junatanmalaga, forthcoming.

4. Derrida (1981:26), nearly paraphrasing Saussure (1959:120), explicates the notion of trace through recourse to the weaving metaphor used above: "this interweaving results in each 'element'...being constituted on the basis of the trace within it of the other elements of the chain or system. This interweaving, this textile, is the text produced only in the transformation of another text. Nothing, neither among the elements nor within the system, is anywhere simply present or absent. There are only everywhere differences and traces of traces."

5. The expressions *phuang-chon chao sayam* or simply *chao sayam* were formerly used to mean 'Siamese' in a legal sense implying citizenship. (See Wan Waithayakon 1932:38).

6. The anthem starts by juxtaposing the expressions phaendin sayam ('the land of Siam') and khon thai ('the Thai people'). In this regard, it is peculiar that some Western scholars have claimed or implied that 'Siam' never appeared as the the the official Thai-language name of the nation. (See Preecha 1988:80.).

7. Unfortunately 'Tai' or 'Tay' has also been used to refer to particular varieties as well, e.g. to one spoken in Vietnam. The Romanized Chinese version of the term is 'Dai', which in China refers to specific speakers in Yunnan, not to the entire family.

8. One meaning of the cognate of *thai* in Lao is 'person, inhabitant', (cp. chao in Thai), so one Lao might refer to another as *thai-ban*, lit. 'person-village', hence 'villager' (Kerr 1972:648). In Thai, the original spelling of *thai* was , later altered to the present form   By Thai current academic convention, the older spelling usually refers to the language family (although occasionally it is used for this). Hence Thai =   , Tai =   ,

9. 'Tai' in this sense follows Fang-Kuei Li (1977), who subclassifies most varieties in Thailand, Laos, Burma, and nearby as belonging to the Southwestern Branch of the Tai family. Hartmann (1980:86) further subclassifies this branch, placing Central Thai in the Lower Subdivision of the Southwestern Tai.

10. Brown (1965:136) called attention to this ability of up-country speakers (or readers); elsewhere (Diller 1979) it has been taken as the basis of a local 'urban hybrid' form of speech. Since Central Thai has gone through sound changes subsequent to the fixing of spelling patterns, in certain features the traditional orthography represents non-Central dialects more closely than it does the normal Central-Thai phonological realization of Standard Thai.

11. The term 'Lao' as applied to language varieties spoken within what is now the Thai nation proper is found widely in Thai literature, e.g. in the poem Khun Chang Khun Phaen, where the term refers to people in the Chiangmai area. In the interests of establishing national unity, this use of 'Lao' has been discouraged since the time of King Rama V. Prince Chakrabongse, in the reign of Rama VI, campaigned vigorously against using 'Lao' for Thai subjects or allowing Lao script to be used; he was also opposed to other regional dialect designations (Vella 1978:200). Thus the later views of Phibunsongkhram, as explained in the introduction to this volume, had clear predecents. Today, one hears the claim that 'Isan' refers to local Northeastern dialect material written in Thai script, rather than in Lao script.

12. Among Thai language authorities writing in Thai, Nidhi Aeosriwongse is one of the few to observe that 'the Isan language is the language of the majority of [Thai] citizens'(1984:31). Also, granting these definitions, far more speakers of 'Lao' would live in Thailand than in Laos. Increasingly, Lao/Isan is a significant linguistic component in the Bangkok metropolitan area. Note that Northern and Southern Thai native residents account for over ten million non-Central speakers.

13. Limited supplementary instruction in, Malay, Chinese, etc. is not currently prohibited, and special exceptions are made for English-medium 'international' institutions.

14. The official or bureaucratic sub-register of Standard Thai is called *phasa ratchakan*, 'civil-service language'. Up-country oral contacts, e.g. in a district post office or train station in Southern Thailand, are frequently conducted in the local non-Central dialect especially when interlocutors are personally-acquainted local people. In the present decade, political campaigning is increasingly heard in non-Central dialects.

15. Also, Thai has lacked a unified officially-enforced Romanization system. Instead, a number of systems and practices compete, even in official documents. The Royal Institute Romanization may be a standard system in theory, but it is not such in practice; e.g. it is not normally taught in schools. It is not impossible that some in authority have fostered this 'chaotic' situation precisely to discourage Romanization as a viable alternative to traditional script for writing the Thai language. Similarly, Thai authorities have opposed missionary transcriptions of hilltribe languages based on Romanization. All of this goes to show the strong sense of national identity felt to reside in the traditional script.

16. For example, she presided over a panel discussion held at the Thai National Library in April, 1990.

17. A recurrent figure in Southern Thai folklore is the learned Buddhist monk who saves the Thai kingdom through accurate knowledge of Pali texts.

18. Modern printed editions of older texts almost always standardize spelling. An authentic source documenting widespread spelling variation in 1685 is the handwritten diary of Kosapan, the Thai ambassador to the court of Louis XIV.

19. See also Nidhi (1984:23) and Sulak (1987).

20. Elsewhere (Diller 1988) more of the early history of Thai formal grammar is summarized.

21. This is stated by Ingorn Suphanwanit (1984:86), who notes a Chulalongkorn University lecture (27 February 1935) in which Phaya Upakit urged all prospective teachers to propagate these forms in schools. There had been some use of *kho' thot* a decade earlier in plays of Rama VI. (B.J. Terwiel, personal communication). As Phaya Upakit (1937) himself observed in a brief essay extolling use of the form *sawatdi*, it originally had occurred as a formulaic

phrase opening inscriptions, and thus seemed to him an appropriate form to be extended as the Thai counterpart of hello-like expressions in Western Languages.

22. A regular radio program called — like the later book — *lak phasa thai* ('Principles of the Thai Language') was organized in 1932; the presenter was a well-known authority, Phra Worawetphiset (Niphon Suksawat 1981:119-122).

23. An Etymological Commission (*niruktisat samakhom*) was set up in 1907 to maintain language standards. As it consisted of four leading princes who, as Vella (1978:239) notes, were 'extremely capable but extremely busy men', little language planning work was actually undertaken. This commission seems to have been eclipsed, in the reign of King Rama VI, by language projects of the king himself, and also by two subsequent associations (*samosan*) he founded: one for literature and one for antiquities. These both had linguistic duties and, according to Sulak (1987:27), they became under Rama VII a 'Royal Council' or 'Royal Academy' *ratchabanditaysapha*, led by Prince Damrong. Prince Bidyalankarana was active in the Academy's censoring of objectionable prose. The post-Revolutionary Royal Institute (*ratchabanditayasathan*) was at first led by Prince Wan Waithayakorn and was charged with the creation of a standard dictionary. Since its founding, a degree of bureaucratic quandary is evident in how the institute has been shuffled between the Prime Minister's Office (from 1942), the Ministry of Culture (from 1952) and the Ministry of Education (from 1958), with periods of comparative autonomy (before 1942 and after 1972; see Royal Institute 1986). Duties mentioned in the Institute's current official act (1986:2) are decidedly nebulous (e.g. 'exchange of knowledge with other academic bodies') and do not even specify language standardization or dictionary-making.

24. Sulak (1987:131) sees the dictionary as a 'mediocre product with hardly any improvement on the 1950 edition' and considers the Royal Institute to be 'perhaps...in a declining state beyond redemption.'

25. One interpretation of this attempt at linguistic leveling might be to see the policies as a widening of opportunities for non-Central citizens of the nation. In this view, the 'Thailand' name change and associated laws might have ... 'downplayed the central Thai-speaking (Siamese) role in the life of the nation' (Wyatt 1982:253), even though Phibun's 'dicta required Thai to...use the national language as opposed to local dialects...' (255). This interpretation would hardly have been shared by Northern Thais whose books were burned; see below.

26. A leading novelist of the day, 'Do'k Mai Sot' (M.L. Buppha Nimmanhemin), wrote, 'I must cease writing because I am unable to use the pronominal forms and particles in my dialogues as the Prime Minister's Office has ordered. To have a child speaking to a father using chan 'I' and than 'you' goes against my feelings and is unbearable.' (Pluang Na Nakhon 1983:43). Similarly, 'Mae Anong' (Malai Chuphinit) wrote, 'If some part of my story is simply cut out, I can accept that, but changing the personalities of my characters along with their mode of conversation, dress, or where they are living — that is tantamount to killing off the whole story' (Trisin Bunkhachorn (1978:163).

27. See also Note 21. The decree was promulgated on 24 January 1943, making the headline of the paper *Thai Mai.*

28. Probably the current norm of *than thang lai* for a collective second-person plural pronominal ('you' in large formal gatherings) is attributable to the Phibunsongkhram policies.

29. In this sense, one sometimes hears it said in Thai that 'English is the *phasa klang* of the world'.

30. In fact, the 1982 edition of the *Dictionary* includes much colloquial and even dialect material (marked as such) and sometimes allows more than one spelling for a given word. Some have even criticised this edition for being too descriptive.

31. *Khana kammakan borihan withayu kracai siang lae withayu thorathat.*

32. Seri Wongmontha (1983:38), in a critical vein, cites controversial decisions on the proper equivalent expression for 'condensed milk' in Thai and how the Thai loan-version of 'strawberry' must be pronounced. One particular translation into Thai of the advertising slogan 'power-press detergent' and another expression meaning 'to remove pimples', both from an English-based source texts, have been censored by the committee, because they were too foreign-sounding.

33. Translation as in Pornpimol Senawong (1989:313). Note that the (then) Prime Minister, Prem Tinasulanonda, was himself a Southerner whose native dialect has a natural and pervasive r/ l distinction.

34. Limited experiments of this sort, using the writing system to represent more spoken styles of Thai, actually go back many years, perhaps to the plays of King Rama VI.

35. 'Certain words, when spoken, do not sound the way they are written, e.g. ...*khao* (written as though rising tone), spoken as *khao* (pronounced high tone)...One should keep in mind that when we speak, we can pronounce [words] in any manner at all, but when we write, we must spell according to the original form' (Panya Borisut 1983:308). This attitude, that written Thai is rule-governed but that Thai as a spoken language is a corruption of 'original' (orthographic) lexemes (*sap doem*) and thus entirely lacking rule-governed order is commonly heard among Thai educators (i.e. among those innocent of linguistic training). Although the claim that Thai orthographic forms are 'original' might be patronizingly dismissed as a quaint but unscientific folk model, in fact the notion is not without a measure diachronic validity, as opposed to claims about an ontogenetic acquisition process.

36. In the English-speaking context, one thinks of Mark Twain, James Joyce (and even of Gertrude Stein), whose revolutionary 'misuse' of Standard English is now read unremarkably as 'literature'.

37. See Charnvit Kasetsiri (1984), who states the hypothesis and Thakoeng Phanthakengamon (1989), who questions it.

38. Suppose that Nakhon Srithammarat (or Korat, Chiangmai, etc.) had become the preeminent seat of Thai power after the Burmese destruction of Ayutthaya in 1767. What would be the national language today?

39. Vichin Panupong of the linguistics department of Chulalongkorn University was an early leader in advocating this position. In 1970 she contended — provocatively, for that time — that in certain (but not all) respects, modern Southern Thai dialects are in a more direct relationship with the traditional orthography than Central Thai is. (See also Brown 1965).

40. This is a mixed local prestige variety, essentially using Southern Thai tones and Central Thai vocabulary and segmentals (Diller 1979). Economic development in the South has already fostered this hybrid variety, which can be easily understood by non-local people.

REFERENCES

Aim-on Truwichian. 1983. 'Address Avoidance in Thai', *Journal of Humanities*, Chiangmai University, 3, 31-40.

Angkab Palakornkul. 1975. 'A Sociolinguistic Study of Pronominal Usage in Spoken Bangkok Thai', *International Journal for the Sociology of Language*, 5, 11-42.

Anon. 1905. *The King's English*. (Compiled by a committee under H.W. Frowde.) Oxford Clarendon Press.

Beebe, Leslie M. 1975. 'Occupational Prestige and Consonant Cluster Simplification', *International Journal for the Sociology of Language*, 5, 43-62.

Brown, J. Marvin. 1965. *From Ancient Thai to Modern Dialects*. Bangkok, Social Science Association Press of Thailand.

--------. 1967. *AUA Language Center Thai Course*. Bangkok, American Universities Alumni Association.

Charnvit Kasetsiri. 1984/2527. 'Samniang thai samai ayutthaya rattanakosin (Thai pronunciation in the Ayutthaya and Rattanakosin periods)', *Silapawattanatham*, 9.9.

Derrida, Jacques. 1981. *Positions*. Chicago: University of Chicago Press.

Diller, Anthony. 1979. 'Tones, Segments and Thai regional society', in *Studies in Tai and Mon-Khmer phonetics and phonology in honour of Eugenie J.A. Henderson*, edited by Theraphan Thongkum, et al. Bangkok, Chulalongkorn University Press, pp.60-93.

--------. 1985. 'High and low Thai: Views from Within' in *Papers in South-East Asian Linguistics No. 9: Language Policy, Language Planning and Sociolinguistics in South-East Asia*, edited by David Bradley. *Pacific Linguistics*, A-67, 51-76.

--------. 1988. 'Thai Syntax and "National Grammar"', *Language Sciences*, 10.2, 273-312.

Diller, Anthony & Preecha Juntanamalaga. Forthcoming. 'A Pragmatic Pagadigm: the Case of Thai "oey" Expressions', *Journal of Pragmatics*.

Gedney, Willian J. 1980. 'A Siamese Innovation'. Paper presented to the International Sino-Tibetan Conference, no. 13. University of Virginia, Charlottesville.

Hartmann, John. 1980. 'A Model for the Alignment of Dialects in Southwestern Tai', *Journal of the Siam Society*, 68, 72-86.

Ingorn Suphanwanit. 1984. 'Nae nam khru phasa thai: phraya upakitsilapasan (Introducing a Teacher of the Thai Language: Phra Upakitsilapasan)', *Warasan Phasa lae Wannakhadi*, 1.2, 80-88.

Kerr, Allen D. 1972. *Lao-English Dictionary*. Washington, D.C., Catholic University of America Press.

Keyes, Charles F. 1987. *Thailand: Buddhist Kingdom as Modern Nation-State*. Boulder, Colorado, Westwiew Press.

Kosapan, Chaophraya Kosathibodi (O'kphra Wisutsuntho'n). (1686) 1986. 'Banthu'k raiwan (Diary notes)', *Silpakorn*, 30.4, 31-95.

Li, Fang-Kuei. 1977. *A Handbook of Comparative Tai*. Oceanic Linguistics Special Publication No. 15. University of Hawaii Press.

Nidhi Aeosriwongse. 1984/2527. 'Phasa thai mathathan lae kanmu'ang (Standard Thai and politics)', *Phasa lae Nangsu'*, 17.2, 11-37.

Niphon Suksawat. 1981. *Wa duai ru'ang baeprian phasa thai (Concerning Thai Language Textbooks)*. Srinakharinwirot University, Phitsanulok.

Omar, Asmah Haji (ed.). 1987. *National Language and Communication in Multilingual Societies*. Kuala Lumpur, Dewan Bahasa dan Pustaka Kementerian Pendidikan Malaysia.

Pallegoix, Jean Baptiste. 1850. *Grammatica Linguae Thai*. Bangkok Assumption College.

Pallegoix, Jean Baptiste. 1854. *Dictionarium Linguae Thai Sive Siamensis; Interpretations Latina, Gallica et Anglica Issustratum*. Paris, Jussu imperatoris impressum. Repr. Farnsworth, England, Gregg International Publishers, Ltd.

Panya Borisut. 1983. 'Wikhro' kho'bokphro'ng kho'ng kanchai phasa thai nai patcuban (An error analysis of modern Thai language usage]', in Samnak soemsang ekelak kho'ng chat (1984:306-316.)

Pin Malakun. 1969/2512. 'Kansu'ksa samai thi mahamat ek phrawo'rawongthoe phrongchao thaniniwat song pen senabo'di krasuang thammakan, (Education when Prince Dhani was head of the Ministry of Instruction) in *Ru'ang kansu'ksa (About Education)*] Funeral volume of Amat Tri Luang Prasitkam. Bangkok, 1973/2516, pp. 23-38.

Pluang Na Nakhon. 1984. 'Khwam kiao kho'ng rawang phasa lae sangkhom (The Interrelationship of Language and Society) in Samnak soemsang ekelak kho'ng chat (1984:276-280).

Pornpimol Senawong. 1989. Sociolinguistic Aspects of Transference from English to Thai. Ph.D. thesis, Monash University.

Prapart Brudhiprabha. 1979. 'Languages of Thailand', in *Papers on Southeast Asian Languages*, edited by T.A. Llamzon. SEAMEO Regional Language Centre, Anthology Series 5. Singapore, Singapore University Press, pp. 293-307.

Prasong Sunsiri. 1983. 'Phasa thai lae khwam mankhong haeng chat (The Thai Language and National Security) in Samnak soemsang ekelak kho'ng chat (1984:245-251).

Preecha Juntanamalaga. 1988. 'Thai or Siam?' *Names, Journal of the American Name Society*, 36.1, 69-84.

Rama IV, King. (1862) 1973/2516. *Prachum Prakat Ratchakan Thi 4 (Collected Edicts of King Rama IV)*. Bangkok, Cremation Volume of Phramahaphothiwongsacan Inthachotthera.

Ratchabanditayasathan. (The Royal Institute.) 1982. *Photchananukrom chabap Ratchabanditayasathan (Royal Institute Dictionary)*. Bangkok, Ratchabanditayasathan.

Rennick, Robert M. 1970. 'Nazi Name Decrees of the Nineteen Thirties', *Names, Journal of the American Name Society*, 18, 65-88.

Riffaterre, Michael. 1978. *Semiotics of Poetry*. Bloomington, Indiana University Press.

Samnakngan Soemsang Ekalak Kho'ng Chat. 1984. *Phasa thai kap sangkhom thai raingan kansammana wa duai phasa thai nu'ang nai kanchaloemchalo'ng 700 pi laisu' thai pho' so.' 2526. (The Thai Language and Society: Report of a Thai Language Seminar Held in 1983 to Celebrate 700 Years of Thai Script)*. Bangkok, National Identity Board, Office of the Prime Minister.

Saussure, Ferdinand De. (1915) 1959. *Course in General Linguistics*. New York, Philosophical Library.

Seri Wongmontha. 1983. Transcribed seminar discussion printed in: Samnak soemsang ekelak kho'ng chat (1984:35-38).

Singkha Wannasai. 1975/2518. *Tamra rian akkhara lanna thai (Manual for Sstudying Lanna Thai Script)*. Chiangmai, Humanities Faculty, Chiangmai University.

Smalley, William A. 1988a. 'Thailand's Hierarcy of Multilingualism', *Language Sciences* 10.2, 345-262.

--------. 1988b. 'Multilingualism in the Northern Khmer population of Thailand', *Language Sciences*, 10.2, 395-408.

Sulak Sivarak. 1987/2530. *Kanchai phasa thai kap khon run mai. (Thai language Usage and the Younger Generation).* Bangkok, Suksit Sayam. Originally published: *Matichon Sutsapda* 28 December 1986 ff.

Thakoeng Phanthakoengamon. 1989/2532. 'Noe: sane ru' saniat thang phasa (Accent: Linguistic Charm or Jinx?)', *Silapawatthanatham*, 10.3, 110-117.

Theraphan L. Thongkum. 1985/2528. 'Minority languages of Thailand', in *Science of Language Papers*, 5, 29-74. Bangkok, Department of Linguistics, Chulalongkorn University.

Trisin Bunkachon. 1978/2521. *Nawaniyai kap Sangkom Thai (The Novel and Thai Society).* Bangkok, Suksit Sayam.

Upakit-Silapasan, Phraya. 1918. 1937/2480. *Lak Phasa Thai (Principles of the Thai Language).* Bangkok, Thai Wattanaphanit.

Vella, Walter. 1978. *Chaiyo! King Vajiravudh and the Development of Thai Nationalism.* Honolulu, University of Hawaii Press.

Vichin Panupong. 1970. 'Kho'khit kiaokap kanriak chu' lae kanbaeng akso'n sam mu (Thoughts on the naming and division of three classes of letters), in *In Memoriam Phaya Rajadhon.* Edited by Tej Bunnag and Michael Smithies. Bangkok, Siam Society.

Wan Waithayakorn, Prince . 1932/2575. 'Phathakatha ru'ang sayamphak' (Lecture on the Siamese Language), in *Pakinaka phim thawai nai wara khlai wan prasut prachansa khrop 80 kho'ng phontri phrachaowo'rawongthoe krommu'n narathipphongpraphan (Lectures Printed for the 80th Birthday Felicitation Volume of Wan Waithayokorn).* Edited by Sathian and Wiwan Sathiansut. Bangkok, n.p. 1971/2514.

Wilaiwan Khanittanan. 1979. 'How much is English influencing the language of educated Bangkok Thais?' in *South-East Asian Linguistic Studies*, Vol. 4. Edited by Nguyen Dang Liem. *Pacific Linguistics*, C-49, 55-9.

Wirot Sararatana. 1987/2530. *Sara samkhan phaen phatthana setthakit lae sangkhom haeng chat chabap thi 6 pho'so' 2530-2534 (Important points in the Sixth National Economic and Social Development Plan, 1987-1991)*. Bangkok: Aksonbandit.

Wyatt, David K. 1984. *Thailand: A Short History*. New Haven, Yale University Press.

Chapter 5

THAI NATIONALISM AND IDENTITY: POPULAR THEMES OF THE 1930S

B. J. Terwiel

Throughout the 1980s the business of promoting Thai culture has been a conspicuously thriving concern. Large organisations, such as the Department of Fine Arts, the Prime Minister's Office and the Department of Education have set up foundations and commissions specifically designed to publicize and foster a positive appreciation of Thai culture. *Ekalak thai*, the newly-coined word for 'identity', became a trendy topic in academic conferences.[1] It was immediately adopted in folklore studies and is now a regularly recurring theme in tourist promotion schemes. The coining of the word *ekalak* and the enthusiasm with which this new term for identity has entered the Thai language may at first give the impression that the awareness and promotion of the concept of identity is a relatively modern development, a recent evolution in the broad field of Thai nationalism. However, the preoccupation with the question 'Who are the Thais?' and 'What does the Thai culture stand for?' has been part of Thai nationalism throughout the history of this movement. In this essay, the way these questions were addressed in the early 1930s is examined.

The study of the early stages of Thai nationalism has been made difficult because the phenomenon is commonly described as one that occasionally arose under the inspiration of a particular head of state, disappearing with the death or loss of office of that individual, only to arise, sometimes decades later, in a new shape when a ruler — such as Field Marshals Phibun Songkhram or Sarit Thannarat — again made it a prominent part of his political platform.

A good example of this standard 'on-off' description of Thai nationalism can be found in Thak's *Thai Politics, 1932-1957*. In this valuable source book on mid-twentieth century Thai political history, Thinaphan Nakhata has edited the documents for the years 1939-1947. He characterises this period under the heading National Consolidation and Nation-Building, and his chapter begins with the following sentences:

> A major political phenomenon between 1939 and 1947 was the attempt to build nationalism in Thai society. Previously, such an attempt was undertaken during the reign of Rama VI....
> (Thak 1978)

Two widely-held assumptions underlie this statement. One is that the attempt at nation building under Rama VI halted with his death in 1925. The second assumption is that in 1939, after fourteen years of neglect, the attempt to build nationalism was taken up again.

These assumptions are based, consciously or unconsciously, upon the idea that Thai history can be meaningfully periodized in the rise and fall of particular individuals (in this case Rama VI and Phibun Songkhram). While politics may indeed respond to such centring upon certain individuals, it is here submitted that the history of concepts that depend upon widespread acceptance — let alone an ideological movement such as nationalism — does not necessarily lend itself to such treatment.

A second reason why the year 1939 is often noted as the beginning of a spell of nationalism is connected with the fact that this nationalism was inspired by German, Italian and especially by Japanese contemporary ideology, one which became intrinsically linked with the lead-up and course of World War II. Those who take the Phibun form of Thai nationalism to commence in 1939 can depict it as a relatively short-lived aberration, lasting a mere

five years, for by July 1944 Phibun was toppled.[2] How ill the
a-priori periodization fits is demonstrated by the fact that the
nationalistic documents for the period 1939-1947 selected by
Thinaphan include extracts from Wichit Wathakan's *Lueat Suphan,
Ratchamanu, Phrachao Krung Thon, Suek Thalang* and *Chaoying
Saenwi,* all written between 1935 and 1938 (Thak 1978:317-21).

One author who dates the nationalist-absolutist Japanese-inspired
state ideology somewhat earlier is B.A. Batson. In one of his recent
articles he takes the growth of the nationalist movement to date
from 1936 onward, following high-level decisions in Tokyo which
focused Japan's attention once more on Southeast Asia. 'In this
same period', Batson states, 'a large number of works published
in Bangkok dealt with various aspects of Japan's modern experience,
including the influence of the *bushido* code.' As an example of
this genre of literature he cites a travel account by Luang
Katsongkhram, published in 1941 (Batson 1980:273-4).[3]

However, even the earlier date of 1936 as the starting point
for this genre of literature may be considered too late, for, as we
shall note, several years earlier the nationalist ideology was already
formulated and its propaganda machinery was in place. Instead
of quoting Luang Katsongkhram's 1941 account of *bushido*, it
would have been more relevant to mention Luang Wichit
Wathakan's article 'Bushido', published as early as 30 April 1933,
in which he informs his Thai public of the importance of the
Japanese martial code. According to this article Wichit had already
in the mid-1920s come into contact with Professor Inazo Nitobe,
and had been deeply impressed.[4] Wichit writes on this topic with
unreserved approval, paraphrasing Nitobe's work in calling this
philosophy the *winyan* or 'soul' of Japan, that which strengthened
Japan and made it into the vigorous and powerful country of that
moment.[5] The roots of the dictatorial period of Thai nationalism
thus go back in the case of Luang Wichit to the 1920s, much earlier
than most historians of Thailand lead us to believe.

Luang Wichit is not the only link between nationalism during the Sixth Reign and that of the late 1930s. Apart from Vajiravudh's plays and articles which continued to exert some influence after his death in 1925, there was W.C. Dodd's posthumous work, *The Tai Race* (Cedar Rapids, 1923), which stresses the importance of the existence of Tai speaking peoples in French Indochina, British Burma and China. Already before the publication of this work Dodd had been considered an authority on the distribution of the Tais (Penth 1968:63). Shortly thereafter W. A. R. Wood's *History of Siam* gave a prominent place to the early history of the Thais, notably the 'Nanchao Period' (Wood 1925). This was followed by Khun Wichitmatra's book *Lak Thai,* which in 1928 won a royal prize and an honorable mention for literature from the Thai Royal Academy.[6]

In contrast with what is usually assumed, it is here argued that the nationalist ideology did not submerge or disappear with the death of King Rama VI. Proponents for a proud national stance continued to state their opinions, inspired by the new information that had been so vigorously disseminated. One prominent figure who accepted a strong nationalistic ideology and translated it into a plan to strive for a re-establishment of the Thai Empire as it was prior to 1893 (thus reclaiming four Malay states, parts of Cambodia and all of Laos) was Prince Boworadet. In 1931, as Minister of War, he submitted a memorandum to the Supreme Council, in which he mooted this idea.[7]

Various observers at the time note that from 1932 onward, when the Thai absolute monarchy was overthrown and the more egalitarian principles of the People's Party began to be implemented, public policy became more directed toward the common people. This is apparent, for example in the redistribution of money within the education portfolio to the less privileged and in the state-led encouragement of home industry and savings. In February 1943

H. G. Deignan, a naturalist attached to the Chiengmai Station of the American Presbyterian Mission in the 1930s, summed it up:

> During the decade just past the Government has initiated a positive program aimed at raising the standards of living of the common people and especially of the peasants who constitute the great majority....
>
> The political aspect of the program leaned heavily toward economic nationalism, in an endeavour to counteract the excessive proportion of foreign capital in the country and to encourage more active participation by the Thai in the building - up of their own land (Deignan 1943:18).

Deignan and other contemporary analysts have rightly identified the advent of economic nationalism with the outcome of the 1932 revolution. The setting up of state enterprises, such as the import organisation of the Ministry of Defence (the Fuel Division) and the Siam Cotton Mill in 1933, are the first practical results of this policy (Suehiro 1989:123). They have failed to observe, however, to what extent this new economic nationalism was linked up both with the much-publicized propaganda of the Sixth Reign and also with the development of a radical form of Thai nationalism. K. P. Landon reports on having attended a performance of Wichit's *Phrachao Krung Thon* but has no observation other than that he was impressed, and that 'a feeling of new energy infused the old patterns and measures' (Landon 1968:181).[8]

Deignan is of the opinion that the laudable Thai economic nationalism was 'perverted by the paid agents of Japanese propaganda and a handful of powerful men within the Thai Government', thus insinuating that the pro-Japanese movement was not popular, and little more than a clumsy attempt by a foreign power to subvert the Thais (Deignan 1943:18). While I am in agreement with Deignan's singling out the decade following the 1932 revolution as one where a policy of economic nationalism became an integral part of state ideology, I consider his view that the Japanese connection amounted to nothing more than the action of 'paid agents' and 'a handful of powerful men' to be ill-judged. Paid Japanese agents there may well have been, just as there were powerful figures backing the *bushido* propaganda. However, Deignan underestimates the alacrity with which the post-1932 governments identified with totalitarianism and the extent to which this movement gained in popular support.

A closer examination of the Thai evidence of the early 1930s suggests that the type of writing which characterises the above-mentioned 'nation-building' period was well into place before 1939, and even before 1936, when Batson deems it to have begun. Chamrat Sarawisut's writing of 1934 and 1935 may be taken as a good example.

Chamrat was apparently a relatively minor official in Bangkok. Hitherto his name has not appeared in history books, for he did not reach the level of political power which would make him a national figure, nor does his writing indicate any degree of literary merit. His booklet *Nangsue rueang chat thai* does not represent original research, being almost entirely cobbled together from previous authors' works. Nevertheless, it is of historical interest, for it is a piece of fiercely nationalistic writing, as the title, *A Book about the Thai Nation,* indicates. The first edition was published in October 1934, the second, expanded edition in March 1935. The second print run comprised no fewer than 20,000 copies for distribution throughout Thailand to village leaders, schools, monasteries, and railway stations. The cost of printing and distributing this second edition was made possible through the generosity of Navatho Phra Chalamphisaiseni, the director of the United Commercial Company.

The first half of *Nangsue rueang chat thai* deals with an overview of the past, beginning six thousand years ago. This whole section is taken directly from Khun Wichitmatra's *Lak Thai.* It tells of a glorious past, culminating in the Nanchao Kingdom and the dispersal of the Thais. After the history there follows an account of numbers of Tai-speakers outside Siam. The Thai race with all its subdivisions listed amounted to 6,750,000 in China, 2 million in Indochina, 1,540,000 in British territory, and 12 million in Siam. The reader is expected to accept several inferences, notably that there is such a thing as a Thai race (with a most honourable pedigree), and that almost half this race lives under colonial regimes bordering Siam.

The final part is entitled *Withi rak chat*, or 'How to Love the Nation'. The statement is a passionate plea to adopt a Japanese *bushido*-style set of attitudes. Apparently Chamrat wrote to Luang Wichit to ask him, as someone who had already published on nationalism, to contribute a section on this topic. Wichit replied by sending him a copy of his work and giving him permission to reprint as much as he liked.[9] The manner in which Luang Wichit is mentioned in *Nangsue rueang chat thai* indicates that Chamrat did not know Wichit personally.

The most interesting aspect of the booklet lies in its style. The text differs notably from the persuasive mode of earlier nationalistic writing, which simply tried to jolt the uncommitted into action. Chamrat's style of addressing the reader is not unlike that of a 'lesser priest' writing to an already-converted audience of acolytes eager to hear of ways to improve their relationship with the Thai nation. The latter part of *Nangsue rueang chat thai* is overtly prescriptive, and intrusions in personal behaviour are justified in terms of the well-being of the nation. In the translated extract appended to this essay it is easy to discern the tell-tale signs of totalitarianism, namely the overriding importance of an *esprit de corps,* the exhortation to complete commitment of all members of the state, and especially the acceptance of the doctrine that the nation has the right to prescribe all aspects of the individual's life. In other words, we find here a form of totalitarian writing in the early 1930s, a genre which historians of Thailand usually associate only with the years 1939-1944. There is a logical sequence from Chamrat's dogma that the nation's welfare is more important than any individual to Phibun's eleventh Cultural Mandate of September 1941, prescribing how Thais ought to divide their working day and what they ought to do in their spare time.

If we accept that *Nangsue rueang chat thai* is a good example of early Thai totalitarian writing, we ought not to lose sight of the fact that it also belongs to the much wider category of Thai nationalist propaganda,[10] a genre of literature that has existed in Thailand since 1893, quite understandably triggered off by the serious external threat to Siam's sovereignty in that year.[11] The study of samples of this genre is more conducive of taking the 'pulse' of ideological history than that which results from a priori periodization. Thus, Rama VI's nationalistic writings, which are often taken as isolated outpourings of a sole person, can and ought to be linked thematically to authors before and after the Sixth Reign.

Nangsue rueang chat thai is in close harmony with the dictatorial state ideology, which was to culminate in the pact with Japan, the declaration of war on Britain and the United States, and a remarkable series of directives from the nation's leadership to the population. This state ideology involved a good measure of propaganda under the inspiration of people such as Wichit Wathakan and Phibun Songkram, but at the same time, these leaders had reasons to believe that their messages and measures would be heard by a willing and sympathetic audience.

By 1934 the basic platform of a state ideology already was in place. Chamrat's booklet covers the chief ingredients of this state ideology. First, it answers the question of 'Who are the Thais?' by relishing in the recently-discovered lengthy pedigree equal to, if not surpassing, other nations in the world. Second, the realisation that there were many 'blood brothers' in China and in British and French-held territories was regarded as precious information. Just as the German and Italian propaganda machinery kept stressing the importance of ethnic groups beyond the borders as providing a 'natural' justification for future incursions into neighbouring territories, so the Thais began dreaming of a vastly enlarged territory. The vision of an enlarged Pan-Thai empire was, as mentioned above, already mooted by Prince Boworadet in 1931. This must not be regarded simply as a personal dream in which Boworadet indulged. Rather, as Batson has indicated, it was a regularly recurring theme in the press in the late-1920s (Batson 1984:178).

While expansionist speculation was not unusual before the fall of the absolute monarchy, it became an increasingly important aspect of the intellectual debate in post-1932 Siam. There can be little doubt but that there was widespread sympathy for the idea of expansion of the borders, particularly at the cost of Cambodia and Laos (Crosby 1945:121). The name change in the first Cultural Mandate from Siam to Thailand may be regarded as part of the irredentist movement. This was clearly recognised by J. Crosby, the British Minister in Bangkok between 1934 and 1942:

> Luang Pibul may appear at first sight to have been making no very great change when he ordained that the word 'Sayam' should be dropped by the Siamese. But the fact that an official change of nomenclature should have been made in coincidence with the launching of the Pan-Thai movement may be interpreted not unfairly as the indication of a desire to familiarise outsiders with the claim of Siam to be regarded as the mother-country of all peoples of Thai race (Crosby 1945:112).

Already as early as 1933, when the League of Nations was in uproar over Japan's invasion of Manchuria, the Siamese government surprised many observers by her refusal to condemn Japan. The abstention of voting against Japan may be seen, not just as a gesture of not wanting to alienate a fellow-Asian nation, but also in the light of Siam's own future ambitions to do similar things. Irredentism, the stated aim to recover 'lost provinces', already was noted in 1934 and 1935 as a trend among the younger military and civilian Siamese.[12]

The popularity of this nationalistic sentiment is reflected in Wichit Wathakan's appointment in 1934 as head of the Department of Fine Arts (Pra'ararat 1985:281; Chaliew 1977:283).[13] Later that same year Phibun Songkhram, at the unusually young age of thirty-seven, became Defence Minister. The fact that the latter just prior to his appointment had published various articles proclaiming an authoritarian form of government has received little attention, but the subsequent appointment may be regarded as implicit approval of his overt dictatorial stance.[14]

During most of the 1930s irredentism was not part of Thailand's formal state policy, but there is evidence that it received high-level government support. In 1936, in the face of British and French dissatisfaction, schools were provided with maps highlighting Siam's 'lost provinces'.[15] The confrontation with French Indochina, culminating in the invasion of parts of Cambodia and Laos in early 1941 and the subsequent annexation of four Malay States as well as part of the Shan States must not be seen as sudden whims, prompted by the opportunities provided by World War II, but rather as the partial fulfilment of ambitions that had been long cherished by many influential government officials and supported by a growing number of the general public (Vichitr 1941).

When Phibun signed a Pact of Alliance with Japan on 21 December 1941 there were three secret clauses attached to the pact, and the first of these clauses read: 'The Japanese Government will cooperate in the realization of Thailand's demands for the return of its lost territories'.[16] The dramatic inroads of Japanese business interests in Siam in the early 1 1930s,[17] the sending of dancers and musicians to Japan in 1933, the curbing of Chinese immigration in 1933,[18] the reintroduction of censorship in 1933 (followed by the strict press control law of 1934), the establishment of the para-military Yuwachon movement in 1935,[19] and the training of Thai military personnel in Japan in 1935, can all be related to a more general drift towards totalitarianism, the ideology that led to Phibun's rise to the prime ministership and thus to the Cultural Mandates.

To take as a starting point for a conference a document such as the promulgation of the first Cultural Mandate on 24 June, 1939,[20] in which the country changed its name to Thailand, unfortunately strengthens the perception that 1939 may be seen as an ideological point of departure. It would be better to see it as the confident outcome of a state-led ideology that had, over the period since 1932, gained wide support among the Thais. While during the 1920s and 1930s there is a steady increase in pro--irredentist Thai writing, in this time it is difficult to find published sources opposing irredentism.

If Chamrat's propaganda may be seen as part of a movement to support the dictatorial type of nationalism that gained momentum from 1932 onward, this may cause us to question the widely-held belief that Thailand differs markedly from other Southeast Asian countries in that it did not develop comparable nationalist movements.[21] With respect to Burma, U Maung Maung calls the period 1931-1936 the 'Gestation Period' of the Nationalist Movements, a phrase that could equally apply to the Thai situation. The circumstances that favoured the rise of Aung San in Burma and Sukarno in Indonesia are not so different from those that propelled Phibun to the fore. In Vietnam the 'Vietnamese Communists were uncomfortably aware of how many intellectuals remained fascinated by the success of militaristic nationalism in Turkey, Thailand, and Japan, not to mention fascism in Italy and Germany' (Marr 1981:320-21). During the late 1930s the national movements supporting Emperor Bao Dai and Prince Cuong De, drawing upon ideas of leadership and national strength not unlike those expressed by Thai military nationalists, experienced a resurgence. The growth of some sub-sects of Cao Dai in the 1930s has also been linked with Japanese-inspired forms of nationalism

(Sacks 1971:44-46). The fact that these and other movements, such as that of the Constitutionalist Party in Cochinchina (Cook 1977), lost against the more radical anti-colonial communists should not prevent us from recognising that an insipient form of Southeast Asian fascism can also be recognised in pre-World War II Vietnam.

CONCLUSIONS

In this essay a particular historical document dating from 1934/35, Chamrat's *Nangsue rueang chat thai,* has been analysed as to its contents and style. It has been found to possess many characteristics of fascist propaganda, a type of literature usually associated with the first Phibun regime (1938-1944). It has been shown that Chamrat's work was not an isolated phenomenon, but that it was part of an increasingly popular dictatorial form of nationalism that had its first adherents in the 1920s. It has also been argued that historians of Thailand have tended to describe nationalism as being a feature of specific reigns and rulers, and that this practice appears to have had a detrimental effect on the study of Thai nationalism as a whole. The history of the various stages of an ideology such as Thai nationalism is not served by this 'on-off' approach. It is much better studied as a phenomenon that, once arisen (and we have argued for its origins to be placed in 1893), moves, changes and develops as one of a range of competing ideologies. Even in the case of particular rulers having an extraordinary preoccupation with nationalism, such as Rama VI, elite-directed nationalism became significant in Thailand's general history mainly because it met with a receptive audience.

In Thai history-writing the 1920s and 1930s have hitherto received scant attention. It appears to be a time of much intellectual debate, in which Luang Wichit and his growing number of followers formed but one of a number of protagonists. It has also been shown that the preoccupation with Thai identity is by no means a recent phenomenon, but that it is an important theme in propagandist literature, as well as of history-writing, during the late 1920s and early 1930s.

Finally, a small attempt has been made to break through the invisible barrier that seems to surround early twentieth century Thai history, isolating it from the history of Thailand's neighbours and preventing meaningful comparisons with events in the rest of Southeast Asia. Largely because of the fact that Thailand was not directly colonised (and the related fact that many primary sources are not available in European languages) it has been treated as the exceptional case in Southeast Asian history. In this essay it has been shown that Thais were part of the same world and partook of the same types of debates. To take note of these shared experiences may assist the historian in throwing light on the region as a whole.

APPENDIX

Translation of the final part of Chamrat's book, entitled *Withi rak chat* (*How to Love the Nation*), pp.36-41.

For this book about the nation I contacted Luang Wichit Wathakan, and expressed the wish to let me have something on *latthi chu chat*[22] or nationalism, a topic on which long ago he wrote and published. However, just now he has very busy government business commitments, and it is impossible for him to sacrifice time to write as he would wish. Instead he sent me a copy of the original *Latthi chu chat,* together with his permission to take and print as much as I needed in this work on the nation.

I would love to print Luang Wichit Wathakan's *Latthi chu chat* again, but I am afraid that it would be superfluous for you, readers, because *Latthi chu chat* is a work that almost all of us already have in our bookcases. Thus it is better to take only certain passages, some advisory words and phrases that may lead the Thais to unite and love our nation, and help us to support the nation according to our ability and strength, for the benefit of the group as a whole, particularly by fostering prosperity, lasting security, and the independence of the nation and the country in times to come.

Luang Wichit Wathakan says: 'The importance of the country and the nation lies in the people. People must love the nation, people must know the way to behave with respect to the nation, and people must consider the nation to be important'.

If you read these few words, these mere two or three lines just quoted, smoothly and flowingly without paying too much attention to the meaning, you may well feel that they are ordinary words of advice, and that there is nothing strange about them, because everybody, even small children, know very well that we must love the nation, must uphold the nation as something bigger than oneself, and so on. But if we stand still and clarify the details bit by bit, then we shall meet various difficult problems. Questions that are not easily answered in a clear and incontrovertible manner are:

1. Why do people have to love the nation?
2. If we love the Nation how do we profit and if we do not love the nation, how does this harm us?
3. Must everyone determine to love the nation in his own way or not?
4. What is this way? If you use force it causes bitterness in the individual. How can we come to regard the Nation as more than we regard ourselves?

If you are able to answer these four difficult questions, then you shall see that the prosperity of the country-nation rests with the people, namely with us ourselves, the basic unit of the nation, as Luang Wichit Wathakan says.

We believe in the truth that lies in the statement that Japan is the most prosperous nation on the Asian continent. This is so because the Japanese nation adheres to the Buddhist religion. In general there is faith and devout belief in behaviour in accordance with Buddhist admonitions, namely, in accordance with the Dhamma. They have the five precepts as their starting point. To this can be added that Japan has the *bushido* doctrine, which is a faith that is good for the nation, for guidance and for the training of the Japanese populace: 1) be direct, honest; 2) be brave; 3) be compassionate; 4) be polite and well organised; 5) love honour; 6) love duty; 7) know how to control yourself. Thus, if all the Thais observe and have faith in the Buddhist religion, together with the practice of Japanese *bushido*, increase diligence, strength, vigour, and grow in a special way, we the Thai nation, the country Siam, will beget not a little dazzling prosperity, equal to that of Japan, for certain.

Friends, bloodbrothers, I invite you to think of the growth of the Thai nation from the earliest beginnings onwards to our present-day existence. If all of us decide to attempt to act according to the words introduced immediately above, every day and together, in a sincere manner, then I boldly can predict the consequences, namely the history and legends of the nation will not change and transform its picture for the worse from this day onwards:

1. Act openly in a good and pleasant way, and at the same time act according to the characteristics of people who are direct, brave, compassionate, noble, polite, honourable, dutiful, and who have self control, diligence, industriousness and energy.
2. Believe the nation to be more important than other matters, and attempt to be useful to the nation at all possible occasions.

3   Be firm in the Buddhist religion.
4.   Respect and venerate the constitution which is the thoughtful and pure soul of the nation.
5.   Attempt to maintain and utilise things that are of the Thai nation.
6.   Cherish unity and help all people of the same nation to think of the nation as something shared, bigger than individuals or constituent groups.

In order to see the Thai nation, the country Siam, namely yourself and your relatives, together with the houses, and the soil, the place of living and where you eat, I implore all you readers respectfully to try and act with self control according to these instructions for a time of only ten or fifteen days, and this will bear fruit and be useful for the country and nation in a satisfactory manner. At the same time this will gain me merit by having introduced this matter,

Faithfully yours, Nai Chamrat Sarawisut

ENDNOTES

1. On the coining of this term see the introduction to this volume.

2. See, for example, how Charnvit Kasetsiri places the sub-heading 'Nationalism' after having described Phibun's rise to power, and how he describes the process in terms of a series of government-inspired activities, dating from 1939 onwards, being foisted upon a reluctant public (Charnvit 1974). A similar message is found in Thamsook 1978.

3. At the same time it ought to be noted that while Batson describes the beginning of this 'aggressive' nationalism as falling in 1936, he also has stated, as early as 1974, that the roots of this nationalism are to be found in the 1920s. See Batson 1974: 89-90. In his *The End of the Absolute Monarchy in Siam,* he provides details, some which will be cited below. See Batson, 1984:177-80.

4. The author of *Bushido, the Soul of Japan,* which Storry reckons to be 'among the best-selling books of Edwardian England'. See Storry 1979:64.

5. Wichit 1933:30. I thank Mr S. Barmé for making available a copy of this article.

6. Khun Wichitmatra is probably better known by his pen-name of Kanchanaphan. *Lak Thai* was inspired by W. C. Dodd's discovery of vast numbers of Tai-speakers in China. Khun Wichitmatra wrote many popular history books, including *Prawat kankha thai* [*The History of Thai Trade*], and *Phumisat wat pho* [*The Geography of Wat Pho*].

7. C. Dormer to J. Simon, Jan. 11, 1934, F.O. 1185/21/40, p.1.

8. This contrasts dramatically with the assessment of Wichit's plays as 'pieces of blatant propaganda' by J. Crosby, F.O. 6378/113/40, p. 2.

9. As far as I have been able to determine, no book *Latthi chu chat* [*Nationalism*] was published by Wichit Wathakan. What is here meant is most probably an article under the same name published in *Duang prathip*, Vol 2, part 36, 25 June 1933, pp.5-6, 10, 23, 27, 28 and 30. I thank Mr S. Barmé for making available a copy of this article.

10. Nationalist writings are defined as those in which the propagation of the concept of a particular nation, the incorporation of the aspirations of all inhabitants of a unified state, is a central concern.

11. The first nationalistic article was found by Rosenberg in the weekly
    Thammasatwinitchai of 23 April 1893 (Rosenberg 1980:84). Recently, apparently
    quite independently, Eiji Murashima has also found this article, and also noted
    its distinct nationalistic character (Murashima 1988:81).

12. C. Dormer to J. Simon, Jan. 11, 1934, F.O. 1185/21/40, p.1. See also J. Crosby
    to A. Eden, F.O. 1909/1909/40, p.8.

13. In contrast, Batson puts his rise to the headship of the Fine Arts Department
    to the 'late 1930s' (Batson 1980:273).

14. C. J. Reynolds has given much thought to Luang Wichit's role in the
    determination of the 'plot of Thai History', citing various of his works through
    the 1920s and 1930s. Reynolds's assessment of Wichit opens new perspective
    and needs to be followed by more detailed work, particularly taking note of
    differences between the Wichit of the 1920s and post-1932 Wichit. See Reynolds
    n.d..

15. F.O. 3754/216/40, dated June 13, 1936, p.2.

16. For details see Swan 1986:234. Swan has shown clearly how the alliance with
    Japan was met with widespread support, and also how various key actors, such
    as Direk Chananam and Phibun Songkhram, after the war described themselves
    as anti-Japanese, although their descriptions do not match contemporary records.

17. According to Landon, in the ten years between 1925 and 1935 Japan's percentage
    of the total Siamese imports rose from 3.41 per cent to 25.56 per cent (and
    this did not include indirect trade with Japan) (Landon 1968:59).

18. Ben Anderson's sweeping statement 'for all the "extreme nationalism" of the
    first Phibun era, nothing was done to limit the influx of golden-egg-laying geese'
    may also be the result of taking the nationalistic period to begin in the late
    1930s (Anderson 1978:212). The measures that indeed severely affected the
    influx of Chinese were taken in the early 1930s and by 1934-35 there was a
    dramatic decrease in numbers. The dramatic change in attitude towards the
    Chinese has been documented by Crosby in his Annual Report, 1934, F.O.
    1931/1931/40, pp.16-17.

19. In 1936 the Yuwachon movement was already established in ten Changwats,
    and had some 3500 members. J. Crosby, F 0. 7676/216/40, p. 2.

20. The date is significant: it was the seventh anniversary of the 1932 overthrow
    of the absolute monarchy, the country's National Day.

21. See Anderson, 1978 on some of the reasons why such comparative questions have been neglected.

22. *Chu* literally 'to lift'. The expression 'nationalism' in modern Thai is *latthi chatniyom*.

REFERENCES

Anderson, Benedict R. O'G. 1978. 'Studies of the Thai State: The State of Thai Studies,' pp. 193-247 in *The Study of Thailand: Analyses of Knowledge, Approaches, and Prospects in Anthropology, Art History, Economics, History and Political Science*, ed. Eliezer B. Ayal. Athens, Ohio, Center for International Studies.

Batson, B. A. 1974. 'The Fall of the Phibun Government, 1944', *Journal of the Siam Society*, 62.2 (July), 89-120.

--------. 1980. 'Siam and Japan: The Perils of Independence' in *Southeast Asia under Japanese Occupation*, ed. Alfred W. McCoy. New Haven, Yale University Southeast Asia Studies. Monograph Series no. 22.

--------. 1984. *The End of the Absolute Monarchy in Siam*. Singapore, Oxford University Press.

Chaliew Phansida. 1977. *Luang wichit wathakan lae ngan dan prawatisat [Luang Wichit Wathakan and his Historical Works]*. Bangkok, Bannakit Trading.

Charnvit Kasetsiri. 1974. 'The First Phibun Government and Its Involvement in World War II', *Journal of the Siam Society*, 62.2 (July), 25-88.

Cook, Megan. 1977. *The Constitutionalist Party in Cochinchina: The Years of Decline, 1930-1942*. Clayton, Victoria, Monash University, Centre of Southeast Asian Studies. Monash Papers on Southeast Asia no. 6.

Crosby, J. 1945. *Siam, The Crossroads*. London, Holis & Carter.
Deignan, H. G. 1943. *Siam, Land of the Free*. Washington, Smithsonian Institution. War Background Series no. 8.

Landon, Kenneth P. 1968 [1939]. *Siam in Transition: A Brief Survey of Cultural Trends in the Five Years since the Revolution of 1932*. New York, Greenwood Press. Reprint ed.

Marr, D. G. 1981. *Vietnamese Tradition on Trial, 1920-1945*. Berkeley, University of California Press.

Maung Maung, U. 1980. *From Sangha to Laity: Nationalist Movements of Burma, 1920-1940*. New Delhi, Manohar. Australian National University, Monographs on South Asia, no. 4.

Murashima Eiji. 1988. 'The Origin of Modern Official State Ideology in Thailand', *Journal of Southeast Asian Studies*, 19.1 (March), 80-96.

Penth, H. G. 1968. 'A Letter by William Clifton Dodd', *Nachrichten der Gesellschaft für Natur- und Volkderkunde Ostasiens*, 103.

Pra'ararat Buranamat. 1985. *Luang wichit wathakan kap botlakhon prawatisat [Luang Wichit Wathakan's Historical Plays]*. Bangkok, Thammasat University Press.

Reynolds, C. J. n. d. 'The Plot of Thai History: Theory and Practice' in *Patterns and Illusions: Papers on Thai Topics in Memory of Richard B. Davis*, ed. Gehan Wijeyewardene and E. C. Chapman, forthcoming.

Rosenberg, K. 1980. *Nation und Fortschritt*. Hamburg, Gesellschaft fur Natur- und Volkerkunde Ostasiens e. V. Mitteilungen der Gesellschaft fur Natur- und Volkerkunde Ostasiens (OAG).

Sacks, I. Milton. 1971. 'Some Religious Components in Vietnamese Politics' in *Religion and Change in Contemporary Asia*, ed. R. F. Spencer. Minneapolis, University of Minnesota Press.

Storry, R. 1979. *Japan and the Decline of the West in Asia, 1894 - 1943*. London, Macmillan.

Suehiro Akira. 1989. *Capital Accumulation in Thailand, 1855-1985*. Tokyo, Centre for East Asian Cultural Studies.

Swan, W. L. 1986. 'Japanese Economic Relations with Siam: Aspects of their Historical Development, 1884-1942'. Ph. D. thesis, Australian National University.

Thak Chaloemtiarana, ed. 1978. *Thai Politics Extracts and Documents, 1932 - 1957*. Bangkok, Social Science Association of Thailand.

Thamsook Numnonda. 1978. 'Pibulsongkram's Thai Nation-Building Programme during the Japanese Military Presence, 1941-1945', *Journal of Southeast Asian Studies*, 9.2 (Sept.), 234-47.

Vichitr Vadakarn [Wichit Wathakan], Luang. 1941. *Thailand's Case*. Bangkok.

Wichit Wathakan, Luang. 1933. 'Buchido [Bushido]' in *Duang prathip*, 30 April.

Wood, W. A. R. 1925. *History of Siam*. Bangkok, Souvenir of the Siamese Kingdom Exhibition at Lumbini Park.

Figure 2   Shrines on the Chiangmai-Chiangrai mountain road.

Shrines for the propitiation of Caw Nang Kaew Hi Luang which lie on the road
between Chiangmai and Chiangrai on the mountain range that marks the boundary
between the two provinces. Nang Kaew is propitiated at many sites throughout
the region and is a fertility deity to whom phallic objects are offered. The road,
upgraded in the late 1970s, was an old caravan route. Since the new road was
built, the shrines, which were situated in a grove slightly below the crown of the
hill, have been dominated by a new Buddha image. More recently, they have been
moved away from the road so as not to catch the attention of tourists. Supplicants
must now remove their offerings once they have performed the ritual.

Chapter 6

THE FRONTIERS OF THAILAND

Gehan Wijeyewardene

INTRODUCTION

This paper emerged as the continuation of work on the Tai-speaking people outside the borders of Thailand and their relations with the Kingdom. The paper reporting on that previous work appears in a collection published in 1990, entitled *Ethnic Groups across national boundaries in mainland Southeast Asia* (Wijeyewardene ed. 1990). The present paper may also be considered a response to a paper given by Thongchai Winichakul at the International Conference on Thai Studies in 1987 entitled 'Siam mapped: A History of the Geo-body of Siam'. I have since then seen his University of Sydney thesis of the same title and should say at the outset that it is an impressive and important piece of work, to be published soon by University of Hawaii Press. The passage in the conference paper which particularly struck me was as follows:

> My study of the geo-body of Siam is a case of how a fact that constitutes the notion of Siam, a nation, was created by a certain geographical discourse ....
> My study shows that even the geo-body of a nation is merely an effect of modern geographical discourse whose technology of representation is a map (1987:159).

The thesis will not allow such cavalier dismissal as the paper may have engendered, and I should try to give an account of his argument, at least in as far as it has bearing on this paper.

AN ARGUMENT ABOUT BORDERS AND FRONTIERS

Thongchai argues that the representation of Thailand as a territory on the earth's surface with demarcated or demarcable boundaries — the 'geo-body' as he calls it — is the product of the modern technology of mapping. The technology went hand in hand with Western ideas about nation-states, political units and their boundaries, a set of ideas quite different from those held by the peoples of Southeast Asia. These were two different ways of conceptualizing space — two different forms of 'discourse', as Thongchai would like to say.

The presentation of the pre-modern (my term, one about which Thongchai has reservations) characterization of space is complex. We do not need to take up at all the ideological characterization inherent in the *Traiphum of Phra Ruang*, the Thai-Buddhist cosmology, which, however interesting it may be as ideology, in my view bears very little relation to the pragmatic, traditional ideas of boundaries and frontiers which are dealt with in this paper.

Thongchai sets out to examine the creation of Thai nationhood as a field of discourse. He writes,

Instead of describing the operations of all discourses which create nationhood, my study will focus on only *one* aspect of nationhood .... The focus is the geo-body of Siam (1988:27).

It is clear throughout that he is opposed to 'the discourse of nationhood' and attempts to show that projection of this 'nationhood' into the past is anachronistic. This latter endeavour, I think, is a convincing piece of historical scholarship.

The characterizations of space were religious, but there were over-lapping conceptions and, these did not exclude more pragmatic ones.

The dominance of Traiphum cosmology and other religious concepts of space in everyday life was great. But the indigenous knowledge of local geography also had a role to play in particular domains (1988:78).

It is to 'boundaries' and 'knowledge of local geography' to which we must now turn. Thongchai, like many other writers on the subject, accepts the convenient distinction between 'boundary' and 'frontier'. The former is a defined line, represented by a line on a map, and the latter a region or transitional zone. I am not entirely happy with this, because it contradicts some general usages of common speech, but will accept it for this paper.

Thongchai's first argument (that is, the first I shall take up) is that prior to the nineteenth century there were no 'boundaries'. His interpretation of the Thai word *müang* is of an urban centre of power and the region over which authority is exercised.[1] Between *müang* is a politically undifferentiated region of mountain and forest not of great concern to the rulers of *müang*. This is the argument of Thongchai's paper. In the thesis this is much elaborated and he represents his argument by four diagrams. These present what he terms a 'natural corridor border' consisting of forested mountain ranges. The plural is important and has to be inferred from his diagram. On either side are frontier towns, and crossings between the ranges are 'passage ways'. Between the frontier towns and the ranges are 'guard-houses' with a delineated distance of a guard's patrol, which marks the 'boundary of authority'.

Because of this constitution of the polity, the Bangkok court did not initially understand the demands of colonial powers for the demarcation of borders, but by the end of the century the court became a party to the new 'discourse'. Previously, the court would take the attitude that borders were the concern of the local inhabitants, not of the royal centre.

Under the pre-modern system the paramount ruler exercised suzerainty over different types of other provinces or *müang*. On the periphery of the domain would be *müang*, usually small, which may in fact have paid tribute and which acknowledged the suzerainty of two or even three other strong centres. These centres were known in Thai as *faai faa*. Even in these cases it was not the borders but the centres that were important. Moreover, these domains of paramount powers were not characterized by national or ethnic identities. Thus there was no concept of a Thai 'nation'. Here Thongchai shows how claims of Thailand's lost territories depicted on maps as well as in history and political polemic are anachronistic. Complementarily, the administrative reform which rationalized the relations of *müang* such as Chiangmai is also anachronistic. It was a completely new process that was set in motion, one that created the nation-state we know today. Administrative construction and the demarcation of boundaries by treaty were new processes, not rationalizations of old ones.

Thongchai also argues that the tendency of both Thai historians and foreign scholars writing from a Thai perspective is to see Thailand (Siam) as being the victim of colonial aggrandisement. He argues that in fact from the point of view of the small *müang* the difference between colonial power and Siam may not be apparent. This analysis of a historical process is most convincing, but to my mind vitiated by the 'theory of discourse', which seems to suggest that the process itself has no real existence apart from the way in which it is talked about. It is also coupled with a strong sense of distaste for nationalism and the nation-state. Much as I, or one, may share these feelings, the 'nation-state' will not go away.

As I have used Thongchai's argument as the entry into my subject, I should make quite clear what I believe to be the fundamental point of disagreement. The argument is relativistic, the identification of the field of discourse seems to be denying the process made up of historical events. In contrast, I take the view that however provisional a statement about the past, or the present, its value lies in a closer approximation to what was, or is, the case. However, it is not always possible to decide how great his commitment is to the 'theory of discourse'.

My first topic, arising from this brief account, is the Thongchai thesis on 'boundaries', but before proceeding a brief word on the applicability of Edmund Leach on the 'Frontiers of "Burma"'(1960). Note that the Thailand of my title is not in quotes as the Burma of Leach's. Thongchai cites this paper as the only previous attempt to look in this way at pre-colonial boundaries, but he says it looked only at ethnic minorities. Leach starts with the proposition that the history of such entities as 'Burma' cannot be seen as that of 'nation-states' with defined frontiers. In the northern regions at least the analogue of 'frontier' is the interaction of two different ecological-cultural adaptations. First, the wet-rice cultivating, valley-based Theravada Buddhist, Indian-influenced polities of charismatic rulers, which are in certain predictable relations with swiddening hill peoples, Chinese-influenced and governed by patrilineal chiefs. Ethnic identity and language are determined by these cultural-ecological adaptations, not by some conjectural history based on linguistic relations.

It is not entirely clear that Thongchai appreciates Leach's ecological argument. Though there is a strong topographical component in Thongchai, the thrust of the argument is semiotic. Thongchai argues that ethnic, linguistic and cultural identity are not relevant to the pre-nineteenth century situation. Leach quite clearly makes a connection between ecology, and linguistic, religious and ethnic identity. For Thongchai the *müang* which were subordinate to more than one paramountcy (*faai faa*) are treated from a purely structural point of view. Cholthira Satyawadhna has treated some cases of these as being typical of small Mon-Khmer groups dominated by neighbouring paramountcies.[2] This raises the possibility that these subordinate, or minority, chiefdoms also may have been of rather different kinds, with different relations to the large valley states. That is, some may have been linguistically and culturally similar, and Buddhist, and at another extreme Mon-Khmer-speaking and pagan.

To return to 'boundaries'. Thongchai identifies two types; those between friendly states where there was a 'golden, silver path' and no hindrance on passing to and fro, and where even settlement near a foreign frontier town was allowed. This contrasted with the situation where hostile states deliberately tried to keep an unsettled frontier region between them, but where intrusion (by non-combatants) into this no-man's-land would not be actively countered.

One further point needs attention. I may introduce this by reproducing a citation Thongchai makes from a Siamese official at the end of the nineteenth century.

We regard the town's walls as the most important.... The watershed on that big mountain is an approximate boundary (1988:165-67).

This example is very difficult to interpret, partly because it is Thongchai's translation of a citation in an M.A. thesis in Thai. Rather than get into extraneous considerations here, I wish only to draw attention to the fact that 'watershed' is treated like any other marker, such as piles of stones, shrines and trees which he claims mark 'approximate boundaries'.

THE *MÜANG*: A POLITY WITH BOUNDARIES

I now make my counter proposals about the nature of traditional frontiers in this region. The disagreement is largely in the nature of domain and boundary, but one first needs to draw attention to a difference of point of view in a most literal sense. Thongchai's perspective is essentially from the court in Bangkok, and subsequently that of Siamese officials. This view is conditioned at least by the nature of the Chao Phraya valley and the change in the topographical implications of the word *müang*. I cannot now remember where I acquired the information, but one of the first things I learned about Thailand was the nature of the *müang*: the river valley bounded by mountains, which was the essential unit of political community, an ecological, agricultural unit in which the watershed and catchment provided the irrigation for wet-rice agriculture, and the mountain passes and the rivers articulated relations with the outside world. This, Cholthira Satyawadhna tells me,[3] is not now one of the things that Thai learn about Thailand. The term 'watershed' is now interpreted by Thongchai as meaning the summit of a single peak, rather than the range, which is such an important topographical and ecological factor in northern Southeast Asia. The Thai term means 'dividing the waters', and the major range separating Thailand from Burma is known as the 'range where the spirits divide the waters' (*phii pan naam*). A very convenient account of the *müang* is given by Hans Penth,

According to northern Thai usage, a *müang* is a populated geographic area the borders of which are formed by the surrounding mountains; it is a state in a valley. A *müang* can have several villages or settlements, one of which would be the principle place with the seat of the local administration. If the *müang* were important enough for a member of the aristocracy to rule it, it had a fortified settlement called *wiang* ... the word is still in common usage because, I believe, it refers to simple geographical patterns which can easily be understood by the least educated.... (1977:180-1)

The *wiang* is the 'town's walls' referred to by the Siamese official. During the whole of the latter part of the nineteenth century Bangkok attempted, through the Chiangmai authorities, to repopulate Chiangsaen (the city referred to by Thongchai) and surrounding areas. The city itself lies on the river, and even when deserted could hardly be thought of as a border outpost. Throughout the period it is certain that the first priority was the building up of population, and one must question Thongchai's using the argument that, because no objection was made to settlers, this implied the absence of any recognition of boundaries. That was not part of the political culture of the period. One might also draw attention to the fact that in 1895 the French established a 25 kilometre *cordon sanitaire* on the right bank of the Mekhong (FO628/17/234) which was recognized by the British in 1896.[4] This meant the depopulation, again, of Chiangsaen, and the establishment of a temporary site outside the zone. At this or earlier periods the acceptance of settlers cannot be taken as evidence of a Thai (or regional) attitude to boundaries. The much cited paper by Kraisri (1965) on 'putting vegetables in the basket, putting people on the *müang*' conveys a quite different message. I have suggested elsewhere that this 'resettlement policy' in the region is even attested to in the sixteenth century (Wijeyewardene 1984-5).

At the centre (political and administrative, if not geographical) is the *wiang*, and at the centre of the *wiang* is a 'city pillar'. In Chiangmai we know that the annual rites at this shrine were, in theory at least, supported by all households in the *müang*. The centre, however, is not at issue. It is the boundaries that matter, and the citation below is an indication of the marking of boundaries in the first half of the nineteenth century.

In the document written on foolscap paper, in pencil, transliterated by Sanguan Chotisukharat and dated by him about 1945 but relating events of over a hundred years before, we have a passage of which I give a rough translation.

> Phracaw Kavila of Chiangmai, when he was still Phraya Mangra Vajiraprakarn Kamphaengkaew, ordered Caw Chiangmai Chang Phüak, when he was still Phraya Uparat (Caw Thammalangka), to inspect the western boundaries of the kingdom up to the eastern bank of the Mae Nam Khong, called the Salaween.

It appears that the country (*müang*) of the Jang Daeng (Red Karen) lies on the west bank and is not subject to the Müang of Ava. Caw Chiangmai Chang Phüak persuaded Phaphor, the Caw Müang of the Red Karen, to be friends with the intention that he would look out for news of Burma's raising troops and let Chiangmai know. They then performed a ritual according to the pagan customs of the Jang Daeng. They slaughtered a buffalo to be eaten with liquor at Tha Sayaa. They split the horn(s) into two, one for the Jang Daeng, the other for Müang Chiangmai to keep in custody, and established a treaty of understanding that as long as the Mae Nam Khong [Salween] did not dry up, the buffalo horn not straighten, the cave of the white elephant not collapse, Müang Chiangmai and Müang Jang Daeng would be friends. (Sanguan 1972:545-46)

This passage also raises the question of watercourses as boundaries, to which I shall return in a moment, but in the meantime we need to consider a phenomenon of which I have written elsewhere (1986). Many northern Thai roads follow old caravan tracks and old practices have endured into the present in somewhat altered form. The highest point of the road, which means the highest point on succeeding ranges, is nearly always the boundary between provinces and is the site of spirit shrines (Figure 2). Today these shrines proliferate, many of them being installed to house the spirits of those killed on the road. In former times the protective spirits were not privatized in this manner, but a shrine could be expected wherever a trade route or path of communication transected a watershed. At a fundamental level, the process at work is the application of human agency to the characteristics of the natural world. In northern Thailand and the surrounding region the creation of social and political boundaries at ecologically significant natural features had taken on the aspect of cultural law.

In 1856 James Barker undertook a journey from 'Amarapoora to the Burmese Shan States on the Salween River and through various parts of those States'. On 31 July his journal records the following:

> ascended the Nat-tiek Pass; ascent very abrupt and difficult; in most parts a rugged surface of granite rock washed bare. On the crown of the Pass a small temple marks the boundary between Burmah and the Shan States.... It is customary with travellers to propitiate the Nat by offerings of fireworks, which they let off at the temple on the summit of the Pass (Barker 1856).

In a paper published in 1972 Andrew Turton proposed a number of contrasts in the ritual system of the northern Thai. For our purposes one of them is relevant. He contrasted the *lak müang* rituals, which symbolized the demanding power of the non-resident 'prince' and propitiated his patrilineal ancestors, with those of the matrilineal domestic spirits ('of a small, bounded local descent group structured by kinship relations'); the fierce versus the domesticated. I have argued elsewhere that from the point of view of the city, the contrast was different. The rituals of the central pillar stood for order and prosperity while the forested border regions were the habitation of wild, uncontrollable spirits. The spirits at the transection of paths of communication were dangerous, but they were also protective (Wijeyewardene 1986: 242).

It has been argued, not only by Thongchai, that the notion of boundary is either alien or only partially applied. Lehman, for instance, suggests that two separate ideas of space, one Buddhist and one Hindu, were found in the region — the Buddhist with recognized boundaries, the other analogous to the mathematical notion of a point field. Without conceding the Hindu/Buddhist dichotomy, one may accept that unbounded political units, like Thongchai's unbounded kingdoms, emerge out of the topographic and demographic characteristics of the region. Against this must be placed the very definite and fundamental notions of 'boundary', both spatial and categorical in northern Thai, and presumably Thai culture. The notion of *khüd*, which may be loosely translated as 'taboo', is fundamentally associated with boundaries. To move a fence or other boundary marker, to add on to a house rather than rebuilding, is *khüd*. Rainmaking in both north and central Thailand often involves the confusion of categories (in the north characterized by the same term). It is therefore not true that 'boundaries', even territorial ones, are alien to Thai understanding.

There are certain difficulties which should not be glossed over. The human boundaries of house and city are easy to recognize. We know, for instance, that the city of Chiangmai, in the nineteenth century was closed over night and all strangers were excluded. Thus, not even other northern Thai traders, visiting or in transit, nor the royal emissary of the king were allowed to sleep within the walls of the city. When the latter was honoured with a *su khwan* ritual, this too was conducted outside the city walls (Schomburgk 1869; Wijeyewardene 1986:136-38). The village boundary may not be so easy to delimit, but this too is ritually marked. It is reported that northern Thai villages were traditionally fenced and forbidden to strangers on the occasion of the sacrifice to the village tutelary spirit at the new year. Many Tai villages in Yunnan are still permanently fenced, though today purely pragmatic reasons may be given. It was very likely this was a much more widespread practice in the past. The *müang*, of course, is different, but it is not difficult to see analogies drawn between city walls, village fences and the natural barriers of mountain ranges. Most important, one should point out that when kingdoms, incorporating many *müang*, developed, borders remained the borders of the *müang*. When small *müang* became subject to more than one paramountcy they were not territorially divided between the taxing states. Almost paradoxically, the integrity of the *müang* is maintained.

THE SIGNIFICANCE OF THE WATERSHED

Let us return to the shrines which are said to 'approximate boundaries' but are not boundaries themselves. That is quite true, but it is a mistake to confound 'watershed' with other signs which act as such markers. I would agree with Thongchai that space, northern Thai space, is ritual, but this does not mean that it is merely a 'point field' of identified shrines. The evidence of chronicles suggests we have to start with the notion that each city is established with a charter, from the Buddha, to preserve and propagate the doctrine. These charters are in my view more important than the cosmology of the *Traiphum of Phra Ruang*. There is some evidence from Chiangmai that, like the sacred city of Anuradhapura in Sri Lanka, the city itself was sanctified by *sima* or boundary markers.[5] The city itself and the territory of the *müang* is dotted with a variety of shrines, Buddhist as well as those dedicated to various supernaturals. The mountain forests are inhabited by dangerous supernaturals, the transections of mountain ranges and human pathways, as discussed above, by protective spirits. The transections mark the points which connect the watershed.   This is a ritual boundary.   It is not unexpected that watersheds are recognized. Like the Sinhalese of Leach's Pul Eliya,[6] the 'people of the *müang*' are constrained by the fact that water flows downhill.   Societies practising irrigation agriculture cannot but be aware of the source of their water.

Let me stress, again, that the disagreement as to the facts is largely a matter of viewpoint. Thongchai's view of the kingdom, its boundaries and the significance of mapping, remain major advances in Thai ethnography. I would only claim that the traditional notions of borders are more complicated and better defined than he appreciates.

Before we leave the question of borders in nineteenth century history, let us return to water courses as boundaries and the manner in which the watershed/watercourse alternation was manipulated. I refer back to the account of the treaty between Chiangmai and the Red Karen to point out that at least in the early part of the nineteenth century the rulers of *müang* were willing to see major water courses as frontiers. It is probably the case that this willingness only applied to major rivers. Otherwise the *müang* doctrine would not make a great deal of sense. There is little doubt, however, that colonial frontline administrators often manipulated the watershed/watercourse choice. The following extracts illustrate this point.

On 20 December 1834, E.A. Blundell, Commissioner of Tenasserim Province instructed Richardson, M.D. Surgeon to the Commissioner, on a mission to Chiangmai and Lampang, to lay down the Thoung Yen as boundary between British and Shans:

> You will explain that their side of that river is equally inviolable to our people and warn our Wood Cutters whoever they may be, that they have not the right of cutting on the other side and can only do so, with the permission of the Shan authorities and on payment of such tax as they may impose.[7] (Richardson n.d.)

On 8 January 1888, Hildebrand, Superintendent, Shan States, wrote to the Chief Secretary to the Chief Commissioner, Burma:

> ... the tracts in dispute are exceedingly rich in teak - that all the streams by which logs can be extracted fall into the Salween and thence to Moulmein ... if these tracts are permitted to form the eastern boundary of what was formerly the dominions of the king of Burma, the watershed of the Salween will be the boundary and not the Salween River itself — this following the almost universal custom in the case of boundary lines between Shan state and state. (Hildebrand 1888)

On 16 April 1898, Beckett, the British Consul in Chiangmai reports to Greville, over a French dispute with the Siamese over salt wells in Nan:

> Monsieur Lugan admits that the wedge in question is not worth ten rupees, but argues that its possession is of vital importance to French Indo-China from a strategic point of view — since, he says, the line of watershed can no more be considered a good strategic frontier than the Salween was so considered by Great Britain when she extended her Burmese frontier across that river. (Beckett 1898)

FRONTIERS TODAY

The next part of my paper is a survey of how the Thai state has handled the problems of the frontiers of that nation state. The problems associated with the northeastern frontier may for convenience be traced to the French occupation of Indo-China. Alastair Lamb suggests that the French were responsible for securing the territorial integrity of both Laos and Cambodia in the twentieth century. Referring to the *de facto* partition of Laos between the right wing and the Pathet Lao in the 1960s, he wrote,

> ... all Laotian nationalists, be they of the right or of the left - find the effective partition of Laos extremely distasteful because it involves the undoing of one of the major achievements of French colonial rule: the creation of Laos as a single administrative unit (1968:180).

Of Cambodia, he wrote,

> The remnants of the Cambodian state, centred on Phnom Penh, survived in a tributary relationship with both Hue and Bangkok. Had the prevailing pattern of Cambodian history been allowed to continue without European intervention, even this small

vestige of the past greatness of the Khmers would most probably have disappeared and a direct boundary between Thailand and Vietnam would have evolved on a line not far to the west of the Mekong (1968:181).

However, to emphasize the continuities rather than the discontinuities, let me continue by referring to the Thai-Lao border and another comment by Lamb.

The process of history which resulted in the evolution of the modern Thai-Laos boundary has produced two major problems which still affect the policy of Bangkok. First: the ruling Thai oligarchy has not entirely abandoned its desire to possess influence over the internal affairs of Laos. The right-wing faction in modern Laotian politics has sometimes assumed the appearance of being, as it were, the Vientiane branch of the Bangkok government. ...the second problem inherent in the present alignment of the Thailand-Laos border [is that] it leaves significant Lao population on the Thai side.... (1968:167)

The interesting point about the Thai-Lao border is that despite the humiliations the Thai suffered when the treaties of the turn of the century were imposed on them, actual conflict over the borders only erupted with the victory of the Pathet Lao and the creation of the Lao Peoples Democratic Republic. Even in the modern period, borders are only of consequence when there is hostility between neighbouring states. As long as 'the right-wing faction' maintained some control of the Lao polity, the regime in Bangkok did not seem to care exactly where the treaties had drawn the boundaries, despite the fact that there was much territory on the right bank of the Mae Khong which had been ceded to France, returned to Bangkok by the Japanese, and subsequently handed back to the French after World War II to become part of independent Laos. I shall return to the Lao border in a moment as we very rapidly move from Thailand's frontiers on the east, across the north, down the west with Burma and in the south with Malaysia.

One of the arguments of this paper is that in the modern period there has been a conscious effort to structure the Thai nation and polity so that it keeps not only abreast, but ahead, of the exigencies of the modern world. The argument can only be maintained by looking at the results of policy — here having to do with boundaries — rather than by examining the process of government and policy-making since 1945. To introduce my argument, I use a section from a newspaper column by Surin Pitsuwan, Democrat Party Member of Parliament and well-known political scientist. The point made is that, at least for some, there are long-term plans based on rational views. Surin's article is concerned with what he saw as an ongoing conflict at the heights of Thai politics between the proponents of a parliamentary democracy under the monarchy and their opponents who were of the opinion that 'an open and free political system could be a threat to national security and some of the nation's highest institutions and values'. He argues that M.R. Kukrit Pramoj in particular has consistently pursued a policy in which the military are placated, development is seen as issuing from the throne and parliamentary processes supported and sustained. He concludes, Kukrit 'is entitled to some personal gratification now that he sees parliamentary democracy with the monarch as head of state is firmly established'.[8] It has been pointed out to me that not least in importance is the fact that the vision is credited to Kukrit, and not elsewhere. The lesson to be drawn by us is that one of the most acute Thai commentators on the polity takes the view that long range aims are a feature of the politically active Thai elite. Surin attributes to Kukrit a conscious formative role in the development of post-war Thai political history. My proposition is that there is likely to have been comparable conscious effort directed towards the definition and maintenance of the Kingdom's territorial integrity. A rather rapid survey of a range of frontier issues sustains this view.

On the Cambodian frontier, the Thai, unhappy with the treaties of the first decade of this century, laid claim to Siam Reap and Battambang which they occupied, with Japanese approval, between 1941-46. Unlike Laos, relations with post-independence Cambodia were not good and the Preah Vihear case before the International Court of Justice symbolized this hostility. For the argument of this paper, two points are worth noting. First, the issue concerned the monument, the ancient monastery, which lay on part of the watershed which by treaty formed the border between the two countries. The second fact is that the Thai accepted the judgment of the Court, admittedly with bad grace. Part of a footnote by Alastair Lamb is most interesting in light of the earlier discussion.

> The 1907 map appeared to indicate that the boundary should depart from the waterparting line so as to place the Preah Vihear temple, an ancient Khmer monument, on the Cambodian (French) side.... During the pleadings before the International Court of Justice, it proved extremely difficult to establish exactly where the waterparting lay; the balance of the evidence suggested that it actually passed through the centre of the disputed temple.... Since receiving the Court's decision, the Thais have, in effect, demarcated unilaterally the boundary in Preah Vihear region by the erection of a high fence. It must be admitted, however, that the main Thai objective was less the desire for boundary demarcation than the wish to spite the Cambodians: the Thai fence spoils the view from the temple. (1968:169)

It should also be mentioned that whereas access to the shrine is relatively easy from the Thai side, it is quite hazardous from the Cambodian.[9]

In a previous paper (1990:59-62) I have discussed at length some of the issues involved in the fighting on the Thai-Lao border, particularly in relation to the battles of Ban Rom Klao. Here we need to go over this material only very briefly. The points that need to be made are first, Thai-Lao border problems only came to the fore after the victory of the Pathet Lao; second, the Thai have in principle accepted the boundaries, in effect, imposed by the French at the turn of the century; third, the recent conflict reduced itself to a disagreement as to the identification of a watercourse and either a mountain range or a single mountain; and fourth, the Thai military reversed their previous stand of hostility to the Lao and effectively carried the nation in establishing a broad agreement with the erstwhile enemy.

The northwestern frontier is rather different. The entire frontier region with Burma has been in insurrection on the Burmese side, and this is of relevance for an assessment of developments on the Thai side. The major insurrections — the Karen, the Shan and the Mon — have had ethnic representation on the Thai side, clearly a matter of great political sensitivity for the Thai government. Until very recently one could say that though the Thai have not satisfied any of the parties concerned, they had not unduly offended them either. However, most recently, there has been rapprochement between the Burmese and Thai military forces and conditions have apparently changed. Another major factor to emerge in 1990 was the success of the National League for Democracy and the subsequent refusal of the Burma Army to relinquish power. The hold on power of the military government seems to have strengthened, but there has also been the development of an understanding between the joint minority commands and the Burman led opposition.

There are four groups in insurrection in Burma which have a direct consequence for Thailand's frontier policy. They are the Mon, the Karen, the Shan and the Kuomintang. Though there is a large Mon community in Thailand, they have not loomed large in Thai frontier politics. The Karen have been much more important, partly because till recently the Karen rebels were supplied through Thailand and were able to conduct their military and taxation policies without much hindrance from the Thai. Neither the Mon (Bauer 1990) nor the Karen (Rajah 1990) in Thailand appear interested in insurrection, though they may give more than moral support to compatriots over the frontier. The Shan and Kuomintang have been more important, largely because of their involvement in the narcotics trade — the Shan, to finance their rebellion, and the Chinese, it seems, for economic gain alone — though it has also enabled them to maintain their ethnic identity. Most important for our discussion is the fact that the Kuomintang operated a major base on Thai territory at Mae Salong.

The Shan insurrectionists were divided into a number of competing groups with conflicting political loyalties. In the late 1970s a major figure emerged, not at first because of his insurrectionist activity, but because of his control of the narcotics trade. This was Khun Sa. In recent years he has headed the Tai Revolutionary Council and the Müang Tai Army, which has claimed to unite all Shan military forces. This claim is disputed by the Democratic Alliance of Burma, which is Karen-led and which recently has included Burmese students fleeing Rangoon, and dissident elements from the Burma Army. Again, the major interest for our discussion is the fact that Khun Sa's headquarters were established on Thai territory, at Ban Hin Taek, until 1982 when it was attacked and taken by the Thai military.

We turn our attention now to Thai territory and the two military strongholds of Mae Salong and Ban Hin Taek. The Thai government has now renamed both these towns — the first Santi Khiri ('the mountain of peace') and the other Thoed Thai ('Thai elevated'). The 1964 *Geographical Encyclopædia of Thailand* mentions neither (Royal Institute of Thailand 1963-66). The recent history of these two towns is revealing. According to the version of history publicly displayed in Mae Salong (Figure 3), the process of finding a solution to the Kuomintang problem began about 1969 or 1970 when a Thai military delegation met with the Taiwan government to discuss the issue. A few years later Kriangsak Chomanand, then, I believe, Army Commander, was responsible for the Ministry of Agriculture investigating the cultivation of tea and pine trees in Mae Salong. The Kuomintang authorities built accommodation for Thai government officials. One informant, who was chauffeur to an Agriculture Ministry official, says that not only was the journey hazardous, the roads disastrous, but also that the population of Mae Salong steadfastly ignored them. When Kriangsak became Prime Minister in 1978, the Kuomintang officials built and dedicated a house to him on the peak dominating the town. The people of Mae Salong renounced the opium trade and were given Thai citizenship. The tea industry seems to be flourishing as are the pine plantations. It is probably the most successful crop-replacement program in Thailand, despite the devastation of forest which characterizes the region. Before 1979 the Kuomintang maintained a military outpost in a Iu-Mien (Yao) village at the foot of the range and radioed permission was necessary to continue on a dirt track to the town. Today there is a first class road, and it is being promoted as a tourist resort. Nevertheless Mae Salong is not yet completely part of Thailand. Effective control is in the hands of the Kuomintang military hierarchy. There is a police station with a lone officer who does not appear to have much to do. There is also a small contingent of a Thai volunteer unit, but this is outnumbered and literally overseen by the Kuomintang unit (which stands on the hill immediately above the Thai post). All Mae Salong males are said to be conscripted for five years at the age of sixteen. They are billed as a tourist protection force and it is true that one of their tasks is to mount patrols, during the day, on the road into the town. The Thai government does have some effective presence, most notably the school, health clinic and *wat*. Till quite recently the school taught in Chinese, but the language of instruction is now Thai. Young children, it is said, are taught Chinese at home. The Thai temple is only a few years old and the foundations of the *cedi* were installed by the Queen Mother in 1988. The health clinic has a Thai staff, but the doctor was 'trained in Taiwan'.

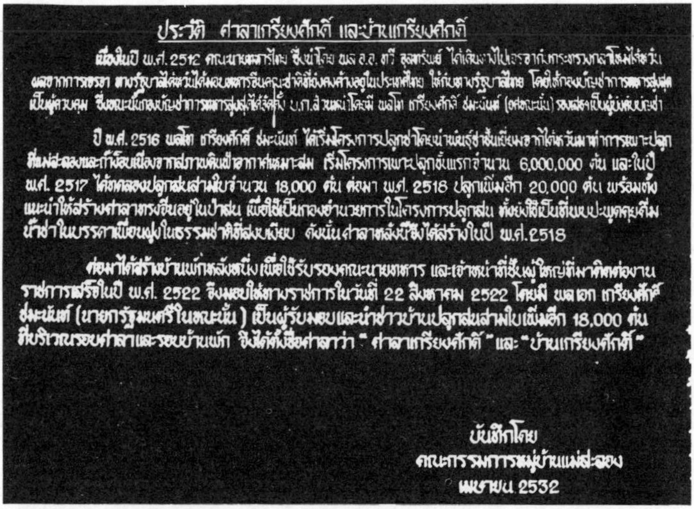

ประวัติ ศาลาเกรียงศักดิ์ และบ้านเกรียงศักดิ์

เมื่อปี พ.ศ. 2512 คณะนายทหารไทย ซึ่งนำโดย พล อ.อ. ทวี จุลละทรัพย์ ได้เดินทางไปเจรจากับกระทรวงมหาดไทยที่ไต้หวัน และจากการเจรจา สาธารณรัฐจีนได้มอบทหารจีนคณะชาติที่ยังคงตกค้างอยู่ในประเทศไทย ให้กับ พวกรัฐบาลไทย โดยให้กองบัญชาการทหารสูงสุด เป็นผู้ดูแลชุม ซึ่งขณะนั้นกองบัญชาการทหารสูงสุดได้ตั้งให้ พล.ท.ส. นามี โดยมี เกรียงศักดิ์ ชมะนันทร์ (ยศขณะนั้น) รวมเป็นผู้บัญชาการ

ปี พ.ศ. 2516 พลโท เกรียงศักดิ์ ชมะนันทร์ ได้ริเริ่มการปลูกชา โดยนำพันธุ์ชามาเลี้ยงจากไต้หวันมาทำการเพาะปลูก ที่แม่สลองและถ้ำงอบเนื่องจากภูมิอากาศเหมาะสม เริ่มโครงการเพาะปลูกตั้งแรกจำนวน 6,000,000 ต้น และในปี พ.ศ. 2517 ได้ทดลองปลูกสนจำนวน 18,000 ต้น ต่อมา พ.ศ. 2518 ปลูกเพิ่มอีก 20,000 ต้น พร้อมทั้ง แนะนำให้สร้างศาลาทรงจีนอยู่ในป่าสน เพื่อใช้เป็นกองอำนวยการในโครงการปลูกสน ทั้งยังใช้เป็นที่แวะพักพูดคุยดื่มน้ำชากันในบรรยากาศเงียบสงบในธรรมชาติที่สงบเงียบ ดังนั้นศาลาดังนี้จึงได้สร้างในปี พ.ศ.2518

ต่อมาได้สร้างบ้านพักหลังหนึ่ง เพื่อใช้รับรองคณะนายทหาร และเจ้าหน้าที่ชั้นผู้ใหญ่ในที่มาทำงาน ราชการที่ที่นี่ในปี พ.ศ. 2522 จึงมอบให้ทางราชการในวันที่ 22 สิงหาคม 2522 โดยมี พลเอก เกรียงศักดิ์ ชมะนันทร์ (นายกรัฐมนตรีในขณะนั้น) เป็นผู้รับมอบและนำชาวบ้านปลูกสนเพิ่มอีกใบเพิ่มอีก 1800 ต้น ที่บริเวณรอบศาลาและรอบบ้านพัก จึงได้ตั้งชื่อศาลาว่า " ศาลาเกรียงศักดิ์ " และ " บ้านเกรียงศักดิ์ "

บันทึกโดย
คณะกรรมการหมู่บ้านแม่สลอง
พฤษภาคม 2532

Figure 3   Public notice in Mae Salong, Chiangrai Province, describing Kuomintang-Thai military friendship, 1989.

Translation: The Story of Kriangsak Hall and Kriangsak House

In the year B. E. 2512 [1969] a group of Thai military led by Air Force General Thawi Chulasab went for discussions with the Ministry of Home Affairs in Taiwan. The result of these talks was that the Government of Taiwan gave into the care of the Government of Thailand those Chinese Nationalist soldiers who were still living on Thai territory, with the Supreme Command Headquarters being responsible. At that time Headquarters had announced the appointment of Lieutenant-General (his rank then) Kriangsak Chomenan as Supreme Commander.

In 2516 [1973] Lieutenant-General Kriangsak Chomanan visited, bringing with him tea from Taiwan for planting in Mae Salong and Tham Ngob, as the climate seemed most suitable. The project first planted sic million bushes and in B. E. 2517 [1974] a trial planting of 18,000 pine trees (Pinus khasya) was made. In 2518 [1975] another 20,000 trees were planted, and the suggestion was made that a Chinese-style hall should be build in the pine forest to be used as an administrative centre for the pine tree project. This is still used as a meeting place for conversation and drinking tea among friends in natural surroundings of peace and quiet. This hall was duly built in the year B. E. 2518 [1975].

Later, a guesthouse was built to receive military officers and senior government servants who came on official business. This was completed in B. E. 2522 [1979] and was officially handed over to the government on 22 August 2522 in the person of General Kriangsak Chomanan, who was then Prime Minister. He then led the people in planting another 1800 pine trees around the hall and the guesthouse. Thus Kriangsak Hall and Kriangsak House acquired their names.

The position of Hin Taek is even more intriguing. The population seems largely Chinese and Shan. The headman says he is Shan (*Tai jai*), but was born elsewhere in north Thailand. He has been (in 1989) headman for over twelve years, which means that he was headman during the Khun Sa period and maintained this position after the 1982 expulsion. There is a Thai Police Station in Hin Taek and a volunteer Thai military post at the main road which is thirteen kilometres away, over a road only barely passable by an ordinary vehicle. Despite this the headman has had enough influence to have electricity connected to the area. Hin Taek is controlled with a locally raised volunteer force. They are nominally part of a force controlled by the Ministry of the Interior, but it seems effective control is entirely local.[10] After the expulsion of Khun Sa the headman formulated a fourteen-point code for the administration of the town. It is of some interest. This is the order in which he recalled them. 1. Obey Thai law. 2. No adultery. 3. No gambling (not even the state lottery). 4. No drugs. 5. Protect the forests. 6. No laziness. 7. No insulting of others. 8. No smuggling. 9. No arms. 10. Moderate drinking. 11. Respect for others' customs. 12. Strangers are forbidden (to be accommodated overnight). 13. Strangers must be reported. 14. All sales must be witnessed. Apart from the electricity, the major presence of the Thai government, as in Mae Salong, is the school.

Mae Salong and Hin Taek demonstrate another set of strategies which Thailand has used to regulate, rationalize and bring control to its frontiers. What seems particularly noteworthy is the very pragmatic use of force and compromise.

The southern frontier is perhaps the most contentious. This is the only one where strong ethnic and religious concerns complicate the situation. It may be stressed here that ethnic and religious issues are of minor concern where Lao, Shan, Chinese Kuomintang and Mon are concerned, and this even seems true with the Khmer. But in South Thailand things are different. The opening paragraph of a long article by the commander of the Fourth Army region encapsulates many of the concerns of the Thai establishment.

There are many sources for the problems of the five border provinces. First there are problems which arise out of natural conditions. There are also the problems which arise out of differences in the ways of thought of some people of the nation, particularly of some groups of Thai Muslims that create strong divisions among citizens which has come down to the present as a chronic problem - that is, the problem of separatism in the south. This arises from the thinking and acts of Thai Muslims who have a partiality for Malaysia. Besides this, there are important problems such as that of terrorists, that of persons with dual nationality, the problem of the education of Thai Muslims, the problems of fishermen, the problem of determining the border between Thailand and Malaysia, and that of boat people. These problems completely disrupt the harmony and the security of the country. We have already in the past lost territories in the south, Mak Island (Penang), we have lost the state of Perlis, Trengganu and Muang Saiburi in the transfer of rights through courts and through embassies to the British during the reign of King Chulalongkorn. But for the Thai to lose the five provinces of Pattani, Yala, Narathiwat, Satun and Songkhla is something to which we cannot agree. For these border provinces have been part of Thailand for a very long time, for many hundreds of years. But the solution to the problem of the southern border provinces has many fine details, particularly the problem of terrorism which arises out of feelings of nationalism and problems of the psychology of society. (Wisit 1988:35-36, my translation)

General Wisit later deals with the problem of the Malayan Communist Party (CPM), but his introductory paragraph makes quite clear that the preponderant concern is with the Thai Muslims and the fear of secession and loss of territory. There has been considerable friction in the past between Malaysia and Thailand, ostensibly on the grounds that the Thai were giving sanctuary to the CPM. The Thai concern of course was that Malaysia was giving succour and sustenance to the Malay separatists. The recent agreement between the Malaysian government and Chin Peng and the CPM[11] must count as a tremendous coup for the Thai. It removes the major source of complaint the Malaysians could tap and allows the Thai to press for reasonable settlement of the border problems.

This brief survey is designed to argue that on all their borders, since the Second World War, the policy of the Thai establishment, and it seems the military part of it in particular, has moved to secure their frontiers and remove grounds of conflict. Thai irredentism as a serious movement seems to have been confined to the writings of Luang Wichitwathakan and the period of the Japanese alliance during the Second World War. Though there are, and continue to be, proclamations about fellow Thai living under alien rule, expansionism has never been a realistic, formulated policy. On the contrary, the Thai have appeared, in many instances extremely legalistic in attempts to elucidate the details of treaties and pragmatic in accepting compromises of various kinds. To return to where this paper began, this is not a matter of 'discourse', but a matter of history.

CONCLUSION

I have argued for two substantive propositions in this paper. First, the notion of territorial boundary is far from being alien to Thai (Tai) understanding, and the *müang* demonstrates this clearly in the political domain. The *müang* is a socio-political recognition of an ecologically and topographically defined unit. The boundaries of larger political units were the boundaries of *müang* on the border. Second, following Thongchai's identification of the point at which the Bangkok monarchy recognized the new principles the colonial powers used in defining the nation state, I argue that there has been deliberate policy of securing the frontiers of Thailand by social and political occupation and through internationally recognized agreement. At a more general level I have argued that Thongchai's discoveries of the 'geo-body of Siam' and the theory of frontiers are not to be seen only as 'discourse', but as finer approximations to what the past really was.

Finally, I would like, briefly, to set this argument in a broader context by citing Philip Morrison reviewing *Catastrophic Episodes in Earth History,* by Claude C. Albritton, Jr.

We have gained important ground even in our indecisiveness. Changes can plainly be fast or slow; we know that now. The old war of method between dominant catastrophe and the application of present experience to the entire past is now best seen as a regional conflict. "We don't need any more doctrinaire labels." Even the assumption that the laws of energy and matter remain unchanged is now a working hypothesis, tentative but tested to high accuracy over the past billion years or so. The historical sciences are able to set themselves an "ambitious end ... a unified theory for the unfolding of the universe." (Morrison 1990:143)

The name most associated with the theories of 'catastrophism', certainly to those of us outside the fields of geology and evolutionary biology, is Stephen Jay Gould. As I understand it, Gould's theory as it applies to evolution is that the evolutionary story is punctuated by unpredictable catastrophes, rather than entirely determined by slow and incremental growth resulting universally in finely adapted organisms. In the Gould picture the consequences of accident loom much larger. An even stronger connection to Gould is in the term 'historical sciences'. Gould sees evolution as a historical process, and it seems to me that as evolutionists have moved towards history, some historians have felt the urge to hide behind semiotics and deconstruction. The reason I say 'historian' and not 'anthropologist' is partly because it is a historian's work I began by discussing, but also because much anthropology may be beyond redemption. The rather grandiose question I would ask is 'Do we take our part in the formulation of "a unified theory for the unfolding of the universe"'?

Craig Reynolds, in a paper still unpublished in English, has taken two major events in Thai history which have 'changed the plot' of Thai history. The first is the 1932 revolution which is interpreted by historians in different ways. He appears to have no difficulty in accepting the importance of the events in themselves. The other is Thongchai's analysis of the emergence of the 'geo-body of Siam', the recognition of which has given to the Thai a 'chunk of territory' about which they can feel emotional. The view that history is a story told for the purposes of the contemporary has a powerful attraction and truth value. There is also the very real question as to whether the constraints imposed by contemporary interests and demands are surmountable. My own position is that the constraints are not insurmountable and that there are non-relativistic positions that may be maintained.

Thongchai's thesis is most valuable because he documents and discusses those crucial, traumatic events that brought the nation-state to Thailand (or as he prefers, Siam; he is a historian and 'Thailand' is an anachronism in the nineteenth century) and Southeast Asia. It may even be seen as a 'catastrophe'. The nation-state was not something which slowly evolved in the consciousness of the Siamese elite or in the political institutions of the country. It was a relatively sudden restructuring of the way in which the Bangkok court apprehended the territory and people it ruled. One view that needs consideration is that a relativism is subsumed within the other, more positivist, view of history. Though the advent of mapping and the recognition of the 'geo-body' may have been a catastrophe in Thai history, to the historian of the world-wide triumph of the ideology of the nation-state it would not necessarily appear as such.

Compare this proposition with recent comments by Gould on the emergence of agriculture in the Levant. He takes exception to the uncritical overuse of the notion of 'adaptation' and points out that intensive foraging in areas which preceded agriculture could in some ways be seen as most non-adaptive. He points out that there is evidence that such areas became grossly overpopulated and 'introduced female infanticide on an extensive scale'. Agriculture in the Levant was a response to catastrophe (Gould 1990:26-27).

The conflict between 'catastrophe' and 'gradual change' as theoretical stances have not, perhaps, been of great moment in anthropological theory, though one must recognize Marxism in its more robust days (as opposed to its gracile, should one say effete, French phase.) But Gould has other lessons for us. In his recent book, *Time's Arrow, Time's Cycle* he looks at the history of geology and, in my view, sets out some important evolutionary lessons. In the first place he demolishes the notion that progress in geology was merely a consequence of greater empiricism. The theories too were important, but it is the nature of those theories that have lessons for us. The major theoretical problem was to cope with the nature of time. What are those laws that remain unchanged and therefore constitute 'Time's cycle' and which phenomena part of Time's unidirectional arrow? Craig Reynolds appears to see the distinction, but does he abandon the latter for the semiotic version of the former? It may well be that semiotic laws are part of Time's cycle, but the arrow, man and society's connections with 'deep time' cannot be abandoned.

Thongchai's discovery of the emergence of the 'geo-body' does not necessarily mean the discovery of universal law; rather, it is an event in history with consequences for the future. We are quite unable to tell what the consequences will be, but we can examine what they have been so far, and part of this examination is most certainly 'deconstruction'. But if deconstruction is premised merely on a notion that any proposition is deconstructible and therefore there is no 'truth' (provisional or otherwise) which is being approached, or even capable of being sought, it is, I believe, a self-indulgence. Thongchai himself appears motivated by the desire to deconstruct and dissipate nationalism and chauvinism. Clearly a laudable aim. Its importance may be epitomized in the fact that the new edition of *In Search of Southeast Asia*, a highly commended university text, has included a new map giving Thailand the borders which Thongchai has just deconstructed. Thongchai's contribution is not to be seen as another plot to be deconstructed, but another correction in the attempt to approximate the trajectory of Time's arrow. Or, to cite Gould, 'narrative explanations in history work differently from lawlike deductions in celestial mechanics, ... the jargon of "modelling" belongs more to the latter, and ... agriculture in the Levant is more a thing than an instance' (1990:27). That is, an object produced by history rather than an outcome, an example, of the working of the laws of celestial mechanics. Our task is to understand the thing, or the event. The 'geo-body of Siam' and the 'frontiers of Thailand' are such things.

ENDNOTES

1. Sulak Sivarak, in his keynote address printed in this volume, interprets Thai history as a conflict between *müang* and *baan*, the first representing political authority, the latter the *gemütlichkeit* of the village.

2. Dealt with at length in her Ph.D. thesis, and briefly in Cholthira 1990:95-96.

3. Personal communication.

4. The legal basis of this appears to have been the Franco-Siamese Treaty of 1893. See Chandran Jeshurun 1977 *passim*, but particularly 'Frontispiece: "The Anglo-French Declaration of 1896"'.

5. It is suggested by some informants that in the past *wat* within the city needed no *bot* and monks could be ordained anywhere within the city walls.

6. '... the Pul Eliya community does not only operate within an established framework of legal rules, it also exists within a particular man-made ecological environment.... The interpretation of ideal legal rules is at all times limited by such crude nursery facts as that water evaporates and flows downhill' (Leach 1961:9).

7. 'Shan' here means the Khon Müang of Chiangmai.

8. This was originally written in that heady decade when many of us thought that parliamentary democracy was in Thailand to stay and successful *coups d'etat* were a thing of the past. But there is evidence that this ideological planning is still alive, despite the coup of February 1991. Professor Boonchana Atthakorn, Chief Advisor to the National Committee on Policy, appointed by the National Peacekeeping Council, said on 28 February 1991:

> Speaking from a historical point of view, we, in Thailand, have had constitutions for 59 years and about 20 coups in 50-60 years, of which about ten have been successful. Even England took 300-400 years before it could have its present-day democracy. With regard to all things we must look to history. In our case I think that within a hundred years, democracy will be better than it is now, because understanding of all circumstances will improve, and our maturity will improve (*Khaw phiset*, 4-10 March 1991, 21-22. My translation).

9. See Le May's description of his journey (1954:130-33). He started at Srisaket by lorry and arrived at the foothills within nine hours. The climb to the foot of the temple took two hours. The first flight consists of 160 steps.

10. For an account of Thai volunteer defence organizations see Suchit 1987:53-58. This may, however, be now somewhat outdated.

11. For an account of this event see Coe 1990.

REFERENCES

Bauer, Christian. 1990. 'Language and Ethnicity: the Mon in Burma and Thailand', in Wijeyewardene, ed. 1990:14-48.

Barker, James. 1856. 'Journal of a journey from Amarapoora to the Burmese Shan States on the Salween River and through various parts of those states', India Foreign [Political] Consultations No. 204, India Office Library.

Beckett, W.R.D. 1898. 'Letter', Public Records Office, Kew, FO/628/17/234.

Chandran Jeshurun. 1977. *The Contest for Siam 1889-1902: A Study in Diplomatic Rivalry.* Kuala Lumpur, Penerbit University Kebangsaan Malaysia.

Cholthira Satyawadhna. 1990. 'A Comparative Study of Structure and Contradiction in the Austro-Asiatic System of the Thai-Yunnan Periphery' in Wijeyewardene ed. 1990:74-101.

Coe, John J. 1990. 'The 1989 Hat Yai accords' *The Beagle: Records of the Northern Territory Museum of Arts and Sciences,* 7 (1), 121-135.

Gould, Stephen J. 1988. *Time's Arrow, Time's Cycle: Myth and Metaphor in Discovery of Geological Time.* London.

--------. 1990. 'Down on the farm' (review of *From Foraging to Agriculture: The Levant at the End of the Ice Age* by Donald O. Henry), *New York Review of Books*, 36.21-22, pp.26-27.

Hildebrand, A.H. 1888. 'Letter to Chief Secretary to the Chief Commissioner, Burma', Public Records Office, Kew, FO/628/12/79.

Lamb, Alastair. 1968. *Asian Frontiers: Studies in a Continuing Problem*. Melbourne, F.W. Cheshire for the Australian Institute of International Affairs.

Leach, Edmund. 1960. 'The Frontiers of "Burma"' *Comparative Studies in Society and History* 3.1, 49-68.

--------. 1961. *Pul Eliya a Village in Ceylon: A Study of Land Tenure and Kinship* Cambridge at the University Press.

Lehman, F.K. 1981. 'On the Vocabulary Semantics of "Field" in Theravada Buddhist Society' in *Essays on Burma, Contributions to Asian Studies*, 16, ed. John P. Ferguson. Leiden, E. J. Brill.

Le May, Reginald. 1954. *The Culture of South-East Asia: The Heritage of India*. London, George Allen and Unwin.

Morrison, Phillip. 1990. 'Review' of *Catastrophic Episodes in Earth History* by Claude C. Albritton, Jr. *Scientific American*, January, 142-43.

Penth, Hans. 1977. 'Historical Notes on the Region West of Chiengmai', *Journal of the Siam Society*, 65.2, 179-88.

Rajah, Ananda. 1990. 'Ethnicity, Nationalism, and the Nation-State: The Karen in Burma and Thailand', in Wijeyewardene, ed. 1990:102-34.

Reynolds, Craig J. n.d. 'The Plot of Thai History: Theory and Practice' in *Patterns and Illusions: Papers on Thai Topics in Memory of Richard B. Davis*. Forthcoming.

Richardson, David, M. D. n.d. 'Missions to Siam 1829-1835', British Library, Additional 30,354.

Royal Institute of Thailand. 1963-66. *Encyclopædia of Thai Geography* (in Thai). Bangkok 4 volumes.

Sanguan Chotisukharat. 1972. 'Report of a treaty of friendship between Chiangmai and *Müang jaang daeng* (Red Karen or Kayah)' (in Thai), *Prachum tamnaan Lannaathai* (*Collected Lanna chronicles*), Bangkok, Odeon Store. Vol. 1, 545-561.

Schomburgk, Robert H. 1869. 'Xiengmai', *Siam Repository* 1, 173-82.

Suchit Bunbongkarn. 1987. *The Military in Thai Politics*. Singapore, Institute of Southeast Asian Studies.

Thongchai Winichakul. 1987. 'Siam Mapped: A History of the Geo-Body of Siam' in *Proceedings of International Conference on Thai Studies*, compiled by Ann Buller, Canberra, Department of Anthropology. Vol. 1, 155-64.

--------. 1988. *Siam Mapped: A History of the Geo-Body of Siam*, Ph.D. Thesis, University of Sydney. University of Hawaii Press, forthcoming.

Turton, Andrew. 1972. 'Matrilineal Descent Groups and Spirit Cults of the Thai-Yuan in Northern Thailand', *Journal of the Siam Society*, 60.2, 217-56.

Wijeyewardene, Gehan. 1984-5. 'Great City on the River Ping: Some Anthropological and Historical Perspectives on Chiang Mai', *Political Science Review* (Chiang Mai University), Series No. 6, 86-112.

--------. 1986. *Place and Emotion in Northern Thai Ritual Behaviour*. Bangkok, Pandora.

--------. 1990. 'Thailand and the Tai: versions of ethnic identity' in Wijeyewardene, ed. 1990:48-73.

Wijeyewardene, Gehan, ed. 1990. *Ethnic Groups Across National Boundaries in Mainland Southeast Asia*. Singapore, Institute of Southeast Asian Studies.

Wisit Artkhumwong. 1988. 'Problems of the Five Southern Border Provinces' (in Thai), *Ratthaphirak*, 30.3, 35-71.

Chapter 7

THAI-BUDDHIST IDENTITY:
DEBATES ON THE
TRAIPHUUM PHRA RUANG

Peter A. Jackson

INTRODUCTION

Buddhism, along with the nation and the monarchy, is one of the officially recognised fundamental institutions (*sathaaban lak*) that underpin the political and cultural identity of the modern Thai polity. Buddhist ethical teachings, ritualistic practices and the institution of renunciate monks or *sangha* together provide norms of individual and collective well-being against which activities in the social and political domains are measured. Thai political processes, in particular, to a significant extent draw their authority and legitimate their claim to the allegiance of the Thai populace by their compliance with Buddhist precepts and principles. The intimate theoretical and ritualistic relationship between Buddhism and all aspects of secular life in Thailand has placed the religion at the centre of recent attempts to isolate, define and promote the features of a distinctive Thai identity (*eekalak thai*).

The search for a unique Thai national identity takes a range of forms in modern Thailand and includes government-sponsored seminars aiming to revive interest in medieval Thai literature; the official promotion of traditional village crafts; the institutionalisation of local cultural forms in annual 'fairs' or *theesakaan* in almost every province as well as the refurbishment and repair of surviving architectural monuments and archaeological sites. However, all of these and other expressions of Thai identity are founded on the assumed identity that to be Thai is to be Buddhist.

The primacy of Buddhism in the definition of 'Thainess' is accepted by all but the non-Buddhist minorities in Thailand, but there is far from universal agreement on just what constitutes the core political and cultural identity of the Thai people. Is this identity founded on urban elite culture or on regional linguistic and cultural forms? Is Thai identity defined by obedience to an authoritarian state relying on the unifying symbolism of the monarchy or is it defined by active participation in the development of democratic political processes modelled on ancient Buddhist paradigms? Is 'Thainess' to be found in acquiescence to the cultural glories of past monarchs and kingdoms or in the transformation of these archaic cultural verities in the creation of a forward-looking popular culture?

In this paper I consider some of the tensions within contemporary efforts to define a unique Thai political identity that integrates both the legitimating symbolism of Buddhism and changing political expectations. In particular, I will outline the relationship between the development of alternative approaches to the interpretation of Buddhist doctrine since the mid-1970s and attempts to develop an indigenous theoretical basis for the democratisation and political liberalisation of Thai society. I will undertake this study by analysing the resurgent interest in a key Thai-Buddhist text, the *Traiphuum Phra Ruang*.

The *Traiphuum Phra Ruang*, composed in the fourteenth century by King Lithai, was one of the most important Buddhist texts in pre-modern Thailand. The Buddhist cosmography described in the *Traiphuum Phra Ruang* was read not only as an account of the structure of the cosmos as a whole but also as a justification for the social and political institutions of the Thai kingdoms of the Sukhothai, Ayutthaya, Thonburi and early Bangkok periods. Despite being subjected to rationalist critiques and a demythologisation of its metaphysical contents in the nineteenth century, the *Traiphuum* has retained a political potency up to the present day. This is because of its symbolic association with the ascribed historical sources of the political and cultural identity of the modern Thai state. In the past decade interpretations attributed to the text by Thai commentators and analysts have reflected a range of conflicting 'conservative' and 'reformist' outlooks within the Thai political and economic elite. Theoreticians aligned with these competing outlooks have sought to legitimise their respective visions of Thailand's political future by referring to early Thai textual and cultural records such as the *Traiphuum Phra Ruang*. This renewed interest in ancient texts such as the *Traiphuum* has to a large extent been spurred by attempts to develop a new Thai-Buddhist 'gospel', that is, an interpretation of Buddhism and of Thai-Buddhist identity that is capable of providing an ethical and religious foundation for emerging democratic political structures in Thailand.

BUDDHISM AND POLITICAL LEGITIMATION IN CONTEMPORARY THAILAND

The important political functions performed by Buddhist teachings and the Buddhist *sangha* in the histories of Thailand and the other Theravada polities of Southeast Asia have been described in a number of studies (F. E. Reynolds 1978a:175; Ling 1976:284-6). In the case of Thailand the historical continuity of the institution of the *sangha* and its close relationship to the Thai state up to the present day has meant that Buddhist doctrines and practices in that country have retained an especially high degree of symbolic significance and relevance to political activities and debates. Fundamental to the ongoing significance of Buddhist teachings, in particular, has been their interpretative plasticity, that is, their capacity to continue to be used to confer symbolic legitimation upon the exercise of political authority and the structures of political power, whether those structures have been founded upon absolute monarchical rule, military rule or upon a popularly elected government.

However, the changing forms of government in Thailand in this century have created new tensions and dissonances within the traditional structures of Thai-Buddhist thought. In their analyses of the relations between Theravada Buddhism and the state in Thailand Keyes and Tambiah, among others, have described a 'crisis of legitimacy' (Keyes 1978:160-1; Tambiah 1984:344) which has afflicted the Thai state since the overthrow of the absolute monarchy in 1932. By this Keyes and Tambiah mean that the overthrow created a disjuncture between the state and the traditional interpretations of Buddhist doctrine and practice which had been referred to in justifying the monarchical political order of the pre-modern Thai kingdoms. These and other scholars (Butt 1978:49) have also noted the continuing quest among *bhikkhus* and lay Buddhists in Thailand to develop more appropriate forms of religious doctrine and practice capable of lending legitimacy to contemporary political processes.

In their analyses of the ongoing efforts to re-legitimise the Thai political order in Buddhist terms Keyes and Tambiah have tended to present the modern Thai state as a single, unitary political unit and have not given much weight to the complex patterns of conflict between the factional groupings of the elite which now vie for political and economic dominance. Recent Thai politics has been dominated by conflicts between, on the one hand, the traditional holders of power — the aristocracy and the civilian and military bureaucracies — and, on the other hand, the increasingly influential groups of business interests and reformist-minded middle class professionals and intellectuals.

I have argued elsewhere (Jackson 1989) that the intellectual and organisational history of Thai Buddhism in the past century should, by and large, be understood in terms of the political and economic history of Thailand during this period. In particular, I maintain that the ultimate provenance of the major disputes about Buddhist doctrine and the administration of the *sangha* in the past one hundred years has lain in the conflicts between competing factions of the Thai political and economic elite. The relationships between the Buddhist *sangha* and the secular organs of state power in Thailand are so intimate and numerous that Thai Buddhism could not avoid being shaken by the waves of political agitation and struggle which have emanated from Bangkok in this century.

At the risk of oversimplification, two broad outlooks on Buddhist teachings and the role of the religion in contemporary Thai society can be identified. I will use the terms 'traditionalist' and 'reformist' to refer to these politico-religious outlooks because of the common use of 'traditions' of Buddhism to support conservative political positions and the use of 'reformist' presentations of Buddhist teachings to support political liberalisation and reform.

Traditional interpretations of Buddhism involve metaphysical formulations of doctrine which emphasise the determining influence of *kamma* and religious merit and demerit on human well-being and socio-economic status. In previous centuries such formulations of Buddhism were used to lend legitimacy to the absolute monarchy. Contemporary metaphysical formulations of Thai-Buddhist doctrine are revealed clearly in the teachings of such conservative monks as Phra Kittiwuttho (Udornkhanaphirak 1986) and such conservative Buddhist movements as the Wat Phra Thammakaay sect (Thattachiwo 1987). In recent years such traditionalist interpretations of Buddhism have commonly been called upon in arguments to support centralised political structures which are patterned after the historical model of the absolute monarchy.

In contrast, reformist interpretations involve rationalist or demythologised interpretations of the religion's teachings which de-emphasise the significance of the doctrine of *kamma* and instead emphasise the capacity of individuals to attain their own religious, and by implication, political liberation. Two of the most prominent reformist Thai-Buddhist thinkers are Phra Phutthathat (Buddhadasa) Bhikkhu (Phutthathat 1978, 1981) and Phra Thepwethi Bhikkhu, formerly Phra Ratchaworamuni (1984a). Such liberal or reformist interpretations are now commonly referred to by middle class and professional groupings in order to support more democratic political structures. Rationalist formulations of Buddhism also emphasise the importance of the individual attainment of *nibbana*. There is a close theoretical relationship between the dual emphasis on the attainment of personal salvation and the development of participatory political forms in reformist interpretations of Buddhism, for both place individuals in an active role, able, at least in theory, to determine their spiritual condition as well as their social and political environment. This view of human existence as the active determination of one's own destiny in accord with Buddhist ethical guidelines contrasts sharply with the traditional, conservative interpretation of human existence. In conservative interpretations of Buddhist teachings the members of the Thai polity are regarded as passive subjects or observers of their spiritual and political fates, accepting personal suffering and political disenfranchisement as *kamma*, the consequences of their immoral actions in previous existences.

Traditional interpretations of Buddhism tend to emphasise collective values of national solidarity and allegiance to central political structures.   In contrast, reformist interpreters place individual salvation and the political rights of the individual at the centre of their theoretical focus and commonly denounce traditional collectivist values and political structures as authoritarian or totalitarian and as being based upon a denial of individual liberty.

Given the diversity of views on the appropriate political direction of the country in recent decades, no single legitimatory structure, that is, no single formulation of Thai-Buddhist doctrine and practice, has been capable of resolving the crisis of political legitimacy in contemporary Thailand. The political visions and objectives of competing traditionalist, reformist and moderate groupings are so distinct as to require markedly different legitimating religious systems. Indeed, in the 1980s political tensions between these groupings of the Thai political and economic elite manifested themselves, among other ways, in the production of a variety of alternative approaches to the interpretation of certain key religious symbols of political legitimacy, such as the *Traiphuum Phra Ruang*.

Despite rationalist criticisms of the text initiated by Prince Mongkut in the nineteenth century (C. Reynolds 1976), the symbolic associations of the *Traiphuum Phra Ruang* with the legitimate exercise of political authority in Thailand were never completely severed. The lasting symbolic power of the *Traiphuum* has been such that even into the 1980s conservative interpreters have attempted to re-assert the primacy of the traditional Buddhist cosmography that the text describes. In contrast, in the past decade reformist interpreters have attempted to bolster the legitimating power of the *Traiphuum*, not by ignoring the subversive impact of rationalist critiques but, rather, by claiming that the true symbolic meaning of the text is in fact consistent with the rationalist view of Buddhism. By arguing for a metaphorical interpretation of the *Traiphuum* reformists attempt to draw on the rich symbolic legacy of the text to lend legitimacy to democratic visions of Thailand's social and political future. These respective conservative and rationalist approaches to the *Traiphuum* represent much more than a mere scholarly debate about approaches to textual exegesis. The competing interpretations of the *Traiphuum* put forward by various ideologues in recent years have all reflected fundamental political conflicts within Thai society and have demonstrated the continuing political significance of Buddhist symbology in general, and of the *Traiphuum Phra Ruang* in particular, in contemporary Thailand.

HISTORY OF THE *TRAIPHUUM PHRA RUANG*

The text which is now called the *Traiphuum [Traibhumi] Phra Ruang* (*The Three Worlds Cosmography of Phra Ruang*) is generally regarded by Thai scholars to have been compiled in A.D. 1345[1] by Lithai,[2] then *uparaja* ('second king') of Srisatchanalai, the second most important urban centre of the early Thai kingdom of Sukhothai.[3] According to popular Thai history, Lithai succeeded his father, Lelithai, as king of the Phra Ruang dynasty of Sukhothai in about A.D. 1346, ruling until his death in about A.D. 1374.[4]

In the *Traiphuum* Lithai describes the conditions and characteristics of the beings which inhabit the various realms of the Buddhist universe. This universe consists of eleven realms in the 'world of desire' (*kamabhumi*), sixteen celestial realms in the 'world with only a remnant of material qualities' (*rupabhumi*), and four higher celestial realms in the 'world without material qualities' (*arupabhumi*). A being's birth in one or other of the thirty one realms of the three worlds (*traibhumi*) is interpreted as being determined by its store of *kammic* merit, *bun*, or demerit, *baap*. Lithai's text concludes with a description of the Buddhist method of attaining salvation from the unsatisfactoriness of the cycle of birth, death and rebirth, which involves liberation from the three worlds of phenomenal existence and the attainment of *nibbana*, which is a condition totally distinct from the thirty-one realms.

Most of the contents of the *Traiphuum* can be described as metaphysical, dealing in detail with the features of the thirty-one cosmic realms of rebirth and the types of actions which ordain beings to be born in one or other of these realms. The text also contains a large central portion dealing with the world of ordinary men and women and includes descriptions of the characteristics of a cosmic ruler, a *mahacakkavattiraja*,[5] and his relations with his subjects. Reformist interpretations of the *Traiphuum* emphasise the sociological and soteriological, that is, the middle and final sections of the text, and attempt to distil meanings with contemporary relevance from these parts while effectively ignoring the long descriptions of the thirty-one cosmic realms. By contrast, conservative interpreters maintain that the emphasis on the thirty-one realms in the *Traiphuum* demonstrate the importance of *kamma* and of merit and demerit in determining individual and collective human well-being.

The oldest surviving version of the *Traiphuum* was inscribed by a monk, Phra Maha Chuay, in a ten-volume palm leaf manuscript in A.D. 1778 during the reign of King Taksin. The source or sources from which the Phra Maha Chuay version was compiled are not known, as no complete copy of the text is believed to have survived the Burmese sacking of Ayutthaya in 1767. The Thai historian Somphong Chaulaem (1985:1) states that the Phra Maha Chuay version was apparently lost or hidden after the death of Taksin, for in 1783 King Rama I directed a group of monks to compile yet another version of the *Traiphuum*. This subsequent text is known as the Phra Maha Jan version, after the principal compiler. However, when he reviewed the resulting text in 1802 King Rama I found it to be inconsistent and stylistically uneven, and ordered that it be rewritten. The resulting text is now known by the title of the *Traiphuumlokawinnitchai* [*Traibhumilokavinicchaya*]. This text appears to have been the only version of the *Traiphuum* known to Thai scholars such as Mongkut throughout the nineteenth century.

The older Phra Maha Chuay version of the *Traiphuum* was brought to light early this century when Prince Damrong directed that large numbers of old manuscripts be collected from provincial monastery libraries and stored for safe keeping in the newly established National Library. The Phra Maha Chuay version is now regarded as the most authoritative version of the text, and it was this version that Prince Damrong chose in 1912, when the *Traiphuum Phra Ruang* was first published in Thailand.[6]

THE POLITICAL FUNCTIONS OF THE *TRAIPHUUM* IN PRE-MODERN THAILAND

The political functions of the text in modern Thailand are based on its long political history and, indeed, a number of analysts regard the motivation underlying the original composition of the *Traiphuum* to have been fundamentally political. Frank Reynolds (1982:10) suggests that Lithai wrote the *Traiphuum* in order to assist in attaining a number of immediate political objectives related to his succession to the throne of Sukhothai and the re-establishment of central Sukhothai authority over nearby principalities. The political intention underlying the composition of the *Traiphuum* is indicated by a number of explicit references as well as by the general structure and tenor of the text. For example, Lithai gives a central place to the notion of the *Mahacakkavattiraja* or universal monarch in the *Traiphuum* and suggests that the teachings of a universal monarch are equivalent to the teachings of a fully realised Buddha. In a review of the history of Thai political thought Sombat Jantharawong and Chai-anan Samudavanija (1980:100) note that Lithai portrays the *Mahacakkavattiraja*, with whom he compares himself,[7]

as being like a representative of the Lord Buddha in this world when a Buddha is not present. 'If in any kalpa (cosmic epoch) there is no self-enlightened Buddha (*sammasambuddha*) or *paccekabuddha* then there is a Phraya Mahajakraphat (*mahacakkavatti*) instead'.

Sombat and Chai-anan (1980:93) maintain that by this association of the monarch with the Buddha, Lithai attempted to lend religious authority and legitimacy to his rule. They note that the socio-political aspects of the *Traiphuum* indicate 'the close relationship between being a person who knows the *dhamma* and being a [political] administrator in the traditional Thai political order'. On this point the literary analyst Somphorn Mantasuut (1981:29-30) has commented that

Lithai's true intention was to instruct the people of Sukhothai in ethics so that they would abide by the *dhamma* and make the state peaceful and prosperous ... and this was for the political benefit of the government of that time, because if the people were well-established in ethics, fearful of sinning and not daring to do wrong, problems such as robbery, assault and other problems of crime would be lessened or might not even arise. This would have the result of permitting the government of the country to proceed smoothly.

The *Traiphuum* continued to be an important text for Thai rulers long after Lithai's particular political concerns had been forgotten. The enduring significance of the *Traiphuum* to the Thai state flowed from its capacity to be interpreted to reflect the political interests of the rulers of the day. Buddhist cosmological conceptions, which as noted above constitute a major part of the contents of the *Traiphuum*, played a central role in the political organisation of pre-modern Thai kingdoms. The socio-political orders of the Thai kingdoms of the Sukhothai, Ayutthaya, Thonburi and early Bangkok periods were self-consciously modelled on the cosmic Buddhist order described in the *Traiphuum*. In these kingdoms the structure of the Buddhist cosmos, especially its hierarchical, merit-determined order, was reproduced at the level of human social and political organisation. Kirsch (1978:55) has observed that even the physical layouts of the capitals of the pre-modern Thai kingdoms were grounded in religious beliefs manifested in the *Traiphuum*.

The continuing socio-political importance of the *Traiphuum* in Thailand up until the early Bangkok period is shown by the fact that King Rama I gave priority to the compilation of a new version of the text when consolidating his power after the turmoil and disarray surrounding the destruction of Ayutthaya in 1767 and the overthrow and execution of King Taksin in 1782. However, Craig Reynolds (1976:203) notes that no Thai king after Rama I commissioned a new recension of the *Traiphuum*. He attributes this to the fact that in the middle of the nineteenth century the metaphysical cosmography described in the text came under increasing attack. From the 1830s onwards the influence of Western ideas on science and cosmology and the more rationalist view of Buddhist teachings promoted by the reformist Thammayut monastic movement established by Prince Mongkut combined to force a new awareness of Thailand's cultural and intellectual traditions on many educated Thais. In the second half of the nineteenth century increasing numbers of the Thai educated elite came to regard supernaturalism and traditional Buddhist metaphysics, including the cosmography described in the *Traiphuum*, as representing obstacles in coming to terms with the empirically-derived and naturalistic systems of knowledge introduced by Westerners. Reynolds (1976:214) comments that in 1851 one Western observer in Bangkok, John Taylor Jones, noted that the *Traiphuum*'s cosmographical descriptions were 'frequently denied by many of the shrewder Buddhists in Siam'.

But while belief in the metaphysical aspects of the *Traiphuum* was shaken by the impact of Western ideas in certain Thai circles, attempts were nevertheless made to retain and re-assert the value of the ethical teachings contained in the text. For example, in his instructional text *Nangsyy sadaeng kitjaanukit* (*A Book Explaining Various Things*) King Mongkut's foreign minister, Jau Phraya Thipphakorawong (Kham Bunnak) (1971), criticised non-empirical explanations of natural phenomena, such as presented in the *Traiphuum,* as being unsustainable. Thipphakorawong nevertheless concluded that the *Traiphuum's* teachings on the ethical aspects of Buddhism, that is, on matters such as *kamma,* merit and rebirth remained valid and true. By this Thipphakorawong acted to retain the symbolic value of the *Traiphuum* by dissociating its socio-political significance from the now increasingly discredited metaphysical aspects of the text, emphasising instead Lithai's ethical teachings. He thus was able to retain some semblance of the text's original symbolic significance by focussing on the purely ethical justification for the socio-political order centred on the institution of the absolute monarchy.

In the twentieth century movements across the political spectrum from pro-monarchists to radical socialists have acknowledged the continuing symbolic importance of the *Traiphuum* in lending legitimacy to political goals, activities and systems in Thailand. All of these groups have found the text too valuable to let questions of the literal validity or invalidity of its cosmographical contents override its long-established function of lending theoretical support to political structures and political aspirations. As a consequence, new interpretative strategies have been applied to the *Traiphuum* which aim to retain the political and symbolic potency of the text in spite of the debunking of the traditional Buddhist cosmography by rationalists and reformists. Two interpretative strategies have been applied to the text in this century. The first has involved the development of selective interpretations of the text, which attempt to avoid the rationally more unacceptable metaphysical sections. The *Traiphuum Phra Ruang* is a complex text, and by the selective emphasis and the careful management of interpretations of its contents it has been able to be used for a range of different and sometimes conflicting purposes. The second interpretative strategy applied to the *Traiphuum* has involved attempts to re-interpret the entire text in allegorical terms, rather than as a literal description of the actual structure of the cosmos. This second interpretative strategy in Thai studies of the *Traiphuum* has been linked with attempts to reveal the underlying symbolic meaning of the text as a whole. This approach has also been associated with attempts to relate the symbolic meaning of the text purportedly revealed by such studies to an idealised interpretation of the historical significance of the political and cultural legacy of the early Thai kingdom of Sukhothai.

CONTEMPORARY CONSERVATIVE INTERPRETATIONS OF THE *TRAIPHUUM*

Reynolds (1976:218) has commented that the demythologisation of the *Traiphuum* by sections of the ruling Thai elite in the second half of the nineteenth century divorced 'the cosmography from contemporary monarchical symbolism'. However, since the late 1950s there have been a number of concerted attempts by political conservatives to re-establish the symbolic link between the *Traiphuum* and the exercise of political authority. Sarit Thanarat's rehabilitation of the Thai monarchy as a symbolic focus of his authoritarian military regime was also associated with a renewed emphasis on the traditional legitimizing symbols associated with the monarchy. As Tambiah (1978:128) has remarked,

the soldiers who captured and exercised power simply replaced the authoritarian and hierarchical system of monarchical times with a structure that manifested the same or similar authoritarianism. There is thus a continuity of political power, although continuity of political legitimacy is problematic.

Sarit and his immediate successors sought in part to resolve this 'crisis of legitimacy' by re-emphasising the traditional political integrative role of the monarchy and by symbolically associating their regimes with the re-imputed legitimacy of the monarchy.

Since Sarit's rehabilitation of the Thai monarchy, after more than two decades of being in official disfavour following the 1932 revolution, an emphasis on the achievements of Thailand's past and present monarchs has become an important component of the promotion of conservative definitions of Thai identity and conservative political structures. In the past three decades there has been a concerted official effort to establish symbols traditionally associated with the absolute monarchy and the elite culture of pre-modern Thailand as an integral part of the definition of modern Thailand's cultural and political identity. The importance attached to establishing this conservative definition is illustrated by the setting up in the early 1980s of the Thai National Identity Board (*samnak-ngaan serm-saang eekalak khorng chaat*) within the Office of the Prime Minister. The primary function of the Board appears to be to popularise traditional elite culture among the Thai populace and to present that elite culture as a national treasure to be valued by Thais in all social strata. Whatever the artistic, literary or intellectual value of the traditional elite culture of Thailand, its official promotion in the contemporary political context simultaneously functions as a medium for reviving and sustaining traditional patterns of respect for political authority. In recent decades Thai military regimes and political parties aligned with or sympathetic to the military have found the manipulation of the symbolism which historically surrounded and supported the absolute monarchy to provide a convenient basis for the centralised and autocratic exercise of political power.

After a period of relative neglect paralleling the period in which the role of the monarchy was de-emphasised in Thailand, the *Traiphuum* has received growing attention and interest from Thai conservatives in concert with the rehabilitation of the monarchy and the official promotion of traditional elite culture. The recent resurgence of interest in the *Traiphuum* in Thailand is shown by the fact that a revised version of the text was commissioned in 1974 by the Director-General of the Department of Fine Arts. This 1974 revision was the first new recension of the text to have been prepared since King Rama I ordered the compilation of the *Traiphuumlokawinnitchai* in 1787.[8] This renewed interest in the *Traiphuum Phra Ruang* reflects an effort to revive and re-establish the symbolic significance of the text so that it can continue to fulfil its legitimizing function. As a cultural product of the kingdom of Sukhothai, and as reputedly the oldest book written in the Thai language, the *Traiphuum* is ascribed the double authority of being associated with the historical sources of the political identity and the Buddhist cultural identity of modern Thailand.

Conservative discussions of the *Traiphuum* have been characterised by a form of intellectual atavism in which the rationalist debunking of the text's metaphysical contents in the last century is all but ignored and the traditional ethical teachings founded on the doctrine of *kamma* are brought to the fore. Such conservative discussions tend to ignore the implications of the rationalist critique of the traditional Buddhist cosmography and involve selective readings of the *Traiphuum* which draw out sections and chapters of the text that appear to support the institution of the monarchy and traditional patterns of respect for authority. The approach of contemporary Thai conservatives to the *Traiphuum* was clearly expressed at a conference on the text organised by the Department of Fine Arts in December 1983 as part of the government-sponsored celebrations of the 700th anniversary of the development of the Thai script by King Ramkhamhaeng, the grandfather of Lithai. The primary emphasis of the papers given at this conference was on the continued relevance of the ethical teachings of the *Traiphuum Phra Ruang* to contemporary Thai life and institutions, including politics, government administration, religion, philosophy and art. The interpretations of the *Traiphuum* presented at this conference emphasised the importance of the text to the officially sanctioned interpretation of Thai identity, to efforts to support traditional institutional arrangements and to 'national security'.

The conservative tenor of the interpretations of the *Traiphuum Phra Ruang* presented at this conference is typified by the comments of one speaker, Associate Professor Sangiam Sawatdikaan, who presented the contents of the *Traiphuum* in their traditional metaphysical formulation. Sangiam (1984:205) stated that,

> The *Traiphuum Phra Ruang* shows us what will result from doing good and performing evil, as well as the results that can be achieved by cleansing the mind [of evil] .... Lithai divides the realms of existence according to the good and bad actions and the *vipaka* [*kammic* consequences] which lead one to be born in one realm or another .... In summary, Lithai shows that [the meaning of the *Traiphuum*] is the law of *kamma*, which cannot be evaded because it is the law of reason — when there is a cause there will be a result.

Sangiam interprets the *Traiphuum* at face value. He presents the traditional metaphysical view of the teaching of *kamma* and implies belief in the literal reality of the various realms of suffering and pleasure described in the *Traiphuum*. His presentation demonstrates the extent to which the *Traiphuum* continues to be interpreted by members of the political establishment and their ideological supporters in ways which re-inforce traditional Thai ethical and political patterns.

THE DEVELOPMENT OF REFORMIST INTERPRETATIONS OF THAI BUDDHISM IN THE 1980s

The re-attribution of traditional metaphysical interpretations to the *Traiphuum* has not gone unchallenged. Since the mid-1970s, and particularly since the beginning of the 1980s, a number of rationalist re-interpretations of the text have been developed as part of a broader effort to counter conservative, officially-sponsored images of Thai identity, and in order to subvert conservative uses of Buddhist symbolism in particular. These interpretations have sought to redefine the traditional religious and political symbolism of Buddhism, and of the *Traiphuum* in particular, in ways that purge them of authoritarian associations, and instead re-orient this symbolism towards the nurturing of a progressive approach to socio-economic development and the revelation of an indigenous political basis for democracy in Thailand. This resurgence of interest in the *Traiphuum* by reformist thinkers is recent and reflects the greater self-confidence of oppositional thinkers in Thailand since 1973, when a broad popular movement forced the dictatorial clique of Prime Minister Thanom Kittikachorn to flee the country.

Reformist re-interpretations of the *Traiphuum* developed in the 1980s drew upon a number of preliminary studies dating from the mid-1970s. These studies attempted to arrive at a more accurate historical understanding of the significance of the *Traiphuum* by locating the function of the text within the political and historical context of the medieval kingdom of Sukhothai. Studies of the Traiphuum by Cholthira Klatyuu (1974:106-121; 1976:2-60), Somkiat Wanthana (1983:89), Somphorn Mantasuut (1981), and by Sombat Jantharawong and Chai-anan Samudavanija (1980), among others, provided a basis of socio-historical information which has been drawn upon in subsequent reformist re-interpretations of the text.

Frank Reynolds (1978b:105) has argued that the traditional Buddhist conception of hierarchical cosmic and social orders in which religious merit (*bun*) determines the socio-religious position of the individual continues to provide the implicit ideological framework upon which Thai society and Thai politics still function. I would qualify Reynold's position by specifying that the traditional Buddhist metaphysic provides the implicit ideological framework for conservative Thai politics. Both the metaphysical formulations of Buddhism and the politically centralised and hierarchical social order which those formulations have historically been used to legitimate are explicitly denied in reformist interpretations of Buddhism (Jackson 1988:96-102).

Nevertheless, there are certain fundamental religious conceptions which characterise both traditionalist and reformist interpretations of Buddhism and which inform the political conceptions of both types of analysis. As Tambiah (1978:123) has observed,

There is a deeply entrenched Buddhist conception of political sovereignty and righteousness as the ordinating principle in society, a conception of political ethics and morality which acts as an enduring yardstick by which to measure political performance and as an inspiring but not wrought-in-detail ideal to which political aspirations of different complexions can equally refer themselves.

It is this notion of righteous sovereignty, variously interpreted by conservative and reformist political theorists, which constitutes the common ideological basis of all Buddhist participants in the Thai political system.

In sharp contrast with the conservative idealisation of the monarchy, reformist Thais regard the symbolism of the absolute monarchy as having unacceptable associations with political authoritarianism and military dictatorship. They maintain that the introduction of more participatory and democratic political political structures is essential for Thailand's further social, economic and political development. Throughout the 1980s a number of reformist Thai theorists have attempted to subvert the conservative manipulation of the symbolism of the Thai monarchy. They have attempted to transfer the *baramii* or charisma of legitimate power traditionally ascribed to the king to a democratically elected government. Reformists have attempted to effect this by emphasising references in the canonical Buddhist scriptures to kingship as an institution founded upon the election of a wise and capable leader by the populace at large.[9] Underlying such analyses of Buddhist accounts of elected kingship is an unstated argument that the modern Thai constitutional monarchy can only retain associations with the legitimate exercise of political authority to the extent that it now becomes a symbol of the canonical Buddhist notion of a popularly elected leadership.

In addition to a generally rationalist stance, reformist critiques of conservative interpretations of Buddhism have two other important features. First, they idealise the political institutions and cultural products of Sukhothai as providing a true Buddhist model of a participatory, liberal form of government. Reformists then attribute the conservative idealisation of centralised forms of government modelled on the absolute monarchy to the purportedly corrupting impact of Khmer Brahmanism on society, religion and politics during the Ayutthayan and early Bangkok periods. Second, reformist critiques of conservative interpretations of Buddhism tend to maintain that the core scriptures of Thai Buddhism, in which some include the *Traiphuum*, were composed in symbolic language that requires careful exegesis to be correctly understood. This methodological approach is linked with the eulogisation of Sukhothai and the denigration of Ayutthaya to construct an argument that literal interpretations of accounts of heaven, hell and other metaphysical notions, such as described in the *Traiphuum Phra Ruang,* are the product of Brahmanical misconceptions dating from the Ayutthaya period. Reformists maintain that those influenced by such Brahmanical notions will fail to appreciate the true intention that Lithai had in writing the *Traiphuum*, namely, to lead the individual reader towards the Buddhist salvation of *nibbana* and to lead Thai society as a whole towards a state of justice and general welfare.

THE IDEALISATION OF SUKHOTHAI

The origins of the modern idealisation of Sukhothai society and culture and the rationalist symbolic interpretation of Thai-Buddhist scriptures can be traced to Mongkut and his reforms of the Thai *sangha* in the nineteenth century. Frank Reynolds (1978b:103) has commented on the value that Mongkut attached to symbols and relics of Sukhothai, noting that Mongkut established

in the royal compound in Bangkok a stele on which the greatest ruler of the ancient and powerful Thai kingdom of Sukhothai [that is, Ramkhamhaeng] had set out a kind of charter for an ideal Thai state.

However, contemporary reformists have adapted this emphasis on the ideal characteristics of Sukhothai to support democratic institutions rather than the institution of the absolute monarchy, which underpinned Mongkut's interest in linking his reign to Sukhothai. It is interesting that in recent decades the rationalist and scripturalist religious trend initiated by Mongkut has been adapted by reformists to support their political demands for more democratic and liberal approaches to government. Efforts to achieve religious reform and political reform are now closely related in modern Thailand.

Reformists regard the Sukhothai period as a golden age of Thai history that has fundamental ethical and political lessons for the present. Reformists also maintain that they uphold the true essence of 'Thainess', an essence whose first historical manifestation they find recorded in that literature of the Sukhothai period which has survived. This idealisation of Sukhothai represents an attempt to develop an indigenous basis for Thai political and religious thought and Thai values which support democracy and social justice. Sulak Sivaraksa (1989:26) summarises the reformist view of Sukhothai as a model of a liberal, just Thai society as follows:

The profound roots of Thai thought are clearly manifested in the first stone inscription of King Ramkhamhaeng of Sukhothai .... This inscription is like pure gold which expresses 'Buddhist-ness' and 'Thai-ness'.... I consider it to be a proclamation of the political, economic and cultural trends which were associated with [Sukhothai] ... and which emphasised liberty, equality and fraternity (*seeriiphaap, samoephaak, phraadaraphaap*) ....

While reformists present Sukhothai as a model of religious purity and political justice, Ayutthaya is, by contrast, associated with the 'erroneous' religious beliefs introduced by Khmer Brahmanism and with the autocratic and tyrannical forms of government that reformists regard as epitomised by the institution of the absolute monarchy. For example, the reformist monk Phra Phaisaan Wisaalai (1986:119-21) claims that the political authoritarianism of Thai governments after the Sukhothai period

resulted from the establishment of Khmer Brahmanism in the [Thai] Royal Palace from the beginning of the Ayutthaya period and the acceptance of the belief that absolute authority based on harsh and strong punishments was necessary for government ....

It can be said that the Sukhothai form of government (which was influenced by the [Buddhist] *dhammaraja* theory) was a government for the benefit and well-being of the people, but the Ayutthayan form of government (which accepted the [Brahmanical] *devaraja* theory ...) was a government for the power of the state.

Reformists have attempted to counter the conservative manipulation of the symbols of Buddhism and the monarchy to lend support to centralised and authoritarian political structures by maintaining that conservative political and religious thought has been infected by the Brahmanically-influenced notion that the institution of the monarchy has divine origins or associations. For example, the reformist critic Krajaang Nanthapho (1985:254-5) has said,

> Buddhism is in contradiction with the principles of feudal or dictatorial and tyrannical government. However, in Thailand the feudal groups have long used Buddhism as a tool in governing and in protecting the power of their own group .... The feudal groups have at all times relied upon ritualistic expressions, which are but the outer coating of religion, to build up the people's belief in the feudal system of government of the group of the supposed *devaraja* [Brahmanical god-king] ....

Reformist Thai-Buddhists maintain that political leaders' steadfast abiding by the true principles of Buddhism, as they interpret them, is important for the maintenance of a just social and political order. It is a corollary of this position that the Thai society which loses its way religiously will also lose its way politically. This argument underlies reformist attempts to discredit Ayutthayan and Ayutthayan-modelled religious and political forms as being polluted by Brahmanical influences. Buddhist reformists also use this same argument — that a just Thai society can only be constructed upon a pure Buddhist base — to explain the occurrence of 'non-Buddhist' political authoritarianism in certain periods of Thai history. In particular, reformists maintain that Thai religion during the period of the absolute monarchy in Ayutthaya and Bangkok and during the military dictatorships in the twentieth century was polluted by Brahmanism. Furthermore, it is proposed that those conservative sections of the Thai political and intellectual elite who today interpret the *Traiphuum* in literalist or 'Ayutthayan' terms, and who support political notions and practices rooted in the authoritarian 'Ayutthayan' tradition, are 'non-Buddhist' and so effectively 'non-Thai'.

Reformist criticisms of authoritarian Ayutthayan political structures and the Brahmanical beliefs regarded as underpinning them have a direct relevance to the present political situation in Thailand. This is because all the monarchs of the Chakri dynasty have regarded the continuation of the traditions of Ayutthaya as an important basis of the modern Thai kingdom centred on Bangkok. In the contemporary Thai politico-legal context, in which the crime of *lèse-majesté* attracts severe penalties, it is not possible to openly criticise the monarchy or the symbolic manipulation of the monarchy by political conservatives. In this context reformist criticisms of the supposedly negative characteristics of the Ayutthayan period in fact represent an attack upon the present Thai political establishment, which supports an Ayutthayan-modelled monarchy in order to legitimate its political position. The contemporary interpretation of symbols linked with Sukhothai and Ayutthaya therefore should not be read as mere scholarly attempts to construct or reconstruct Thai history. These interpretations also represent attempts to construct a symbolic legitimation of present political structures. At the level of theory the contemporary political and ideological conflict between reformists and traditionalists is being waged in the form of a symbolic battle between the two extinct kingdoms of Sukhothai and Ayutthaya. The spirits of the long dead kings of these two kingdoms are being invoked to engage in a battle whose combatants seek the right to determine the form of the religious and political identity of the Thai nation in line with their respective alternative and competing political visions.

METAPHORICAL READINGS OF THE *TRAIPHUUM*

Literal interpretations of the metaphysical aspects of Buddhism, which at least in a superficial reading appear to be the dominant theme of such texts as the *Traiphuum Phra Ruang*, are explicitly rejected in reformist analyses. This is because, given their commitment to alternative, democratic political structures, reformists seek to undermine the historical use of Buddhism's traditional cosmographical symbolism to support the traditional hierarchical Thai social order. Current discussions about the *Traiphuum* among reformist Thai intellectuals instead focus on the assumed creative intention of its author, Lithai, which, it is claimed, was to present a Buddhist model for a just social order.

Nevertheless, there is not universal agreement on the symbolic value of the *Traiphuum Phra Ruang* among all Thai analysts who oppose conservative interpretations of Buddhism. Sulak Sivaraksa, for example, maintains that the *Traiphuum*, despite being a literary product of the Sukhothai period, has closer associations with the political authoritarianism of the Ayutthaya period and so should be rejected by Thais seeking to develop progressive formulations of Buddhist teaching. Sulak (1989:26-7) has said,

Afterwards [in the Ayutthaya period] the *Traiphuum Phra Ruang* almost completely obscured this fundamental current of [Sukhothai] thought [expressed in the Ramkhamhaeng inscription]. Even though the *Traiphuum* quotes the words of the Buddha and relates these to the ending of suffering in accord with Buddhist teachings, it nevertheless overemphasises *pubbekatapuññata* [reaping the benefits of meritorious deeds performed in a previous life]. It speaks too much about heaven and hell and places too much stress on teachings which encourage the people to be subordinate to the ruling class. Furthermore, it introduces supernatural [*saiyaasaat*] cosmological beliefs as if they were scientific.

The impact of the thought expressed in the *Traiphuum* of Sukhothai was compounded by the fact that Ayutthaya accepted supernatural beliefs from Cambodia when we [Thai] repeatedly attacked the Cambodian capital. This led to a decline in the 'Thainess' of our thought, a reduction in liberty and equality ....

However, others, such as the prominent reformist monk Phra Thepwethi,[10] disagree with those who repudiate the text because of its imputed Khmer Brahmanical influences and its associations with political authoritarianism, and have developed an alternative political analysis. Rather than simply rejecting the *Traiphuum*, Thepwethi attempts to interpret the text in symbolic terms as presenting reformist ideals in covert form. He criticises not the *Traiphuum* itself but the methods of interpretation which have traditionally been applied to it and, by implication, those conservatives who have used these methodological approaches. This methodological critique achieves a similar political objective to the outright rejection of the *Traiphuum*, namely, the criticism of the use of Buddhist teachings and symbology to support authoritarian political structures. By developing a symbolic interpretation of the text Thepwethi presents an alternative view of the *Traiphuum* and its rich symbolic associations with the supposed roots of Thai-Buddhist identity, which directly counters the traditional interpretations which have historically been used to support conservative socio-political positions. He attempts to redirect the legitimizing power ascribed to the *Traiphuum* from bolstering authoritarianism and monarchism to supporting democratic political structures.

In his study of the text Thepwethi emphasises its individual soteriological and ethical aspects rather than its cosmographical descriptions. He re-interprets the *Traiphuum* in terms of the activist outlook of contemporary Buddhist reformists and maintains that the text does not, as maintained in conservative studies, teach that *kamma* determines all of human existence. Rather, he argues that the text in fact teaches about the need to transcend worldly fetters and to attain the ultimate spiritual salvation of *nibbana*. Thepwethi says that even though the text is called the *Traiphuum* (The Three Worlds), its true objective is in fact a fourth realm, *lokuttara* or the transcendence of the three worlds of phenomenal existence. Thepwethi (Ratchaworamuni 1983:9) claims that Lithai's intention in writing the *Traiphuum* was to show a way out of the suffering of phenomenal or worldly existence in the three *lokiyabhumi*:

> I wish to emphasise the significant point that the fact that Lithai speaks of *lokuttarabhumi* shows that the objective of his text, the *Traiphuum*, was to lead the reader or the person who listened to its teachings to see ... the harm [*dosa*] of the three [worldly] *bhumi* in order to liberate them from those three *bhumi* and so attain the fourth *bhumi*, namely, *lokuttarabhumi*.

Indeed, Thepwethi (Ratchaworamuni 1983:52) says that he regards the proper name of the *Traiphuum Phra Ruang* to be 'The *Traibhumi* and Liberation from the *Traibhumi* (into *Lokuttarabhumi*)'. Thepwethi maintains that the Buddhist notion of *kamma* denotes the possibility of liberating action which leads one out of the strictures of social classes and castes. He says that Buddhism does not emphasise the enslaving aspect of action but rather the liberating potential of understanding the relations between cause and effect mediated by intentional action. Thepwethi (Ratchaworamuni 1983:37) contends that,

> The line of explanation [in the *Traiphuum*] leads us to see that Lithai intended people to consider their good and bad actions which will lead them to meeting with good and bad consequences in the future. He did not intend pointing out evil actions in the past so that people accept either their own or others' present situation.

Thepwethi says that traditionalists interpret the *Traiphuum* statically, as a description of how things came to be the way they are, while he interprets it dynamically, as indicating a process of liberation from the present order of things.

While Thepwethi maintains that the objective of the *Traiphuum* is to lead the reader or listener towards *nibbana,* he says that Lithai's line of approach in the text was to begin by speaking of the more immediately comprehensible matters of *kamma* and the fruits of actions (*vipaka*). He is critical of those who concentrate on these superficial aspects of the text and who fail to appreciate what he regards to be the original spiritual intention underlying its composition. Thepwethi (Ratchaworamuni 1983:22) says,

We have now forgotten that [original intention]. People nowadays have become narrower [in their understanding of Buddhism] than in the past [era of Lithai]. Now we speak only of heaven, but people in the past also spoke of *nibbana,* and this point should be noted well.

Another analyst, the academic Suthiwong Phongphaibun, has also given a reformist interpretation to the *Traiphuum.* Like Thepwethi, Suthiwong (1983:123) claims that the *Traiphuum* was written in a symbolic form which, when deciphered, reveals the true intention of the author as being to lead the reader to ultimate salvation,

The *Traiphuum Phra Ruang* was written in a style which used symbols .... That is, it used a method of taking one thing to stand for a line of thought, which enables an intelligent and capable person to interpret it very broadly .... This style of writing can be regarded as having been very far ahead of its time ....

Suthiwong claims that, contrary to traditional literalist readings of the *Traiphuum* which interpret it as referring to metaphysical phenomena, it is in fact a text which supports a modernist and rationalist Buddhist world view.

In their criticisms of traditional metaphysical readings of the *Traiphuum* Suthiwong and Thepwethi also attempt to counter conservative interpretations. Thepwethi, in particular, extracts elements of what he interprets as a compassionate, Buddhist social policy from the *Traiphuum*. One section of the text dealing with the virtues of the *cakkavattiraja* or universal Buddhist monarch describes the ideal ruler as teaching that no living being should be killed pointlessly, and that no matter how evil a person's deeds they should be instructed in the *dhamma* and should not be executed for their crimes. Thepwethi (Ratchaworamuni 1983:32) comments that, 'This point shows that King Lithai did not support execution as a form of punishment'. However, he adds that

> afterwards in the Ayutthaya period this principle [of compassion and leniency in the punishment of wrongdoers] was changed because of the influence of Brahmanism, which has a system of meting out severe and violent punishments .... We can see that in subsequent periods in Thailand [that is, the Ayutthaya and Bangkok periods] the ruling circles also resorted to increasingly severe punishments. Could it be that this principle came from Hinduism, especially given that that religion developed [its influence] in the Ayutthaya period?

According to Thepwethi's reformist analysis of Thai political and religious history Brahmanical influences on Thai society and government have led to tyranny. Furthermore, according to this view of Thai history, if a just form of government is to be realised in Thailand true Buddhism, that is, a radically doctrinal or rationalist interpretation of Buddhist teachings, must be supported and promoted.

Thepwethi reveals the political motivation underlying his analysis of the *Traiphuum Phra Ruang* when he expands on his analysis of Lithai's text by noting *Jataka* stories which maintain that if a monarch causes difficulties for his subjects and fails to uphold the *dasarajadhamma,* the ten ethical principles appropriate for a king, the people should rise up and protest, forcing the monarch to reconsider his actions and edicts. Thepwethi (Ratchaworamuni 1983:45) maintains that this scriptural reference can be regarded as

an origin of the contemporary idea of demonstrating. This comes from the period of the *Jatakas,* and the *Jatakas* cite a large number of instances of [the people] demonstrating in this way. This is the Buddhist system of government.

In other words, Thepwethi maintains that Buddhism condones popular unrest against an unjust ruler. He also observes (Ratchaworamuni 1983:37) that the primary political emphasis of the *Traiphuum Phra Ruang* is on the responsibility of the state to the people, rather than of the people to the state, which has been the predominant ideological emphasis in Thailand's recent political history.

Apart from the severe consequences of doing wrong to one's parents, to a *samanabrahmacariya* and to a monk upholding the moral precepts, and to old people, which have already been mentioned many times [above], the *Traiphuum Phra Ruang* also emphasises the severe consequences of the evil actions of rulers, or of public officials who oppress and exploit the people or govern unjustly. No mention is made of the responsibility of the ruled to their rulers.

LIMITATIONS OF THE *TRAIPHUUM PHRA RUANG* AND THE NEED FOR A NEW THAI-BUDDHIST 'GOSPEL'

Despite the significant theoretical and re-interpretative efforts of reformist thinkers such as Thepwethi, there are limits to the extent to which the *Traiphuum* can be interpreted as lending support to modernist views of Buddhist doctrine and to a liberal, democratic political order. Even those involved in efforts to revive and sustain the ancient symbolic power of the text admit that their interpretative strategies may ultimately fail. Reformist analysts of the *Traiphuum*, such as Thepwethi and Suthiwong Phongphaibun, do countenance the possibility of a not too distant end to the centuries-long legitimizing function of the text, and they also refer to the consequent need to find a religious text which can replace the *Traiphuum* and provide a Buddhist basis for contemporary Thai society and government.

It is noteworthy that in developing his interpretation of the teachings of the *Traiphuum* Thepwethi emphasises the comparatively shorter section of the text dealing with the attainment of *nibbana* rather than the much longer sections dealing with the suffering experienced by those beings living in the various Buddhist hells and the joys experienced by those beings inhabiting the various heavens. Thepwethi's is a selective reading arrived at by emphasising specific aspects of the text. However, given the large amount of space that Lithai devoted to descriptions of the retributions of hell and the rewards of heaven in the original text, it would appear difficult not to regard such matters as having been prominent in the author's mind at the time he compiled the *Traiphuum*. This is particularly so given the almost incalculable eons over which Lithai maintains that heaven is enjoyed and over which hell is suffered. Suthiwong Phongphaibun makes just such a criticism of the *Traiphuum* in his concluding remarks on the text. Suthiwong agrees that the *Traiphuum Phra Ruang* contains true Buddhist teachings about salvation and *nibbana*. However, he criticises (Phongphaibun 1983:124) the presentation of materials in the *Traiphuum*, saying that Lithai's attempt to convey Buddhist teachings in symbolic form was not successful because the symbols became so complicated and involved as to obscure the original underlying ideas:

The final result was that the core [of spiritual ideas] was swamped and disappeared under the superficial coating [of material symbols]. For example, when Lithai refers to *narakabhumi* [hell] he explains it thoroughly and in detail ... complete with numerals and examples piled upon examples. In the end the reader or listener becomes lost, remembering only the numbers and the examples and unable to return to the core [idea of *nibbana*]. Lithai explains in great detail that beings which are born in *Sanghatanaraka* [hell] remain there for 2,000 years. In *Sanghatanaraka* one day and one night is equivalent to 145,000,000 human years .... When he explains in such detail the unthinking reader will believe it all and his thought will remain stuck at the level of the numbers and names of the hells. He will forget to translate and interpret the symbols in terms of *dhamma* [i.e. symbolic] language.[11] Thus Lithai conveyed only the numbers and the belief in hell as a legacy for his descendants. This indicates the failure of the *Traiphuum Phra Ruang* to lead Buddhists to the higher *dhamma*.

Suthiwong concludes (1983:124) that 'this book can consequently be regarded as an obstacle to propagating the *dhamma* in a form which can lead people to the highest truth'. Suthiwong maintains that the *Traiphuum* does indeed contain Buddhist truths about salvation hidden within its complex symbolism, truths which are acceptable to contemporary reformist Buddhists. However, he criticises Lithai for failing to successfully convey these truths. It should be noted, however, that this is not a criticism of the meaning or literary intention underlying the *Traiphuum* but rather of Lithai's literary method. It is a criticism of the failure of the text to achieve what is interpreted to be the author's true goal of attempting to convey Buddhist truths. Thus, Suthiwong's criticism does not represent a debunking of the ascribed literary intention of the author, which is lauded and retained, but rather of Lithai's symbolic literary style, which is rejected.

Despite his broad support for the teachings of the *Traiphuum Phra Ruang*, as he has interpreted them, Thepwethi also criticises Lithai for having placed too much emphasis on the severe consequences of evil actions instead of the positive consequences of good actions. He maintains (Ratchaworamuni 1983:38) that if Lithai had given greater emphasis to analysing good actions, such as showing

> the good consequences of assisting people, being established in justice and fairness, etc., then [the *Traiphuum*] may have been able to become a forerunner or prototype for the wider development of more constructive and positive thought and action in the succeeding centuries.

Because of this inadequacy in the *Traiphuum* Thepwethi concludes his analysis (Ratchaworamuni 1983:57) by suggesting that the text may need to be replaced by a Buddhist analysis which is more appropriate for contemporary Thai society.

> Even if society is changing markedly the principle of salvation [taught in] the *Traiphuum* ... can still be an appropriate ideal and ideology for Thai society. [The *Traiphuum*] can be used as a trail blazer in correctly developing Thai society in accord with *dhamma*. But it may have to be revised and the obscuring factors may have to be removed so that it can be clearly understood. If for one or other reason the old version of the *Traiphuum*, which has been prepared from commentaries and post-canonical texts, proves inappropriate for the contemporary situation we may also have to consider the possibility of developing a book similar to the *Traiphuum* as a new text which is able to lead the thought of contemporary people today.

In this statement Thepwethi gives further insight into the reasons for the resurgent interest in the *Traiphuum* in Thailand today, namely, the need to develop new sources of legitimating Buddhist authority. This need has led traditionalists and reformists alike to return to traditional sources of religio-political authority in an attempt to adapt them to contemporary purposes. However, Thepwethi points out that such texts as the *Traiphuum* may not be able to be successfully adapted to meet contemporary needs and he raises the possibility of developing the equivalent of a new Thai-Buddhist gospel capable of meeting the need for new sources of religious and political legitimacy in Thailand today. Thepwethi proposes that the *Traiphuum* may have to be superseded by a more amenable contemporary theoretical medium for the expression of the original democratic and liberal intention that he regards as having underlain the foundation of the Thai state. Significantly, Thepwethi's own definitive study of Buddhist doctrine, the thousand plus page opus *Phutthatham* (Ratchaworamuni 1984b), is in the process of becoming a new Buddhist gospel for many progressive Buddhists. *Phutthatham* is a scholarly work with the potential of becoming a modern *Visuddhimagga*,[12] a new standard text on Buddhist doctrine among Thai intellectuals. In his above statement Thepwethi perhaps reveals the motivation which underlay the writing of his great scholarly effort.

CONCLUSION

Craig Reynolds (1976:220) has described the *Traiphuum* as a relic. This description is particularly apt for a text whose antiquity enhances its contemporary value and significance. Though the text can be compared to a revered religious relic whose age enhances its contemporary value and significance, the *Traiphuum* is certainly not an antiquity empty of meaning for modern Thais. The rationalist debunkings of the text's metaphysical contents in the nineteenth century did not mark the end of its political history. Ideologues aligned with the conservative political establishment in Thailand, by their support for traditional readings of the text, demonstrate that political might is still capable of overriding considerations of mere logic or reason. The military overthrow of the Chatchai government in early 1991 will almost certainly confer added impetus and immediacy to conservative interpretations of the text.

In contrast, the metaphysical contents of the *Traiphuum* are now largely irrelevant to the message being attributed to the text in reformist analyses. In these analyses the *Traiphuum* is presented primarily as a symbol, however imperfect, of the purported formative intention of the founders of the first Thai kingdom to create a just Buddhist state. The contemporary symbolic value of the *Traiphuum* for reformists lies not so much in its contents but rather in its simple existence as a reminder of the hope that Lithai purportedly had for a perfect Buddhist social order. The *Traiphuum* is taken as revealing the hidden and long lost political essence and the true meaning of Thai identity, which reformists maintain was distorted and lost in the Ayutthaya and early Bangkok periods. This is the 'truth' that the historical roots and the true nature of being Thai is to be democratic, and that political authoritarianism, whether of an absolute monarch in the past or of a military dictator in recent decades, represents a perversion of the true character of Thai identity.

ENDNOTES

1. The Thai historian Wannau Yuuden (1984:30) maintains that, given the limited archaeological and literary information currently available, the composition of the text cannot be precisely dated. Wannau suggests that the Traiphuum was composed some time between A.D. 1347 and A.D. 1376.

2. In contrast with popular Thai historiography, Michael Vickery (1974:275-84) has attributed the Traiphuum to Lithai's successor and grandson, Sai Lithai.

3. In this article I use the Thai term Traiphuum to refer to the text ascribed to Lithai, and the Sanskrit term *traibhumi* to refer to the notion of the three worlds which constitute the Buddhist universe, namely, *kamabhumi* (the realm of sensual desire), *rupabhumi* (the realm with a remnant of material factors) and *arupabhumi* (the realm without material factors).

4. Wannau Yuuden (1984:30) dates Lithai's reign as A.D. 1354-1376.

5. *Mahacakkavattiraja* - The Great Wheel-turning Monarch.

6. The *Traiphuum Phra Ruang* was first printed in Thailand as a cremation volume for the funerals of Phra Ong Jau Prasansrisai and Phra Ong Jau Praphaisrisa-at in 1912.

7. Note Lithai's formal title upon coronation was Mahadhammaraja, Great King of the Dhamma.

8. Phithun Maliwan (1983, Introduction), head of the editorial committee, prepared the revised and emended version of the *Traiphuum* by comparing three versions of the text, the Phra Maha Chuay version written in 1778, the Phra Maha Jan version written in 1787 at the direction of King Rama I, plus another incomplete manuscript thought to date from the late Ayutthaya period.

9. Somboon Suksamran (1984:19), a political scientist, traces the origins of the Buddhist theory of popularly elected leadership to the Agañña Sutta in the canonical Theravada scriptures.

10. Phra Thepwethi (Prayut Payuttho) formerly held the clerical title of Ratchaworamuni, and this is the name that appears on most of his earlier publications, including those referred to in this article.

11. Suthiwong adopts the symbolic method of interpreting the Buddhist scriptures in terms of '*dhamma* language' developed by the reformist monk Phutthathat (Buddhadasa) (1974).

12. The Visuddhimagga, written by Buddhaghosacariya in the fifth century of the Christian era, has been the most influential interpretation of Buddhist doctrine in Theravada countries for many centuries.

REFERENCES

Butt, J. W. 1978. 'Thai Kingship and Religious Reform (18th-19th Centuries)' in Smith 1978.

Chothira Klatyuu, 1974. 'Traiphuum phra ruang raakthaan khorng udomkaan thaang kaan-myang thai [The Traiphuum Phra Ruang: The Basis of Thai Political Ideals]', *Warasaan thammasat* 4.1 (June-September).

--------. 1976. *Wannakhadi khorng puangchon [Literature of the Masses]*. Bangkok, Khlet Thai.

Jackson, P. A. 1988. *Buddhadasa: A Buddhist Thinker for the Modern World*. Bangkok, Siam Society.

--------. 1989. *Buddhism, Legitimation and Conflict: The Political Functions of Urban Thai Buddhism*. Singapore, Institute of Southeast Asian Studies.

Keyes, C. F. 1978. 'Political Crisis and Militant Buddhism in Contemporary Thailand' in Smith 1978.

Kirsch, T. 1978. 'Modernizing Implications of Nineteenth Century Reforms of the Thai Sangha' in Smith 1978.

Krajaang Nanthapho. 1985. *Mahanikay thammayut khwaam-khat-yaeng phaay-nai khorng khana song thai [Mahanikay - Thammayut: The Internal Contradictions of the Thai Sangha]*. Nonthaburi, Samnak-phim Santitham.

Ling, T. 1976. *The Buddha: Buddhist Civilisation in India and Ceylon*. Harmondsworth, Penguin.

Phaisaan Wisaalai Bhikkhu, Phra. 1986. *Phutthasaasanaa kap khun-khaa ruam samay [Buddhism and Contemporary Values]*. Bangkok, Muunnithi Koomon Khiimthorng.

Phithun Maliwan, ed. 1983. *Traiphuumikatharyy traiphuum phra ruang phra raatchaniphon phra mahathammaracha thii 1 phraya lithai chabap truat sorp chamra mai [The Traibhumikatha or Traiphuum Phra Ruang: A Royal Composition of Phra Mahadhammaraja I, Phraya Lithai, Revised and Emended Version]*. Bangkok, Krom Silpakorn.

Phutthathat (Buddhadasa) Bhikkhu, Phra. 1974. *Two Kinds of Language*. Ariyananda Bhikkhu, trans. Bangkok.

--------. 1978. *Thamma nai thaana latthi kaanmyang [Dhamma as a Political Ideology]*. Bangkok, Samnak Nangsyy Thammabuuchaa.

--------. 1981. *Nipphaan [Nibbana]*. Bangkok, Samnak Nangsyy Thammabuuchaa.

Ratchaworamuni, Phra. 1983. *Traiphuum phra ruang itthiphon tor sangkhom thai [The Traiphuum Phra Ruang: Its Influence on Thai Society]*. Bangkok, Chumnum Syksaa Phutthasaat lae Prapheenii Mahawitthayalay Thammasaat.

--------. 1984a. *Khaa-niyom baep phut [Buddhist Values]*. Bangkok, Samnak-phim Thianwan.

--------.   1984b.   *Phutthatham chabap prap-prung lae khayaay-khwaam [Buddhadhamma, Amended and Expanded Version].* Bangkok, Thammasathaan, Chulalongkorn University.

Reynolds, C. 1976. 'Buddhist Cosmography in Thai History with Special Reference to Nineteenth-Century Culture Change', *Journal of Asian Studies*, 35.2 (February), 203-20.

Reynolds, F. E. 1978a. 'The Holy Emerald Jewel: Some Aspects of Buddhist Symbolism and Political Legitimation in Thailand and Laos' in Smith 1978.

--------.   1978b. 'Sacral Kingship and National Development in the Case of Thailand' in Smith 1978.

Reynolds, F. E. and M. Reynolds, trans. 1982. *The Three Worlds According to King Ruang: A Thai Buddhist Cosmology.* Berkeley, The Center for South and Southeast Asian Studies. Berkeley Buddhist Studies Series no. 4.

Sangiam Sawatdikaan. 1984. *Sarup phon kaan-samanaa ryang traiphuum phra ruang [Summary of the Proceedings of a Conference on the Traiphuum Phra Ruang].* Bangkok, Krom Silpakorn.

Smith, Bardwell L., ed. 1978. *Religion and Legitimation of Power in Thailand, Laos, and Burma.* Chambersburg, Pennsylvania, Anima Books.

Sombat Jantharawong and Chai-anan Samudavanija. 1980. *Khwaam-khit thaang kaan-myang lae sangkhom thai [Thai Political and Social Thought].* Bangkok, Thammasat University, Thai Khadi Institute. Research Document no. 6.

Somboon Suksamran. 1984. *Phutthasaasanaa kap kaan-pliang-plaeng thaang kaanmyang lae sangkhom [Buddhism and Political and Social Change]*. Bangkok, Chulalongkorn University Press.

Somkiat Wanthana. 1983. 'Traiphuum phra ruang din korn diaw nai din-daen [*The Traiphuum Phra Ruang*: A Single Piece of Earth in the Land]' in Ratchaworamuni 1983.

Somphong Chaulaem. 1985. *Traiphuumikatha chabap khooy yang chua [Traibhumikatha, Improved Version]*. Bangnkok, Suan Aksorn Sakhaburi.

Somphorn Mantasuut. 1981. *Wannakam sangkhom lae kaan-myang [Social and Political Literature]*. Bangkok, Odeon Store.

Sulak Sivaraksa. 1989. *Naew-khit thaang pratyaa thai [Thai Philosophical Thought]*. Bangkok, Khana-kammakaan Saasanaa Phya Kaan-phatthanaa.

Sutthiwong Phongphaibun. 1983. 'Traiphuum phra ruang kap khwaam-chya lae prapheenii thaang phutthasaasanaa [The *Traiphuum Phra Ruang* and Buddhist Beliefs and Customs]' in *Phutthasat [Buddhist Teachings]*. Bangkok, Thai Watthana Phanit.

Tambiah, S. J. 1978. 'Sangha and Polity in Modern Thailand: An Overview' in Smith 1978.

--------. 1984. *The Buddhist Saints of the Forest and the Cult of Amulets: A Study in Charisma, Hagiography, Sectarianism and Millennial Buddhism*. Cambridge, Cambridge University Press.

Thattachiwo Bhikkhu, Phra. 1987. *Luang phor thorp panhaa [Luang Phor Responds to Problems].* Pathumthani, Muunnithi Thammakaay.

Thiphakorawong Mahakosathibodi, Jau Phraya. 1971. *Nangsyy sadaeng kitjaanukit [A Book Explaining Various Things].* Bangkok, Ongkaan Khaa Khorng Khurusaphaa.

Udornkhanaphirak (Kittiwuttho) Bhikkhu, Phra. 1986. *Ryang phra sayamthewathirat [Concerning Phra Sayamthewathirat].* Bangkok, Saphaa Sangkhom Songkhror Haeng Pratheet Thai.

Vickery, M. 1974. 'A Note on the Date of the Traibhumikatha', *Journal of the Siam Society,* 62.2 (July), 275-84.

Wannau Yuuden. 1984. *Prawat wannakhadii samay sukhothai lae ayutthaya [History of the Literature of the Sukhothai and Ayutthaya Periods].* Bangkok, Thai Watthana Phanit.

Chapter 8

THAI IDENTITY IN THE ASTROLOGICAL TRADITION

Nerida M. Cook

To a large extent astrology claims a part in Thai life and culture by appeal to tradition. Thais are said to have relied on the selection of auspicious times for the correct performance of a whole range of activities, from weddings and royal rituals to going into battle, for as long as they care to trace their historical origins. As is the case with some neighbouring countries (e.g. Burma, see Aung Thwin 1982), Thai historical records are replete with references to astrological and other divinatory auguries and practices; so is much of Thai classical literature. Indeed, the oldest known recording of horoscopes in Thai literature can be traced back to the Traiphuum Phraruang (Uean Monthianthong 1981:24)[1], an early work of continuing, indeed renewed, political and cultural importance for Thai intellectuals (see Jackson this volume). It is the perceived longevity of the practice of astrology and its integral role in the activities of the country's royal rulers that leads many to argue that astrology is an intrinsic part of Thai thought and of the Thai way of life.

Thai astrologers[2] have a unique contribution to make to the question of Thai identity in two related ways. The first is that they have the ability to provide advice and a sense of direction to individual clients on the basis of analysis of natal horoscopes. Second, they have the ability and, some would argue, the duty to understand and interpret the implications of the horoscope of the nation. A national horoscope, of course, provides clues to the identity of the nation. Just as the horoscope drawn up for the birth of an individual contains indications of the life, character and predispositions of that person, so the horoscope of a country indicates the nation's individual characteristics, as well as the conditions influencing it and its people. Thailand's horoscope, drawn up by the astrologers of the founding king of the present dynasty, continues to be the subject of much interest among Thai astrologers. Present-day experts use the recorded time of the original to construct their own versions of the horoscope, and become familiar not only with the features of the horoscope itself, but also study the recent analyses made of the horoscope by others.

Astrology, further, has something to say about national identity because astrologers undertake the task of interpreting Thai history in the light of the national horoscope and the influences of the movements of the planets as they change in relation to the planetary positions embodied in the national horoscope. Being primarily concerned with conceptualization of fate or destiny, astrology provides a basis for analyzing history as an indication of the destiny, and therefore the identity, of the nation: destiny is identity manifested over time. The Thai astrological view of history therefore seeks to establish those features of the Thai past and present which are indicative of the intrinsic qualities of Thai nationhood, qualities which, by implication, will also extend into the future. It is not surprising, therefore, that astrological interpretations of history are often articulated in terms of events, concepts and nationalist ideals already very well known to the Thai public.

ASTROLOGY AND THAI HERITAGE

The most commonly cited exemplars of the wise and moral use of astrology in the responsible conduct of affairs are the past monarchs of Thailand, who are believed to have used the services of their court astrologers for the important aspects of their duties. The royal palaces - and even provincial court centres - had departments of astrologers. The duties of the king's astrologers in the *krom hoon* included drawing up official annual calendars, calculating auspicious times for court events of importance, and paying constant attention to any celestial movements or other omens which might have significance for the human realm. Severe penalties could be applied for mistakes made in the performance of these duties (Wales 1971:11). Astrologers continue to be employed in the Royal Palace, in a limited capacity, and this can be interpreted as a sign of recognition of the continuing importance of astrology in traditional Thai culture.

Well-known stories from the chronicles confirm royal interest in and knowledge of matters of prognostication and the importance recognised by kings of heeding warnings and acting in response to divinatory advice. Popular historical anecdotes recount how the reigns of several Thai monarchs, the founder of the present dynasty included (Gesick 1983:98), followed prophecies intimating their accession to power. Astrologers and lay enthusiasts argue that Thailand's prosperity and long independence are partly due to the wise counsel of astrologers who advised the kings on royal ritual, supplied them with predictions of future events, and guided their successful armies into battle. Naresuan's celebrated victory against the Burmese Crown Prince in 1593 is said to have followed on from encouraging astrological advice (Worayaphorn 1976:12). Similarly, it is argued (e.g. S. Satcayan 1982), Thailand's continued independence under the present dynasty is essentially due to Rama I's carefully selecting a horoscope for the current capital which would ensure a long life for the city and impregnability against enemies. Further, Thai astrology is frequently characterised as having helped shape Thai history and as having been an integral part of national independence and success from 'ancient times' (e.g. Somrocana 1981; Prathip 1981). This perceived role, the fact that astrology can be said to have been a constant guide for past kings in all matters of importance, lends astrology considerable authority and relevance for both contemporary individuals and for the interpretation of current political events.

The long history of astrological and divinatory thought in Thai history, and the prominent part sophisticated astrological beliefs played in the elite culture of the royal court, have served to enhance the prestige of astrology despite more recent Buddhist, rationalist and scientific arguments brought against it. Moreover, the fact that astrology was once an intrinsic part of the statecraft of Thai monarchs specifically contributes to the appropriateness of continued use of astrology in the political sphere in the view of some politicians; and this can be supported by those who seek to preserve specifically Thai social values and political culture, both at an individual level and via such bodies as the National Identity Board (e.g. Somrocana 1981). Astrological associations such as the prestigious Astrological Association of Thailand[3] actively promote this conservative view of astrology.

ASTROLOGY AND PERSONAL IDENTITY

Sophisticated astrology, based on the use of birth horoscopes, was available only to members of the elite in the days before the advent of widespread literacy and access to accurate time-measurement. Now, however, the use of such horoscopes, enabling an interpretation of personal identity to be created soon after birth, is widespread among urban middle- and upper-class groups. This also appears to be the case in other Theravada Buddhist countries (e.g. Ceylon, see Gombrich 1971:148). This pattern of interest in astrology is probably related to the wider range of options and comparatively ambitious expectations of -or insecurity regarding - the future among these groups as compared with, say, the less socially mobile farmers and urban poor, who in Thailand generally evince less interest in fortune-telling (Suntaree and Snit 1979:328). On the whole, patterns of interest in astrology is highest among the middle class, urban and more educated sections of Thai society (Suntaree and Snit 1979:311, 328). A survey of Thai values has found what appears to be significantly less interest in traditional religious behaviour and beliefs, and concomitantly less fatalism, in urban Thai society than in the more religiously active and highly fatalistic rural population (Suntaree 1985:180). Interest in astrology therefore appears more important for what has been found to be a comparatively self-centred and achievement-oriented section of Thai society (Suntaree 1985:180). Nevertheless astrology has at least some following amongst all social groups.

In Thai astrological consultations general ideas of karma, specific planetary influences or more nebulous notions of fate can be used to account for the 'why' of the client's experiences, while the movements of the planets with the passage of time account for the 'when'. Personal identity is associated with the natal horoscope, a representation of the configuration of planetary positions as they appear against the heavens at the time of birth. The various phases of life are then analyzed as they are affected by subsequent changes in the positions of the planets in relation to this original configuration.

In the West astrological analysis is popularly conceived of as providing insight into personal identity, supplying the individual with a description of his or her own characteristics and propensities, as well as the possibilities for the future which these imply. Such analyses can provide a sense of individual importance and self-assurance. In Thailand also, popular astrology provides the basis for coming to terms with individual identity, although as Bechstedt also points out in this volume it is necessary to modify the Western notion of 'identity' for the Thai case. As has been argued elsewhere, in Thailand

individualism is apparently *not* rooted in a differentiated inner world; it is not based on the individually articulated experiences of, and attitudes towards the outside world. On the contrary ... the preference is for traditional and universal formulas. (Brummelhuis 1984:42)

These are derived from Buddhist or other explanations. In effect, therefore, when individuals explore what their horoscopes reveal, as with other forms of self-examination, their 'preoccupation is not so much with self-realization and autonomy as with adaptation to the social or cosmological environment' (Brummelhuis 1984:44). Suntaree confirms this attitude is a significant part of the Thai value system, in that, generally,

> to be successful and to "achieve" in Thai society does not depend so much on one's competence as on one's ability to perceive and choose the right means and opportunity that lead to success in the society.... In short, achievement in Thai society does not mean hard [work] or task orientation. To quite an extent, it is more of a "social achievement". (Suntaree 1985:179-180)

This orientation is evident in astrological consultations, where the individual clients are likely to spend much time enquiring about the options available given their immediate social situation. Future possibilities are canvassed less in terms of the individual's innate propensities and abilities than as the result of the dispositions of others, especially superiors and close family members, towards the client as well as whether the horoscope indicates a change in life or not. Understanding one's social environment and its potential for one's personal future has come to take on some of the connotations of proper and successful behaviour for the competitive and highly stratified society of modern Bangkok. Knowing one's situation, possibilities and likely fortunes as indicated by a personal horoscope is one framework which allows the individual to orient him or herself to a place in the differentiated Thai social order.

Sometimes taking astrological advice furthers the fulfilment of obligations entailed in social relationships. It is commonly asserted that prospective marriages are often abandoned if astrologers employed by the parents to check the couple's compatibility advise against the match. During Sarit Thanarat's period as Prime Minister, many of his government officials followed his lead by regularly visiting astrologers at the monastery where one of Sarit's key astrological advisers resided either to seek astrological advice or simply to keep abreast of the situation (Mosel 1966:198).

Knowing the future or contemplating future options enables an individual to maintain key psychological states such as resoluteness and self-possessed forms of demeanour highly valued in Thai social life. Consultation with a fortune-teller or astrologer is commonly believed to provide the psychologically troubled with a measure of restored calm and confidence, to the extent that these practitioners are often explicitly equated with psychological counsellors in the West. This is in part attributed to their capacity to encourage the client to think about when good fortune can be striven for, or at the least, when alleviation of suffering can be expected, providing psychological comfort or even a morale boost. Such active orientation towards the future therefore helps to maintain socially approved optimism and diligence which are thought to be the appropriate expression of the realisation of personal identity.

It is often suggested by the sceptical that the popularity of fortune-tellers can be attributed to their willingness to tell the client what he or she may want to hear, thereby lulling them into the much desired feeling of *sabaai cai* (contentment, mental ease). Yet it is also likely that the weighing up of alternatives and possibilities that forms a prominent feature of consultations helps clients to maintain such highly culturally valued attitudes as patience, imperturbability and tolerance in any unfortunate circumstances they may find themselves in. Many clients state that, when trouble is foreseen by the astrologer, they prefer to be told about these difficulties in advance. A person is thereby in a position to prepare him- or herself psychologically, and to be able to maintain some degree of the all-important quality of cool-heartedness (*cai yen*) and composure in the face of his or her adversities. In its turn, predicted good fortune can be met with similar equanimity.

Graceful acceptance of one's place and also of one's 'fate' can thereby be facilitated by astrological consultations.

Astrologers and fortune tellers can even be regarded as informal moral police, in a position to nip incipient crime in the bud and encourage clients to choose the morally and socially correct path (Worayaphorn 1976:14). In one extreme case, an astrologer used the example of his experience of trying to dissuade a distraught wife from taking violent revenge on her unfaithful husband to remind his fellow practitioners that it is the astrologer's prime duty to emphasize aspects of their horoscopes and to direct courses of action in ways which will be in their client's best long-term interests. He stressed that this should pre-empt any desire on the part of the astrologer to show off talents for prophetic accuracy by entertaining less socially acceptable alternatives in their prognosis (Caran 1979).

Further, many Thais who favour the use of astrology look upon foreknowledge of one's personal future not only as providing useful personal and social benefits but also as clearly promoting moral duty as a Buddhist. This argument stems from an accommodation popularly made between astrology and the Buddhist theory of karma. While some Buddhist critics argue that fortune-telling and the various ceremonies performed to alleviate misfortune go against the central Buddhist doctrine, many clients of fortune-tellers feel that prior awareness of what the future holds brings home the message of the importance of karma, and encourages people to remember to behave in a morally desirable way in order to avoid or mitigate what might otherwise befall them (e.g. Worayaphorn 1976:11).

Astrologers often stress the non-deterministic nature of what their methods foretell, and some suggest Buddhist merit-making activities for those for whom future misfortune is a likelihood, thereby simultaneously advocating a familiar source of comfort to the client and linking their own activities to the teachings and practices of popular Buddhism. This is especially important for the many monks whose astrological services are sought by the laity, since there is considerable criticism, from both within and outside the order, of monks who practise forms of fortune telling for their lay followers. An eminent monk-astrologer at a prestigious *wat* explained the benefits he saw in his provision of astrological knowledge with the example of a young couple coming to seek an auspicious time for their wedding. Calculating the auspicious time gives him the further opportunity to impress on the couple their future responsibilities towards each other and the right attitudes which Buddhism advocates for a successful marriage. In this way Buddhist social ethics can be presented as the true basis for future success, and the monk can consider his role of instructor in the dhamma extended.

More generally, the frequent rationalization of the horoscope as representing the results of the individual's past karma reinforces consciousness of the Buddhist doctrine and the need for the recognition of individual responsibility for actions and their consequences, a key social ethic. Bangkok astrologers now analyze the finer points of the relationship between astrological theory and karma, and often develop an explicit professional ethic concerning their duty to help the client realize the Buddhist implications of their situation. This allows astrologers to ally themselves and their profession with the dominant religious tradition and distance themselves from astrology's inferior and increasingly discredited Brahmanic roots.

ASTROLOGY AND NATIONAL IDENTITY

In analysis of the national horoscope the same pragmatic emphasis placed on the appropriateness of certain future trends and actions can be discerned as is the case with personal horoscopes. It is possible to suggest that political astrologers often adopt for themselves the same constructive social and psychological role in political predictions as astrologers display in personal consultations. Astrological analyses of the national destiny are generally optimistic in overall outlook, despite their common orientation towards the crises of the time, and create and reinforce notions of an appropriate, enduring, essential 'Thainess' for their audience.

In contrast to the confidence of method which Thai astrologers bring to the analysis of personal horoscopes, mundane or political astrology, that branch of astrology which predicts events for nations or politically organized groups, is sometimes described as currently little known and understood in Thai astrological circles, despite the antiquity of the subject. This dearth of experience may be related to the fact that popular astrology at present is mostly practised professionally in relation to individuals. It may also be related to the caution with which political predictions have to be made in the Thai legal and political context, where predictions likely to incite disturbance among the public are illegal, and where public political predictions can be discouraged. Nevertheless there is a discernible commonality of views in relation to the Thai national horoscope shared by many of the Thai astrologers who choose to write on topics of political significance.

The decline of official use of court astrology and the extension of astrology into the popular sphere since the decline of the absolute monarchy have had some notable consequences for Thai political astrology. There are inherent difficulties in knowing how to draw up horoscopes for politically organised groups, especially nations, since the moment of inception of such entities is open to interpretation and is of necessity frequently judged by the perceived role or nature of the given entity in the present. Even when the dates and times of significant foundation events are known, therefore, there still remains the question of which event best represents the emergence of the country or nation-state in its present form.[4]

However, in those countries where astrology has been actively maintained as part of the practice of statecraft, as was the case with Siam under the absolute monarchy, these inaugural historical events were deliberately marked as part of public, official ceremonies. There was no astrological problem with the founding of Bangkok, since the decision as to the moment of establishment of the new socio-political entity was consciously chosen and marked with appropriate ritual by those who were founding both a new rule and a new centre of power. The long-established use of astrology in the political sphere meant that the identification of the polity with a particular horoscope was believed to be dictated by recognised political and astrological practice. It is understandable that the first Cakkri king's attempt to reinstate many of the symbolic and ritual forms of legitimate monarchical rule included attention to the longstanding tradition of the inaugural installation of a city pillar, one of the formalities apparently ignored by his unfortunate predecessor Taksin. The horoscope of the new capital was established for the moment of the ceremonial raising of the city pillar, the *lak mueang*, on 21 April 1782. The raising of this pillar signalled the founding of the new capital of the new Cakkri king, occurring within a very short time of the accession of the new monarch and preceding, logically and temporally, the construction of the royal palace and the monasteries of the city.

The city pillar is closely associated with the ruling dynasty. As an institutional site marking the temporal era and spatial centre of power, the pillar has continued to be maintained and ceremonially venerated by the country's reigning monarchs. The shrine for the pillar's guardian deity is also a popular site of veneration and source of supernatural assistance and protection for ordinary citizens. Astrologers today continue to analyze the implications of the factors influencing the selection of an appropriate auspicious time for this site. The horoscope of the original city pillar, the *duang mueang*, is publicly cited as evidence of the wisdom, foresight and benevolence of the founding monarch, as is reflected, for example, in the choice he is believed to have personally made to select a

time for the horoscope which would ensure that the Burmese would
not ever be able to destroy the new capital. However other less
propitious compromises are also said to have been made. Phuu
Phaakphuum (1978:28) mentions the oral tradition suggesting that
the selection of the horoscope entailed a choice between the
dynasty's longevity and the common people's prosperity. Rama
I's astrological perspicacity is celebrated by astrologers (e.g. S.
Phlainoi 1982:6), especially because he paid careful attention to
omens concerning the city horoscope and took appropriate action
for the protection of his city (Thep 1981:4-15).

At the time of the inauguration of the new capital, the *duang
mueang* was known as the horoscope of the city at the centre of
new royal power. However, as the capital has since become the
formal political centre of what is now the nation-state of Thailand,
the horoscope of the city has *ipso facto* come to be regarded as
in effect the horoscope of the country. By implication, therefore,
the horoscope is now seen as also representing the time of the
emergence of the nation in its modern form. The astrological
implications of the horoscope of the capital have eventually come
to define the nation as a whole as contemporary astrologers now
understand it, even though some astrologers realise that this cannot
really be seen as identical to the original political conceptions of
the city's founders.[5]

Nevertheless the profound social and political changes which
have transformed the nation in the intervening two hundred-odd
years have posed some conceptual and practical challenges for
modern astrologers. For example, a question now raised within
Thai political astrology is that of whether this original horoscope
is the only appropriate one on which to base astrological
interpretations for contemporary Thailand. While it seems the
vast majority of astrologers follow tradition in using this official
marker, there is some dissension from the assumption that the
original city pillar horoscope is still the sole relevant occasion in
the emergence of the nation as it is now.

It can be argued, for example, that the much-needed improvement in foreign relations during the reign of Rama IV, eventually resulting in the signing of trade treaties and the importation of medical knowledge, was the result of Mongkut's timely installation of a new city pillar. The new horoscope for this pillar was selected to avert imminent dangers relating in part to the potential encroachments of European powers (Phansak 1986:222).[6] Moreover it can be seen to be this second city horoscope, rather than the original, which was badly affected by transiting planets and therefore of considerable relevance for the coup d'etat against the absolute monarchy in 1932. Nevertheless the fact that this occasion was bloodless can be related to the fact that there were no adverse planetary transits affecting the original city horoscope at the time (Phluu Luang 1968:46).

The change of government as a result of the so-called Revolution of 1932 represented, symbolically and supposedly in practice, a major change in the nature of the political identity of Siam. By the end of the decade, as we know, the name of the country had been formally changed; and the commencement of the Thai year was also brought into line with international practice to emphasize the nation's new direction (Thamsook 1978:235). Astrologers sometimes suggest that the decisive change in the government of the country, especially that which ended the absolute rule of the monarchy which had established the city horoscope, is the time at which the contemporary situation commenced, and that therefore the horoscope of this time ought now to be used in conjunction with the original horoscope in analyzing the destiny of the nation. This suggestion has logical links with the former practice of using the horoscope of the reigning monarch in addition to that of the capital in the analysis of predictions concerning the country as a whole. On the whole, however, astrologers prefer to use only the original, royally sanctioned horoscope as a basis for interpretation. While a few astrologers argue for the importance and relevance of a horoscope for the 1932 change of government, however, they do not suggest that this supplant the 1782 horoscope but merely supplement it. For Thai astrologers, modern Thailand commences with the Cakkri dynasty (cf. Chula 1982:80).

There are a number of factors at work in the retention by most astrologers of the original horoscope of the founding of Bangkok. The historical continuity of the capital as the centre of power and of the central importance of the monarchical institution naturally play a role. The destruction of Ayutthaya was recognised by some as the fulfilment of an earlier prophecy and has often been portrayed in terms of the time of the city having run out. Obviously there has been no parallel in the case of Bangkok. There is also a range of astrologically based reasons relevant to the rejection of the June revolution horoscope. Whether the 1932 horoscope is rejected as having lasting significance because, as one conservative police officer-astrologer argued, those who came to power in 1932 are no longer in government (Camrun 1976:25); or because, as another astrologer pointed out, there can only ever be one major ritually significant foundation post (i.e. as for a house), it is generally accepted among astrologers that the horoscope which still identifies the nation is that of 1782. This decision enables them to retain features of the earlier understanding of the astrological view of the national identity.

There is yet another reason why the change of government in 1932 has been discounted by astrologers. This has to do with the well-known prophecy ascribed to Rama I that the dynasty he founded would last for one hundred and fifty years. This prediction was revived in the months preceding the overthrow of the monarchy in 1932, and with hindsight, many astrologers now argue that the change of government in June of that year is evidence of the accuracy of the prophecy predicting a change in dynastic fortunes at that time. While Rama I may not have foreseen the exact nature of the changes that took place in that year, his prescience is interpreted by astrologers as having been accurate in terms of the timing of the eventual political change. The fact that the change was apparently predicted by the founding monarch lends it a kind of royal benediction similar to that bestowed by Rama VII on the People's Party after the restitution of the king as titular head of a constitutional government. It is ironic that such a prediction, which is thought to have been deliberately used in 1932 to justify the coming revolution as a legitimate end to the absolute monarchy, is now used to incorporate the change of government as part of a longer, royally conceived historical trajectory, one which subsumes the change of government as an intrinsic part of the national destiny as it was envisaged by the nation's royal founder. Precisely because it can be argued to have been destined in terms foreseen from the start, in the astrological view the change of government in 1932 forms part of the nation's original destiny, rather than signalling the start of a new era, and with it a new destiny and a changed identity.

What of the *duang mueang* itself, and the identity it is thought to signal for the nation? Current astrologers can make educated guesses as to the original intentions of their predecessors. They construct their horoscopes based on the recorded time used for the original and provide their interpretations of what can be predicted for the future from the horoscope embedded in the city pillar. Although some of the more historically minded astrologers try to be guided, for their suppositions concerning the intentions of the founding monarch's astrologers, by the state of Thai astrological knowledge at the time of the establishment of Bangkok, most of them simply employ their favourite theories and schools of thought in their own interpretation of what the horoscope signifies for the identity of the Thai national community and for the impact changing planetary positions will have on the country. Nevertheless, although there are mainly minor variations in the calculations of horoscopes for the city pillar, in terms of analysis there is much general agreement about national characteristics and historical destiny.

A few examples of analyses over the last few decades will indicate that interpretations vary and cannot be characterised as being uniform over time. It also appears that astrological analyses often borrow quite heavily from other past and contemporary sources of interpretation of national destiny, including topical views of history. For example there are some interesting parallels with the nationalist writings of Luang Vichit and the political rhetoric of the Sarit period in the analysis of 'Aacaan' Thep in the mid-1960s. While detailed ideas and Thep's method preferences link his analysis to the particular preoccupations of the period, however, this influential writer's overall analysis illustrates features of what is a prevalent understanding of national identity based on interpretation of the national horoscope.

Thep's 1965 analysis elaborated on the themes of the paramount protection offered to diverse subjects by His Majesty the King; the excellence and vigilance of the army's leaders in their valiant defence of the nation; the inevitable defeat of all of the country's enemies whether from without or from within; the abundance of the country's natural resources; the co-operation and support Thailand always receives from friendly powers; the strength and eminence of Thai Buddhism internationally; and the containment of the Chinese in Thailand -all clearly indicated in the horoscope of the capital, and, in the author's view, intentionally ensured by the early royal astrologers (Thep 1967:140-162).[7]

Later, however, during the 1973-1976 'democratic' period, when 'the unfulfilled expectations of 1932 resurfaced' (Reynolds n.d.:5), another astrologer put forward a rather different picture of the nation's strengths and weaknesses. In Phluu Luang's interpretation the nation's youth was seen to be the source of national fame, as evidenced by the actions of the younger generation on 14 October 1973. On the other hand, the writer was not sanguine about the benefits for the country of national rulers when they had been in power for some time. Unlike Thep, and unlike the interpreters who later provided predictions towards the end of the interregnum (see below), this analyst argued strongly that the position of the military planet of Mars indicated that the army was a source of deterioration in and danger for national politics and the economy (Phluu Luang 1975:21). Significantly, in the view of this liberal historian-astrologer, the horoscope of the June Revolution has not been as auspicious for the country or its people as was the original city pillar horoscope (1977:4-6).

Soon after the abrupt and violent end to the democratic period this same astrologer argued vigorously for a more comprehensive basis for the astrological analysis of indications for the national destiny, suggesting that the horoscope of the 1932 Revolution must be seen to have had great significance for subsequent events, and should therefore be used in conjunction with the city pillar horoscope in constructing national predictions. Other issues raised in Phluu Luang's attempts to suggest astrological reorientations in the way national destiny be analyzed included incorporation of interpretation of the horoscopes for the times of various constitutions introduced subsequent to the 1932 change of government. He suggested these be analyzed in terms of what each portended for the subsequent success of democracy in the country, in effect suggesting an ongoing, 'developmental' approach to the nation's astrological identity, rather than the fixed and limited approach implied in the sole use of the original city horoscope (Phluu Luang 1977).[8]

The original 1782 horoscope is the basis for another well-known, more recent prediction: that the country is destined to be ruled by 'people in uniform'. This forecast is understood to mean an expectation of military rule, or rule by those in military uniform, since the military is one of the primary associations of the planet Mars. During the ascendancy of right-wing elements towards the end of the 1973-1976 interregnum this prediction was publicly tied to the idea that Thailand could only be saved from a takeover by communists if 'those in uniform' were in power (Morell and Chai-anan 1981:249).[9]   On the other hand rumours circulating about the escalation of violence, which culminated in the killing of students at Thammasat on October 6, linked the trend to a dire prediction thought to have been made in August of that year concerning the longevity of the royal dynasty (Phuu 1978:16).

Other elements of popular conceptualization of Thailand's weaknesses are apparent in features ascribed to the original *duang mueang*, such as evidence for chronic corruption in government, a poor record in educational achievements, and the suspicion, usually communicated privately, that the horoscope contains little grounds for hope for improvement for the mass of the Thai people. By contrast, in the late 1970s and early 1980s the obvious strength indicated in the national horoscope of the three institutions of nation, religion and monarchy was a popular lecture topic at the astrological associations.

The practice of astrology in political circles has its own popular logic. The fact that astrological calculations are widely associated with coups, but far less with elections, reflects popular attitudes concerning those in competition for power. Achievement of power by coup d'etat, an unscheduled event rather than part of a due process, is dangerous but relatively clear cut. Auspicious timing is thought to be a prerequisite for success, as is the case with any undertaking of great import. Moreover astrology is thought to be more practically geared to the analysis of changes in individual fortunes than in any more systematic analysis of governments and political parties. Unexpected changes in power, such as those achieved by coup d'etat, are easily accounted for astrologically by periods of strength or weakness in the horoscopes of individuals and perhaps of the country. By contrast the complexity of elections, and of Thai coalition governments, is not so easily analyzable in the same way. It is perhaps also significant that it is widely thought that military officers are among the most avid followers of astrological advice in political circles, and that some of the recent successors to power by coup have the reputation of being strongly influenced by astrology. This list would include Sarit, Thanom,

Thanin and Kriangsak, all of whom have also been reported to have disapproved or attempted suppression of predictions that their length of stay in office would be prematurely ended.

CONCLUSION

Astrological interpretations of personal and of national historical destiny come under attack in Thailand for a variety of reasons. Among some educated groups and reformist Buddhists astrology in general is coming to be viewed as a form of superstition without rational or moral foundation. It is, in this context, criticized as inappropriate as a basis for action, especially for those having power over, and responsibility for, others. It is also, therefore, seen as inappropriate as a basis for interpretation of the actions of the politically powerful. In this view the astrological interpretation of national identity cum destiny is at best anachronistic, based in an intellectually and politically archaic framework, and lacking any of the social scientific sophistication which now informs the educated view of history (Reynolds n.d.:1), politics, and the role of the individual in society. At worst, it encourages fatalism and masks the real economic and political causes underlying social conditions (e.g. Anut 1976:122-123). Nevertheless, as I have argued, for the population at large the prominence of astrology in the Thai past lends it peculiar attractiveness as a source of identity and reassurance at both the personal and the political levels. In particular astrological accounts appeal to popular self-conceptions by describing experience depicted as being unique to Thailand and to Thais, evoking the sense of a destiny not shared by other nations or peoples.

It may well be the case, as is often expected - at least by astrology's detractors - that astrological predictions of political affairs have much to do with suggesting certain attitudes and points of view rather than simply reflecting access to arcane knowledge. Political astrology in Thailand borrows concepts and assumptions from the wider concerns and debates of the moment, at the same time as it allows astrologers to avoid or refute óther perspectives and arguments. To some extent the popularity of this kind of astrology depends on the ability of astrological writers to locate their predictions in the context of well-known references to national problems and ideals. For this reason, astrological writings and rumours concerning astrological predictions of political matters are not restricted in their circulation to those who place faith in astrology itself, but allow communication based on shared cultural conceptions to reach a much wider audience. In this sense astrological analyses and predictions are not necessarily 'read' as revelations arising out of arcane knowledge but can equally be accepted as oblique and allusive, yet singularly suggestive accounts of the relationship between past, present and future. The familiarity and versatility of astrology help promote the continued vitality of astrological expressions of identity and destiny and provide some scope for dissent from, as well as reinforcement of, the prevailing orthodoxies.

Thai astrology provides a vehicle for popular, opportune, lay articulations of personal as well as social, political and economic concerns at any given time. Just as the accepted pattern of resort to astrology at the individual level largely involves consultation with astrologers in times of trouble or uncertainty, so, at the political level, the Thai media present more astrological opinions at times of social unease or political upheaval. The deliberations within Thai political astrology reflect many of the ambiguities and uncertainties that arise in the vexed questions of national identity and of the directions the Thai nation has already taken in the past and is likely to take in the future.

ENDNOTES

1. These horoscopes are for the most significant moments of the Buddha's attainment of the three kinds of Nibbana (see Reynolds and Reynolds 1982: 330-331), indicating the very close links between Buddhist and astrological concerns in the mind of the royal author (Andaya 1978:10).

2. As is the case with many aspects of belief supposedly closely linked to the 'Thai world-view', astrology is a controversial topic in Thailand, and it is necessary therefore to emphasize that this paper only discusses one side, the pro-astrology view, of the debate concerning the role of astrology in Thailand. The arguments used to support astrology in Thailand are usually implicitly or even explicitly designed to refute the Buddhist, rationalist and modernist arguments brought against it by those who argue that astrology is intellectually, morally and politically an anachronism in modern Thailand. Although there is only space to consider the astrologers' views here, therefore, it is important to remember that such views are always expressed with reference to a broader context. A further discussion of this broader context can be found in Cook 1989.

3. The Astrological Association of Thailand is the best-known society of astrologers in Thailand. It was established in 1947. Founding members included the then Chief Royal Astrologer and other eminent elite astrologers of the time. The association, housed at the prestigious Thammayut sect's Wat Bowornniwes, is well known for its provision of daily consultation services, which appear to be regarded as reliable and reasonably priced, and a little less well known for its weekend classes in astrology, palmistry and numerology. The Association also publishes a long-running monthly astrological magazine, with some limited distribution beyond its own membership. In 1983 its increasing popularity had created a membership of approximately 2,300 nationwide. An analysis of its consultants' usefulness to its largely educated middle-class clientele is provided in Philairat 1981. There are at least two other major astrological associations of a similar kind in Bangkok; all three are located in Buddhist monasteries.

4. For a discussion of how this difficulty has affected Western astrologers wishing to draw up a horoscope for modern France, for example, see Campion 1988:128-134. The history of Germany, and indeed of many other nations, provides similar problems.

5. Naturally, horoscopes for nations have also only recently been developed in Western astrology in which, as with the Thai case, astrologers were accustomed to using horoscopes for cities, politicians, royalty and coronations prior to the development of the modern nation-state concept (Campion 1984:95).

6. For further discussion of the astrological legacy of Mongkut's reactions to the international situation of the time see Cook n.d.

7. 'Aacaan' Thep Sarikabutr is a very well known astrologer, expert on Indian astrology, and writer on Brahmanic practice and belief. He has been a prolific writer over the past several decades, and was a very influential member of the Astrological Association of Thailand during the sixties and seventies, during which time he wrote many articles on contemporary political events. He was reportedly a close associate of Field Marshal Sarit Thanarat. Thep was appointed to the House of Representatives on 20th August 1957, when Phibulsongkhraam was Prime Minister. A month later Sarit seized power, and Thep was reappointed to the Assembly soon afterwards (see Prasoet 1974:883, 887). Thep's analysis is included in a collection concerning the national horoscopes of the major powers: the United States of America, Russia and China, together with that of Thailand.

8. 'Phluu Luang' is the astrological pen-name of Prayun Uluchada, a well-known art historian and former lecturer of Sinlapakorn University whose prolific writings cover many fields. As an artist, writer and teacher he has been active in intellectual circles for several decades. Phluu Luang has an eclectic interest in foreign astrological and divinatory traditions and has developed his own innovatively modified basis of interpretation which does not appear to be commonly used by other Thai astrologers, although his works are apparently widely read.

9. It is sometimes thought that Thanin Kraivixian's efforts to enforce the wearing of official uniforms by civil servants during his term as Prime Minister (1976-77) was an attempt to substitute government official for military uniforms in response to this prediction, presumably as a way of prolonging the security of his government (Morell and Chai-anan 1981: 249). However the military significance of the term is the one popularly understood. From the late 1970s through the early 1980s left-wing political magazines published interviews with a well-known political astrologer in which he reaffirmed the inevitability of this aspect of national destiny. The astrologer, Poramet Wacharapan, who apparently regards himself as the originator of this prediction, is the son of the former astrologer Prachuab Wacharapan, who is still remembered as the 'personal fortune-teller' of Sarit Thanarat during the latter's term as Prime Minister. Poramet makes extensive use of original Indian texts in his astrological interpretations.

REFERENCES

Andaya, Barbara Watson. 1978. 'Statecraft and the Reign of Lu Tai of Sukhodaya (ca. 1347 - 1374)' in Bardwell L. Smith, ed., *Religion and Legitimation of Power in Thailand, Laos, and Burma.* Chambersburg, Pennsylvania, Anima Books.

Anut Aphaphirom, 1976. 'Khwaam khit thii pen witthayaasaat [Scientific Thinking]' in *Sinlapatham sangkhom niyom, kham toop waa duai satcatham, sangkhom niyom kap kaan sueksaa, khwaam khatyaeng nai faai sangkhom niyom, khwaam khit thii pen witthayaasaat.* Bangkok, Khom Chai.

Aung Thwin, Michael. 1982. 'Prophecies, Omens and Dialogue: Tools of the Trade in Burmese Historiography', in David K. Wyett and Alexander Woodside, eds., *Moral Order and the Question of Change: Essays on Southeast Asian Thought.* Monograph Series No 24. New Haven, Yale University Southeast Asia Studies.

Brummelhuis, Han ten. 1984. 'Abundance and Avoidance: An Interpretation of Thai Individualism' in Han ten Brummelhuis and Jeremy H. Kemp, eds., *Strategies and Structures in Thai Society.* Amsterdam, Anthropological-Sociological Centre, University of Amsterdam.

Campion, Nicholas. 1984. 'The National Horoscope: Mundane Astrology and Political Theory' in Michael Baigent, Nicholas Campion and Charles Harvey, *Mundane Astrology.* Wellingborough, Northamptonshire, The Aquarian Press.

Campion, Nicholas. 1988. *The Book of World Horoscopes*. Wellingborough, Northamptonshire, The Aquarian Press.

Camrun Watthanamongkhol. 1976. 'Duang chataa pratheet thai [Thailand's Horoscope]', *Phayaakornsaan*, 30.9 (December), 22-34.

Caran Phikul, 1979. 'Moo duu maen maen [Accurate Fortune Tellers]', *Phayaakornsaan*, 33.8 (November),41-44.

Chula Chakrabongse, H.R.H. Prince. 1982. *Lords of Life. A History of the Kings of Thailand*. Bangkok, DD Books.

Cook, Nerida M. 1989. 'Astrology in Thailand: The Future and the Recollection of the Past'. Ph.D. dissertation, Australian National University.

Cook, Nerida M. n.d. 'A Tale of Two City Pillars: Mongkut and Thai Astrology on the Eve of Modernization', in G. Wijeyewardene and E.C. Chapman, eds., *Patterns and Illusions: Papers on Thai Topics in Memory of Richard B. Davis*. Forthcoming.

Gesick, Lorraine. 1983. 'The Rise and Fall of King Taksin: A Drama of Buddhist Kingship', in L. Gesick, ed., *Centers, Symbols and Hierarchies: Essays on the Classical States of Southeast Asia*. Monograph Series No 26. New Haven, Yale University Southeast Asia Studies.

Gombrich, Richard F. 1971. *Precept and Practice. Traditional Buddhism in the Rural Highlands of Ceylon*. Oxford, Clarendon Press.

Morell, David and Chai-anan Samudavanija. 1981. *Political Conflict in Thailand.* Cambridge, Massachusetts, Oelgeschlager, Gunn and Hain.

Mosel, James N. 1966. 'Fatalism in Thai Bureaucratic Decision-Making', *Anthropological Quarterly*, 39, 191-199.

Phansak Pradapkaew. 1986. 'Kaan bancu duang phrachataa mueang krungtheep khrang thii soong [The Second Installation of a Bangkok City Horoscope]', *Dichan*, 10.230 (September), 220-224.

Philairat Ruciwanichkul. 1981. 'Kaansueksaa panhaa sukkhaphaapcit khoong phuu maa rap borikaan caak moo duu: sueksaa chapho koranii phuu maa rap borikaan caak moo duu khoong samaakhom hoon haeng pratheet thai [A Study of the Mental Health of Fortune Tellers' Clients: Specifically the Case of the Clients of Fortune Tellers at the Astrological Association of Thailand]'. M.A. dissertation, Thammasat University.

Phluu Luang. 1968, 'Phracomklaw kap hooraasaat thai [King Mongkut and Thai Astrology]', *Sangkhomsaat Parithat*, 6.2 (September-November), 43-50.

Phluu Luang. 1975. *Hooraasaat phichai songkhraam - duang mueang [Phichai songkhraam Astrology - National Horoscope].* Bangkok, Kasem Bannakich.

Phluu Luang. 1977. 'Wiwatthanakaan khoong duang mueang [The Development of the National Horoscope]', *Phayaakornsaan*, 30.12 (March), 1-9.

Phuu Phaakphuum. 1978. 'The Ninth King: A Tale of Palace Intrigue in Modern Thailand', *Ampo*, 10.1-2, 20 - 29.

Prasoet Pathamasukhon. 1974. *Ratthasaphaa thai nai roop sii sib soong pii (2575 - 2517)* [*The Thai Parliament over Forty-Two Years (1932 - 1974)*]. [Bangkok: the Author?].

Prathip Akkhara. 1981. 'Patithin hoon soong baep [Two Types of Astrologers' Ephemeris]', *Phayaakornsaan* (n.s.), 2.6, December (1981) 12 - 31.

Reynolds, Craig J. n.d. 'The Plot of Thai History: Theory and Practice', in G. Wijeyewardene and E.C. Chapman, eds., *Patterns and Illusions: Papers on Thai Topics in Memory of Richard B. Davis*. Forthcoming.

Reynolds, Frank E. and Mani B. Reynolds, trans. 1982. *Three Worlds According to King Ruang: A Thai Buddhist Cosmology*. Berkeley Buddhist Studies Series 4. Berkeley, University of California.

S. Phlainoi. 1982. 'Hooraasaat kap raatchasamnak [Astrology and the Royal Court]', in *Kotphayaakorn haeng hoon sayaam*. Bangkok, Astrological Association of Thailand.

S. Satcayan. 1982. 'Duang mahatsacan [Miraculous Horoscopes]', in *Kotphayaakorn haeng hoon sayaam*. Bangkok, Astrological Association of Thailand.

Somrocana Sawasdikul Na Ayutthaya, Khunying. 1981. 'Hoon kap chiiwit thai [Astrologers and Thai Life]' (Radio Broadcast in series by the National Identity Board, 27 November 1981), in *Yuu yaang thai bot witthayu*. Bangkok, National Identity Board.

Suntaree Komin. 1985. 'The World View Through Thai Value Systems' in *Traditional and Changing Thai World View*. Bangkok, Chulalongkorn Social Research Institute.

Suntaree Komin and Snit Smuckarn. 1979. *Khaaniyom lae rabop khaaniyom thai khrueang mue nai kaan samruat wat* [*Values and the Thai Value System: Measurement Indicators*]. Bangkok, National Institute of Development Administration.

Thamsook Numnonda. 1978. 'Pibulsongkram's Thai Nation-Building Programme during the Japanese Military Presence, 1941 - 1945', *Journal of Southeast Asian Studies*, 9.2 (September), 234-247.

Thep Sarikabutr. 1967. 'Khamphayaakorn taam lak hooraasaat thaksaa lae mahaathaksaa [Predictions According to the Principles of Astrology, Dasa and Greater Dasa]' in Pracuap Wacharapan, Piam Bunyachot, Thep Sarikabutr and Siri Phongthat, *Chumnum hoon thamnaai chataa mueang chataa look*. Bangkok, Utsaahakam Kaanphim.

Thep Sarikabutr. 1981. *Hooraasaat nai wannakhadii* [*Astrology in Literature*]. Bangkok, Sinlaphaa Bannakhaan.

Uean Monthianthong. 1981. 'Tanuseet pen hooraasaat thai borisut koet korn raahuu [Tanuseet is Pure Thai Astrology, Appearing Prior to Rahu]', *Hooraaweet*, 7.84, (March), 24-31.

Wales, H.G. Quaritch. 1971. *Supplementary Notes on Siamese State Ceremonies*. London, Bernard Quaritch.

Worayaphorn Saengnaphabuan. 1976. 'Kaanphayaakorn chataa chiiwit mii prayoot rue mai phiangdai [Is Life Prediction Useful, and to what Extent]', *Phayaakornsaan*, 29.12 (March), 9-16.

Chapter 9

THE CASE OF THE PURLOINED LINTEL:

THE POLITICS OF A KHMER SHRINE AS A THAI NATIONAL TREASURE[1]

Charles F. Keyes

MONUMENTS AND NATIONAL CULTURE

In association with colonial expansion Europeans introduced into Southeast Asia a new notion of the state whose subjects constituted a people or a nation. This notion was to prove subversive both to traditional Southeast Asian conceptions of the state and, ultimately, to the colonial enterprise itself. The colonial powers imposed clearly defined geographical boundaries not only on their dependencies in Southeast Asia but also on independent Siam which bordered on their domains. These boundaries were then taken as demarcating 'nations' located within them. These 'nations' were not, however, given in some natural way; rather, they had to be imagined (Anderson 1983). That is, the past of the peoples living within the boundaries of states like Siam (later Thailand) and Cambodia (also known as Kampuchea)[2] had to be consciously reflected on to determine what aspects of it constituted a national heritage.

A national heritage is an abstraction, but it is made concrete by being linked to physical objects which can be pointed to as national treasures because they represent some significant aspect of the past which has been accorded national significance. Handler (1985:194) refers to the 'fetishism of material culture that animates governments, citizens, and museum curators [and, I would add, conservators of monuments and art historians] alike in their zeal to preserve their "heritage"'. '*Whose* heritage', Handler continues, 'a particular collection [or monument or other national treasure] represents is often open to question; but the idea that objects, or material culture, can epitomize collective identity — and epitomizing it, be considered as the property of the collectivity — is rarely disputed' (Handler 1985:194; emphasis in original).

Prior to the European-inspired quest for a national past, the objects which had most epitomized imagined communities in precolonial Buddhist Southeast Asia were relics of the Buddha enshrined in stupas (cf. Keyes 1975) and certain images of the Buddha linked in myth with the power of Buddhist rulers. The Emerald Buddha, arguably the most famous of all images in Buddhist Southeast Asia, had been claimed at various times by rulers of different Tai[3] and Khmer principalities (see Reynolds 1978). Ruins of older capitals, even those with Buddhist remains, held no interest, however, other than providing evidence of the Buddhist truth that all is change.

Europeans coming to Southeast Asia found romantic fascination in the ruins of the region. In 1860 the French naturalist, Henri Mouhout, 'discovered' those of Angkor located near the Great Lake in what is today northwestern Cambodia. Angkor was soon to be compared with some of the other great ruins of the world, including those of the Mayans in central America, of Machu Picchu in Peru, of Barabudur in Java, and of Pagan in Burma. The 'lost' civilization of Angkor, although never, of course, lost to peoples in the region, then entered into the historical consciousness of people outside of Southeast Asia. The international value placed on Angkorean civilization by Western explorers, scholars, and travellers set the stage for making the history of Angkorean civilization a part of the national heritage of a people living in a modern Southeast Asian state. Cambodia (Kampuchea), which would seem to have the only legitimate basis for such a claim, has found itself in competition with Thailand (Siam) over this heritage.[4]

COMPETITION FOR THE HERITAGE OF ANGKOR

When the French established a protectorate over Cambodia in 1863, Cambodia did not include the provinces of Battambang and Siem Reap, the latter containing the Angkorean ruins both had been under the rule of Siam since the 1790s. King Norodom, the first Cambodian monarch to reign under the French, did not seek the restoration of these provinces during his reign (1863-1904). He had close ties with the Siamese court and, moreover, was preoccupied with French encroachments on his authority. His successor, Sisowath, however, made the retrocession of the two provinces the major endeavor of his reign. Chandler (1983:149) writes:

The number of pages in Sisowath's chronicle devoted to the return of Battambang and Siem Reap suggests that the compilers, like the French, considered this to be the most important event of the reign, even though the king had little to do with it beyond providing the *résident supérieur*, in 1906, with a "history" of Thai occupation. The importance of the retrocession was probably connected with the importance that Angkor and especially Angkor Wat, retained for the Cambodian monarchy throughout Cambodia's dark ages.

After the Siamese were persuaded to cede control over Battambang and Siem Reap to French Cambodia in 1907, French archaeologists, supervising Khmer laborers, undertook to 'recover' Angkor through research and then to 'restore' it. The results of research on Angkor, and the restoration which took place after the end of the Pacific War until the chaos of the 1970s made further work impossible, made Angkor well known to the Western world. The more that Western scholars and visitors acclaimed Angkor as one of the great civilizations of the world, the more Khmer pride in their being the inheritors of that civilization grew.

Angkor became and remains the dominant symbol of the Khmer national heritage. When Cambodia became independent in 1954, an image of Angkor Wat was given sole prominence on the new national flag.[5] While the country has been torn apart since 1970 by conflicts between republicans and monarchists and by rival factions of the Cambodian Communist Party, the national flags of successive regimes have all incorporated an image of Angkor Wat. Even though Angkor belongs to an empire of the distant past, it still symbolizes for Khmer their distinctive legacy (Keyes 1990). As Myrdal and Kessle (1970:165) have written in reflecting on Angkor: 'Cambodia has a history of its own. A specific history. It is not "Indochinese" history.'[6]

The heritage of Angkor does not, however, belong unequivocally to the Khmer; it has also been claimed by the Thai. The legacy of Angkor is especially closely linked with the Thai monarchy. In the middle of the fourteenth century a new kingdom, Ayudhya, ruled by Tai and located in what is today central Thailand began to challenge the dominance of the Khmer empire. But despite a long period of warfare between Ayudhya and Angkor, leading in the fifteenth century to the abandonment of Angkor, the rulers of Ayudhya looked to Angkor for their principles of statecraft. As Wyatt (1984:71-72) has written:

> Such men spoke Khmer and from the beginning [of Ayudhya] buttressed the majesty of the throne with a special court vocabulary based on Khmer and Sanskrit. For them, a truly royal king should be raised far above the level of his subjects, insulated by layers of officials from direct contacts with them, and wrapped in a cloak of mystery and sanctity compounded out of the brahmanical religion from the cults of Siva and Visnu.

While the Brahmanical cults of the Siamese court were subordinated to Theravada Buddhism, they remained important not only for the rulers of Ayudhya but also for the kings of the Chakri dynasty which has ruled from Bangkok since the late eighteenth century (see Wales 1931).

The legacy of Angkor for the Siamese court is especially evident in the identification of these kings with Rama, an avatar of Visnu and the hero of the Indian epic *Ramayana*, which in its Thai version is known as the *Ramakian*. This equation of a king with Rama had been asserted strongly by a number of Angkorean kings, including the early twelfth century ruler, Suryavarman II, whose magnificent Angkor Wat contains extensive bas relief scenes from the Khmer version of the *Ramayana*. The Siamese rulers of Ayudhya were influenced by Khmer ideas about Rama as the exemplary monarch and their successors who ruled from Bangkok accorded them even more prominence. The founding king of the Chakri dynasty, known posthumously in English as Rama I (1782–1809), wrote a version of the *Ramakian* which is considered to have been the chief literary monument of his reign (Wyatt 1984:153).[7] In equating themselves with Rama, the kings of Siam have not sought, however, to supplant Buddhism with Hinduism. In the epilogue to his *Ramakian* King Rama I wrote: 'This romance of the *Ramakien* ... should not be regarded as of basic value, but is merely a part of His Majesty's dedication to the glory of the Master's [the Lord Buddha] teachings' (quoted in Prince Dhani 1963:24). Nonetheless, the Angkorean conception of a king closely identified with a Hindu divinity persisted at the Siamese court.[8]

The murals depicting the *Ramakian* which line the cloisters surrounding the most sacred shrine of the Thai kingdom, the temple of the Emerald Buddha at the Grand Palace in Bangkok, have their prototype in the bas reliefs of Angkor Wat. While modern Khmer kings have also perpetuated the same tradition, they have taken it not directly from Angkor but from the Thai court. The palace at Phnom Penh, built at the end of the nineteenth century, with its murals depicting the *Reamker*, the Khmer version of the *Ramayana*, is modeled directly on the grand palace at Bangkok and, thus, only indirectly on Angkor Wat.

King Mongkut (r. 1851-1868), before becoming king and while still a monk, had begun to investigate the historical origins of Siam. He 'discovered' the importance of the kingdom of Sukhothai, which had flourished in the thirteenth and fourteenth centuries, an importance that had been forgotten since the incorporation of Sukhothai into Ayudhya. He also 'discovered' the importance of Angkor as an antecedent to modern Siam. This importance was made manifest in a model of Angkor Wat which he had constructed, after becoming king, near the shrine of the Emerald Buddha at the grand palace. Mongkut began to lay the foundations for modern Thai nationalism and for the determination of what was to constitute the history of the Thai nation. In this history the Angkorean legacy had an important place, especially as it related to the monarchy.

Even after Siam gave up control of Angkor as a consequence of the retrocessions in 1907, Angkor did not disappear from Thai historical consciousness. In 1924, Prince Damrong Rajanubhab, King Mongkut's brilliant son who was at once an architect of the modern Thai state and the father of modern Thai historical scholarship, made a trip to Angkor. His book, *Nirat Nakhon Wat* (*Journey to Angkor*) (Damrong 1971), first published shortly after his trip, describes his impressions of Angkor (as well as of Phnom Penh and Saigon) as a tourist. Tourism for him was not, however, recreational travel; rather, he looked at tourist attractions with the eye of one who could find in a monument an embodiment of the spirit of a nation. This book, as well as Prince Damrong's other accounts of travels around Thailand and to neighboring countries, became sources for what later Thai governments would determine officially constituted the national heritage.

In 1941, on the eve of the Pacific War, Thailand engaged the French in Indochina in a small-scale border war. Following Japanese mediation, the Thai reclaimed some parts of northwestern Cambodia as well as some territories in Laos which had also been under Siamese rule prior to 1907. Although Angkor itself remained within French Cambodia, the Thai move into northwestern Cambodia signalled a renewal of an ancient claim that their kingdom is the successor to the Angkorean empire. Thai control over northwestern Cambodia was, however, short-lived, for in 1946 Thailand was required, in the aftermath of the defeat of Japan, to return all lands taken in 1941 to French rule. Again, this loss did not spell an end to efforts to claim the Angkorean heritage for the Thai national tradition; rather, attention shifted from Angkor itself to Angkorean monuments still under Thai rule.

A recent controversy over one of these monuments — Phanom Rung in Buriram province in northeastern Thailand — reflects the continuing importance which some attach to the Angkorean roots of Thai national culture. Ostensibly the controversy centered on criticism of the United States government for not assisting in the return of a lintel which had been stolen from Phanom Rung in the 1960s. I maintain, however, that it was rooted at a deeper level in an attempt to make the restored ruins of Phanom Rung a concrete manifestation of the linkage between the Thai monarchy and the Angkorean heritage. As the monarchy is the major national institution in Thailand, the controversy also entailed a claim on the Angkorean tradition as part of the national heritage of Thailand.

THEFT OF A NATIONAL TREASURE

In February 1988 the following advertisement, addressed 'With Respect to the American People', was placed in English-language newspapers in Bangkok:

> For almost a thousand years, a magnificent stone lintel carved with the image of Vishnu Asleep on the Water remained over the entrance of the main shrine of the Phanom Rung Hindu Temple in Buriram Province.

In the 1960s, thanks to the special privileges enjoyed by US forces, the lintel was removed without hindrance with the use of US military equipment and spirited abroad.

Within a few months, it reappeared at the Art Institute of Chicago, where it remains on display today.

The Thai Ministries of Foreign Affairs and of Education sought its return in 1973 without success because no cooperation was given to [by?] the US government.

Though far from wealthy, the Thai people have used their own funds and technological expertise to restore this majestic archeological site, which is to be officially opened by HRH Princess Maha Chakri Sirindhorn early this April.

We know that Vishnu Asleep on the Water was once an integral part of the Phanom Rung temple, we know exactly where it was located and we know that today, it is on public display in the United States of America.

The Thai people have learnt that we cannot expect help from the US government. We therefore turn our appeal to our friends, the American people, to bear pressure so that this cultural treasure may be returned to its rightful owners...so that a part of our cultural heritage can be replaced in its rightful setting for future generations of Thais and mankind to admire.

We believe you, the American people, will not remain unmoved by our plea. We believe that you will support us against this act of transnational theft.

The advertisement was signed 'The People of Thailand'.[9]

Shortly after the advertisement appeared, the American embassy issued a statement saying it was investigating how the lintel arrived at the Art Institute in Chicago and indicated that the 'U.S. government wants a satisfactory and speedy resolution of this issue and will keep the Thai government informed about any information obtained on the lintel' (quoted in *The Nation*, 9 February 1988). Despite this commitment, and the fact that evidence regarding the lintel's removal to the States had been available to the American government for a decade and a half, a resolution was not found in a 'satisfactory and speedy' manner.

At first it appeared that an agreement had been reached whereby the Thai government would provide another Thai art object in 'exchange' for the lintel. Several members of the Thai National Assembly protested strongly, however, maintaining that there should be no exchange for a national treasure which had been stolen from the country. Negotiations which had been taking place between the Institute and the Thai Fine Arts Department were now complicated as both parties had to deal with the parliamentary Committee on Culture and Tourism. When H.R.H. Princess Maha Chakri Sirindhorn presided over the ceremony for the opening of the Phanom Rung Historical Park (on 21 May rather than in April as originally planned) the lintel was conspicuously not in place. On 4 July 1988 student activists organized a protest demonstration at the American embassy in Bangkok. In late summer 1988 negotiations became bogged down when the Chicago Art Institute insisted on being given something by the Thai government as a replacement for the lintel. Finally, an agreement was reached whereby the Thai government would 'loan' a piece to the Institute following the Institute's return of the lintel, and the lintel was returned to Thailand in November. It was then placed back at the shrine in its original location.

On the surface the controversy might seem as but another example of a people in a Third World society seeking to recover a significant art treasure which had been taken from their country by powerful Westerners. There can be little question that the Phanom Rung lintel should not have been taken away from Thailand. It is known that the lintel was still at the shrine in the early 1960s. In a survey carried out in 1960-61, the lintel was photographed by a team from the Fine Arts Department (Fine Arts Department 1967:12, 49 and figures 10 and 11); it was then on the ground where it had apparently fallen along with other pieces of the shrine.[10] Sometime in the early or mid-1960s the lintel disappeared from Phanom Rung. It reappeared in 1967 when a Mr. James Alsdorf presented it as a loan to the Art Institute of Chicago where it has remained ever since; in 1983 the Alsdorf Foundation made the lintel a gift to the Institute. Alsdorf said he had purchased the lintel in 1967 from an art dealer in New York. Another art dealer in Bangkok may have had the lintel in his possession at an earlier stage since in 1965 the Fine Arts Department confiscated the right end of the lintel from this dealer (Quinn-Judge 1985:66; Paisal Sricharatchanya 1988:48).

During the 1988 controversy, 'A senior official of the Fine Arts Department of Thailand said it is believed that the best way to smuggle such a big, heavy object out of the country was to use US aircraft at the U-tapao airfield — a former US base during the Vietnam War' (*The Nation*, 14 February 1988). It is not unreasonable that the lintel was shipped as part of the belongings of some American with official or military status without Thai customs officials knowing since many other art objects (most notably, prehistoric painted pottery known as Ban Chiang ware) are known to have made their way out of Thailand in the 1960s and early 1970s by such means. The American embassy in Bangkok denied, however, the allegation that there was official complicity in the movement of the lintel from Thailand to America.

However it was transported to the U. S. A., the lintel was illegally acquired and removed from Thailand. Prince Suphadradis Diskul, Thailand's leading art historian, and other representatives of the Thai Fine Arts Department tried since at least 1973 to have the lintel returned, but they were rebuffed by both the Art Institute and Alsdorf. An American embassy spokesman said in 1988 that while the U.S. government was sympathetic with the case, it was 'difficult for the U.S. to return the sandstone to Thailand, which has not ratified a 1970 convention of the United Nations Education, Scientific and Cultural Organization' (*The Nation*, 14 February 1988) which prohibits illicit import, export, and transfer of ownership of cultural property.[11] So long as the lintel was simply an art object, the Thai government made only a modest effort to seek the return of the lintel.

In 1988, however, 'the People of Thailand' declared the lintel to be a 'cultural treasure' and made a public issue of the theft. Both the content of the advertisement and the name chosen by those who produced it to identify themselves indicate that the return of the lintel has become a point of national pride.[12] The controversy stems, I maintain, not simply from outrage over the illicit traffic in art objects taken from Thailand, but from a heightened significance given to the shrine of Phanom Rung -as well as other monuments from the same historical period -as part of the national heritage of the Thai people.

There is a seeming paradox involved in the recognition of Phanom Rung as a shrine of national significance, for it was built not by Thai but by Khmer at a time when much of what is today northeastern and east central Thailand was under the control of the rulers of Angkor. Moreover, the shrine is not a Buddhist one, but was dedicated to the Hindu god Visnu and incorporates elements associated with the cult of Siva as well. After the early thirteenth century (from which the last inscriptions at Phanom Rung date), there is some evidence of introduction of Mahayanist Buddhist elements, but the shrine seems to have lost any connection with Angkor by the middle of the thirteenth century when Angkor declined in power and the populace of the Angkorean empire increasingly turned to Theravada Buddhism (Prathip Wahin n.d.:7; Fine Arts Department 1988:96, 98). Phanom Rung did not attract the attention of the rulers of the major Buddhist kingdoms which emerged in the place of the Angkorean empire, although it probably retained some significance for the local people living in its vicinity since in the late nineteenth century an annual festival was being held at it (Aymonier 1897:232). What led to the incorporation of the localized shrine of Phanom Rung into a 'totality' in which 'local and national history bear a functional relationship to each other' (Hanks 1967:255)? What led Thai Buddhists to give such national attention to a Khmer Hindu shrine?

These questions cannot be answered by viewing the controversy solely as one involving outrage toward the United States for condoning an art theft. Indeed, there are hundreds, perhaps thousands, of valuable pieces of art in the United States and Europe and probably in Japan which were removed from Thailand by illegal or extralegal means.[13] Rather, one must look deeper for the reasons why the lintel was deemed in early 1988 to be a 'cultural treasure' by 'the People of Thailand' and why a restored Phanom Rung (still lacking the lintel) was opened by Princess Sirindhorn on 'Thai cultural preservation day' on 21 May, 1988. To answer these questions it is necessary to understand the evolution of official Thai attitudes toward the Angkorean heritage.

PHANOM RUNG AND THE ANGKOREAN WORLD

The monumental ruins on the hill known as Phanom Rung[14] stand as testimony to the past power of a cult which represented the potency of local geomantic forces. These forces had been given form in Indian-derived iconography and architecture and they had been linked to the authority of a temporal monarch who ruled at Angkor. Although the earliest inscription at the shrine is dated 890 A.D. (No Na Paknam 1986:70), what Paul Mus (1975:21) has termed a 'cadastral cult' almost certainly existed at the place before that time. This first inscription, in Khmer, shows that by the late nineteenth century local people had begun to worship *linga* which were at once a representation of Siva, an embodiment of fertility, and a symbol of the reigning monarch. A provincial shrine such as Phanom Rung was, moreover, a model of the sacred center, the *nagara*, which in the Khmer version of the Sanskrit term became *angkor*.

The shrine in the form that has remained appears to have been built in the early eleventh century:

> In its lonely grandeur, its position on the slope of a hill, its lay-out in successive courts instead of concentric enclosures, its series of stairways and causeways, with their mile-posts and naga balustrades and in other respects, it bears a close resemblance to the monuments of the latter part of the reign of Surayavarman I [1001-1050] - to which period it probably belongs ... (Briggs 1951:182)

An inscription from the reign of Suryavarman II (1113-1150) found at Phanom Rung (Coedès 1930) gives the lineage of a king, Jayarvarman VI (1080-1107), who usurped the throne of Angkor and set up a new dynasty. The family of this king ruled at a place called Mahidharapura, located on the Khorat plateau, perhaps at Phimai where today there are the most impressive remains in Thailand dating from the Angkorean period. 'Jayavarman appears to have been a vassal prince from the upper Mun valley near Phimai, as most of the early inscriptions of his reign come from that region' (Briggs 1951:178). The inscription tells of the father of Jayavarman VI, Hiranyavarman, who may have been the builder of the main sanctuary (No Na Paknam 1986:70). It also tells of Hiranyavarman's father, Narendraditya, a hermit (*rsi*) for whom the shrine may have been built originally. Jayavarman also had an elder brother Dharanindravarman, who was later to become king of Angkor as Dharanindravarman I (1107-1113). The inscription continues through to the reign of Suryavarman II, who is well known for having built Angkor Wat and having promoted the worship of Visnu.

The cult of Visnu is clearly evident at the shrine not only in the now famous image on the missing lintel,[15] but also in numerous other representations of the deity as well as in scenes from the Ramayana (with Rama being an avatar of Visnu) (No Na Paknam 1986:70). Even as the shrine was made to serve the cult of Visnu the earlier dedication of the hill to Siva was not abandoned, as is evident in the image of a dancing Siva on a lintel on the main sanctuary above the one where the stolen lintel should reside, as well as other images of Siva elsewhere (Srisakra Vallibhotama 1986:58). 'Prasat Phanom Rung is a Hindu religious complex' (No Na Paknam 1986:69), but this Hinduism is syncretic as it is at many of the other shrines of the Angkorean world. Suriyavudh Suksvasti, who wrote a doctoral dissertation on Phanom Rung, summarizes the iconographic evidence about the religious purpose of the shrine as follows:

> We know that the whole complex was built for the worship of the two Hindu gods of Siva and Vishnu, as well as to represent some historical events concerning the hermit called Narendraditya. In particular the scenes depicting Narendraditya are important, because they are the earliest examples of historical carvings made earlier than the battle scenes of Suryavarman II along the gallery of Angkor Wat. (Suriyavudh Suksvasti 1985:110)

Although the so-called libraries at Phanom Rung appear to date from the reign of Jayavarman VII (1181-1215) (Suriyavudh 1985:110), the shrine had begun to decline in significance by the end of Jayavarman's reign. Jayavarman himself promoted a new cult centering on the Buddha-raja which was shaped by ideas drawn from Mahayana Buddhism, but the populace of the Angkorean empire were increasingly turning toward another new religion, that of Theravada Buddhism. This religion proved to be subversive to the older cults in which the king was seen as either an avatar of a Hindu god or a Bodhisattva.

By the end of the thirteenth century Tai-speaking peoples had become sufficiently strong to form new polities in the northern part of mainland Southeast Asia and to challenge Khmer supremacy in the region. By the middle of the fourteenth century, Tai kingdoms had replaced Angkorean rule in what is today central Thailand while another Tai kingdom, apparently with Angkorean help, had been established in the middle Mekong area in what is today Laos. The rulers of the new Siamese kingdom of Ayudhya, founded in 1350, soon felt they had the power to attack Angkor itself. In the 1430s Ayudhyan forces sacked the city; Khmer rulers felt compelled to abandon the old capital (indeed, they may have done so some years earlier). With the defeat of Angkor by the Tai and the conversion of the Khmer population to Theravada Buddhism, both the shrines at Angkor itself and those like Phanom Rung which also belonged to the Angkorean world lost their significance as representations of a cosmic order and of ancestors linked with the Hindu gods.

FROM LOCAL TO NATIONAL HISTORY

By the time of the collapse of the Angkorean empire in the fifteenth century, Phanom Rung had already become a shrine of purely local significance. The Khmer people living in surrounding villages must at some point have been converted to Theravada Buddhism, presumably in the same period as were their neighbors. This change did not, however, eliminate the sacred significance of Phanom Rung to the peoples living nearby. In 1883, Etienne Aymonier (1897:232), one of the first, if not the first, Westerners to leave a record of a visit to the shrine, found that local villagers held an annual Buddhist festival at Phanom Rung at the time of the full moon of the seventh lunar month.[16] In his brief time at the ruins in March of 1883, Aymonier met a large group of local people who had been visiting the shrine and a Buddhist temple-monastery located nearby, which he said had recently been abandoned. Despite Aymonier's great interest in the antiquities of the Khmer,[17] he makes only a single laconic observation about

Phanom Rung: 'Son ossature est en grès avec quelques pierres noires et dures' (Aymonier 1897:232). It appears the shrine at this point did not figure as more than one more ruin among the dozens he visited in the area.[18]

Aymonier noted that some of the villages surrounding Phanom Rung were populated by Khmer, some by mixed Khmer and Siamese, and some by people who knew their ancestors were Khmer but who now spoke Siamese (Aymonier 1897:227). These observations attest to the fact that the area had long been under Siamese rule. This rule dates from at least the eighteenth century, when Siamese kings are recorded as having extended their control over an area known as the 'forest Khmer' (*khamen padong*) area of the Khorat Plateau. It is probable that the peoples living near Phanom Rung had been part of the domain of Khorat which had been under Siamese rule for at least a century (see Toem Wiphakphacanakit 1978:11ff and 167-8; also Paitoon Mikusol 1984). Neither the rulers of Ayudhya nor their successors at Bangkok showed any particular interest in Phanom Rung, however. The shrine was relegated to local history until the late 1950s and early 1960s.

In 1959 and again in 1960-61 the Thai Fine Arts Department undertook a 'survey and excavations of ancient monuments in North-eastern Thailand' (Fine Arts Department 1960, 1967). There could be little question but that the archaeological remains on the Khorat Plateau hold great interest for scholars of the region. An aerial survey made by the British Royal Air Force during World War II had shown that the region contained a large number of settlement sites which subsequently have been shown to belong to the protohistoric period — that is, to what Thai scholars have termed the Dvaravati or ancient Mon period. Subsequent work at Ban Chiang and other sites has established the region as the locus of some of the most important prehistoric remains in all of mainland Southeast Asia. The majority of the remains surveyed in the late 1950s and early 1960s were not from these early periods, however;

rather, they were from the period which Thai scholars then termed 'Lopburi' after a town in central Thailand which contained important remains from the period of the eleventh-fourteenth centuries.

The very use of the label 'Lopburi' is indicative of an effort to appropriate these monuments for the Thai heritage rather than for the Khmer. This is also evident in the way in which Thai archaeologists discussed these monuments for Thai audiences. While Dhanit Yupho, then Director of the Fine Arts Department, in the English translation of the introduction to the second report on the survey uses the term 'Khmer' in reference to the monuments of the 'Lopburi' period, he employs the term *khom* in the Thai version (Fine Arts Department 1967:2, 42). While the term *khom* is simply an ancient term used by Thai for Khmer,[19] it was used in the 1960s in the popular press — with semi-official backing — to disassociate the modern Khmer from the heritage of Angkor. From the Thai perspective, the *khom* had as much or more connection with the Thai than they did with the Khmer.

The report of the 1959 survey points especially to the importance of the ruins at Phimai and Phanom Rung:

> The Phimai Temple in Korat, and the stone sanctuary on Phanom Rung Hill, Buriram, are not second in quality to monuments in Cambodia. If they were restored, and were made easily accessible they would be visited by many people.

> The local citizens of north-eastern Thailand would also prosper financially from the tourist trade. Moreover the knowledge of their ancient and civilized heritage would make them more conscious of defending their country and its traditions. (Fine Arts Department 1960:55-56)[20]

Given the imprimatur of the Fine Arts Department, these monuments were raised from local to national significance.

It is by no means coincidental that at the time when the Fine Arts Department was carrying out its survey of archaeological remains in northeastern Thailand, the Thai were growing increasingly hostile toward the newly independent government of Cambodia under Prince Norodom Sihanouk. In 1954 when Cambodia, as a consequence of the Geneva conference, had gained acceptance as an independent state, the Thai government had initially developed good relations with the new government. After 1957, however, when Sarit Thanarat became military dictator in Thailand, relations quickly deteriorated both because Sarit was moving Thailand into a closer alliance with the United States while Cambodia was attempting to maintain a neutral foreign policy and because Sarit took a strong personal dislike to Prince Sihanouk. In 1961, following a speech in which Sarit spoke in insulting terms of Sihanouk, Cambodia broke off diplomatic relations with Thailand (Nuechterlein 1965:222).

The two countries soon also found themselves in a conflict which centered on claims to a monument of the Angkorean period. Shortly after gaining independence, Cambodia laid claim to a shrine which in Khmer is known as Preah Vihear and in Thai as Phra Wihan.[21] The shrine, then under Thai control, is located in the Dangrek mountains on the border between Cambodia and northeastern Thailand and is more accessible from the Thai than the Cambodian side. Thailand had agreed to have the dispute settled by the International Court of Justice, apparently on the assumption that the claim would never be sustained. The decision in 1962 to award the shrine to Cambodia came as a powerful shock to the Thai. Nuechterlein wrote of the decision that 'the news hit the public like a thunderbolt'.

Few issues have aroused such widespread public indignation, among even peasants and villagers, as did this decision of the court. In dealing with the popular outburst of emotion against the Cambodians, the Sarit government had to use all the power and persuasiveness at its command to keep the situation under control and to prevent dissident and subversive elements from using it to try to discredit and perhaps to upset the regime. (Nuechterlein 1965:250)[22]

While the truth was perhaps more that the government encouraged public antagonism toward Cambodia than sought to restrain it, the fact remains that the decision forcing Thailand to cede the Preah Vihear/Phra Wihan shrine to Cambodia made the Angkorean-era ruin a major political issue.

The Preah Vihear/Phra Wihan conflict stimulated the Thai government to make a place for the Angkorean legacy in the Thai national heritage. In the next two decades the Thai government allocated significant monies to 'restore' the two major Angkorean period shrines still under Thai control. In 1964 the Fine Arts Department, with the assistance of French experts who had worked at Angkor, began reconstruction of Phimai, the more accessible and architecturally more complex shrine near the city of Khorat. Once this work was completed, reconstruction was begun in 1971 at Phanom Rung. In the early 1970s, when the war in Cambodia brought tourist visits to Angkor to a halt, the Tourist Authority of Thailand began to promote Phimai and Phanom Rung as alternatives to Angkor and an increasing number of cultural tourists began to make their way to the ruins.

Even with the increased attention given to these monuments, their importance as elements of the Thai national tradition still was vastly overshadowed by those connected with the Buddhist kingdoms built by the ancestors of the Thai. As Sophie Quinn-Judge (1985:67) noted: 'There is said to be little interest among Thais in the restoration of Khmer temples'. In January 1985 and again in January 1987 I led cultural tours organized by Archaeological Tours of New York which included visits to both Phanom Rung and Phimai. I was struck by the fact that our Thai guide, one of the most respected in the country and a man who was very expansive in his descriptions of the old Siamese capitals of Ayudhya and Sukhothai, had little to say about the Angkorean monuments. Phanom Rung (along with Phimai) had, however, been selected to become a national monument and in 1988 the process incorporating the now restored ruins into the pantheon of material objects deemed to embody the national heritage reached a climax.

In early 1988 the lintel of the sleeping Visnu from the Phanom Rung monument became a national *cause çelèbre*. The immediate reason for the timing of the affair lies in the fact that HRH Princess Maha Chakri Sirindhorn was scheduled to open the shrine after completion of its reconstruction in May 1988. The Princess had by 1988 become well known for her efforts to promote and preserve the Thai cultural heritage. She had a particular interest in historical archaeological sites because she had taken a Master's degree in archaeology at the Fine Arts University. It was, morever, especially appropriate that she should (re)dedicate the monument given the particular connection of the Angkorean legacy with the Thai monarchy. As a representative of the monarchy — she is, in fact, second in line of succession to the throne — her anticipated role was what gave Phanom Rung the marked national significance that prompted the effort to gain the return of the lintel.

This affair came at a time when the prospects of a settlement of the 'Cambodian question' began to seem possible for the first time since Vietnamese military forces ousted the Khmer Rouge in 1979. If such a settlement should occur, tourists would again be able to travel to Angkor. Even without a settlement, by the late 1980s the People's Republic of Kampuchea (after 1989 officially renamed as the State of Cambodia) had already begun a modest promotion of tourism to Angkor.[23] With increased tourist attention, as well as with the renewed restoration efforts which were being undertaken with assistance provided the People's Republic of Kampuchea by the governments of India and Poland, Angkor could once again become the focus of Khmer national pride in the eyes of the world (cf., in this connection, Keyes 1990). One wonders what the Thai government might do if a request should come from authorities in Phnom Penh, perhaps backed by public demonstrations, for assistance in recovering the many significant pieces of Angkorean art which have been removed from Cambodia over the past decade and taken to be sold in Thailand.[24]

Of the many pieces of Angkorean art which have passed through the hands of antique dealers in Bangkok, the Phanom Rung lintel became the focus of a major campaign for its return not because it is the most valuable piece to have found its way into Western collections but, rather, because the shrine from which it was taken had been raised from one of local historical importance to one representing an Angkorean heritage which Thai have incorporated into their national tradition. The controversy over the lintel took on added meaning because it occurred at a time when some in Cambodia were once again bidding to have international recognition for an exclusive claim by Khmer to this heritage. The Thai who made an issue over the theft of the lintel and its presence in an American museum were seeking implicit validation from the West for a Thai claim to the legacy of Angkor. The case of the purloined lintel from Phanom Rung demonstrates well that the construction of a national history is always a political act.

ENDNOTES

1. This paper is dedicated to the memory of Professor Lucien Hanks. Professor Hanks's paper on 'Bang Chan and Bangkok' (Hanks 1967) first stimulated me to reflect on the relationship between local and national history. I have benefitted from comments made on previous drafts of this paper by David Chandler, Ben Anderson, Craig Reynolds, Jane Keyes, May Ebihara, and David Wyatt.

2. The name 'Siam' was used until 1939 when it was replaced by 'Thailand'. 'Kampuchea', although closer than 'Cambodia' to the Khmer designation for their country, has been used officially only since 1975. In 1990, all competing factions, save for the Khmer Rouge, returned to using 'Cambodia' as the official English-language name of the country.

3. Following scholarly convention in English, I use the term 'Tai' to refer to any people speaking a Tai language and to principalities ruled by Tai-speaking people. The term 'Thai' is used to refer to the people of the modern state of Thailand.

4. A Lao claim on the Angkorean legacy is also manifest in the designation of Wat Phu in southern Laos as a national monument. The historical significance of Wat Phu derives from its connection to Angkorean civilization. Although Vietnam has not attempted to appropriate the heritage of Angkor for Vietnamese national culture, there have been attempts to assert Vietnamese superiority to that heritage. In the late 1980s when tourism to Angkor began to become possible again after the long period of conflict in Cambodia, the state tourism agency in Vietnam began offering trips between Saigon and Angkor. Very quickly, the state tourism agency in the People's Republic of Kampuchea, even though the PRK was supposed to be a client state of Vietnam, moved to ensure that tourists made the trip via Phnom Penh.

5. David Chandler (personal communication) informs me that a flag with an image of Angkor first became the national flag when Cambodia was given partial independence in 1947. Prior to that time, a flag with an Angkorean motif had served as the royal standard.

6. Myrdal and Kessle's account of their visit in 1967 is one of the most curious ever written about Angkor. It consists of reflections on the 'meaning' of Angkor with reference, on the one hand, to an environmental determinist view of why

Western colonialism, including the contemporary American effort in Vietnam, would fail because Westerners are ill-suited to the tropics, and on the other, to Marxist 'laws' of history which makes the collapse of Angkor the same as the fall of Rome or the French Revolution. In light of what happened to Cambodia in the 1970s, the book, especially as it is dedicated to Samdech Norodom Sihanouk, can only be read ironically, although the irony was hardly intended by the authors.

7. Wyatt writes of this work: 'This is no blind translation of an Indian text, but rather a recasting of a classic central to Indian civilization in such a way that it was domesticated into Siamese tradition. The central figure in the *Ramayana* is, after all, a Rama (not completely alien to Rama I) who lives in a city called Ayodhya (or Ayudhya) and ascends his throne through virtue and bravery after a long dark period of dangerous warfare. The point is, however, that the characters and setting of the *Ramakian*, no less than the language, are clearly Siamese' (Wyatt 1984:153-54).

8. Although the older idea of Angkorean kings as a *deva-raja*, a king who is also an incarnation of a Hindu deity, most strongly promoted by Coedès (see, for example, Coedès 1963), has been effectively challenged by Kulke (1978), the fact remains that Angkorean kings were situated symbolically within the realm of the gods.

9. The advertisement appearing in *The Nation*, from which the quote is taken, was a half page in length and appeared with a picture of the lintel superimposed on what looks like some stones from the shrine and together with a picture of the shrine. A Thai language line at the bottom of the advertisement indicates it was published with the assistance of the newspaper. The three dots in the quotation are in the original and do not indicate any ellipsis. I did not have the opportunity to check Thai language newspapers to see if the ad also appeared there, but the main audience to whom the ad was directed was clearly American, not Thai.

10. Sophie Quinn-Judge (1985:66), has reported a more dramatic account of how the lintel became detached from the shrine. Using information provided by a Fine Arts Department official stationed at Phanom Rung, she reported that the lintel 'was dynamited away in 1959'. Paisal Sricharatchanya (1988:48), writing in the same journal after the controversy developed, reports that the lintel is 'believed to have naturally fallen off the eastern entrance to the Hindu temple's main shrine'. Paisal's source was Professor Srisakra Vallibhotama, an archaeologist and the son of Manit Vallibhotama who had conducted the survey in 1960-61.

11. Paisal Sricharatchanya (1988:49) observed that 'the government [of Thailand] has been reluctant to join the 1970 Unesco Convention on the Means of Prohibiting and Preventing the Illicit Import, Export and Transfer of Ownership of Cultural Property—on grounds that it can ill afford to "buy back" any stolen objects'.

12. Paisal Sricharatchanya (1988:48) reports that the advertisement is 'believed to be the handiwork of a group of journalists dedicated to arts and culture'. The group involved were probably connected with *The Nation*, one of the two English-language newspapers, *Matichon*, a Thai-language paper read mainly by the educated elite, and *Sinlapawatthanatham* (*Art and Culture*), a monthly journal for intellectuals which often publishes articles on the politics of art.

13. Among these are many neolithic ceramic pieces which are known as Ban Chiang ware after the most famous site in northeastern Thailand from which many have come. In addition, many Buddha images, including ones from the earliest period of Buddhist art (sixth-nineth centuries) in Thailand, are also found outside of Thailand. Thailand has also been the major source for hundreds, perhaps thousands, of pieces of Angkorean and other Khmer art from Cambodia and Burmese art which certainly constitute cultural treasures of these countries.

14. In Thai the name means 'rainbow hill', but Prathip Wahin (n.d.:1), in a mimeographed summary history of the shrine which I obtained from monks at the Buddhist temple-monastery near the Phnom Rung, says that the *rung* in the name is really the Khmer word *rung* meaning 'cave'. In Thai the Khmer term *phnom* is pronounced *phanom*; since I am writing with reference to Thai sources, I use the transliteration Phanom Rung rather than Phnom Rung.

15. The scene on this lintel has been labeled not only 'Vishnu Asleep on the Water', but also 'The Birth of Brahma with Reclining Vishnu on Water'.

16. In 1883 the full moon of the 7th lunar month in the Lao calendar would have occurred on 22 April. In 1988 an annual festival, now held at the time of the traditional New Year (13-15 April), was still being held (Levine 1978:197).

17. Aymonier combined a deep intellectual curiosity about Khmer culture and history with a commitment to the French colonizing mission. He was to write a number of books which are still of great value to anyone interested in Cambodia and was later to become the Director of the École Coloniale. He had begun his career in the country, however, as assistant to Jean Moura, the French representative in Cambodia from 1868 to 1879, at a time when the French were consolidating their control over their new protectorate (Osborne 1969:37, 47-48,

55-56). His scholarship contributed to French efforts to extend their control over territories which they could claim as traditional parts of Cambodia and Laos.

18. In a subsequent work, Aymonier (1900-03) mislabeled the shrine as Buddhist (see Briggs 1951:182), thus indicating that he had paid more attention to the contemporary practices at the shrine than to the evidence of the ruins themselves (also see Lajonquière 1907:208).

19. Until the reform of Buddhism in the nineteenth century, most texts in the Pali language found in temple-monasteries in central Thailand were written in a script which Thai referred to as *khom* but which is the same as Khmer script.

20. In the Thai version of this passage (Fine Arts Department 1960:11) the term *maiphae* is used in comparing Phimai and Phanom Rung to ruins in Cambodia. This term, which can be glossed as 'not less than', implies that the Fine Arts Department considered Phimai and Phanom Rung to be at least equal to any monuments found in Cambodia. It is interesting that Angkor is not specifically referred to in this passage.

21. The name also sometimes appears as Khao Phra Viharn. The name means the 'sacred *vihara*' or image hall. While it has a name which implies it is a Buddhist shrine, it was also a Hindu shrine.

22. The reaction in Cambodia was, as might be expected, quite different. David Chandler, who was then serving in the American Embassy in Phnom Penh, has written (personal communication) that 'joy spread through Cambodia — or Phnom Penh at least — when the decision was announced'. This joy was indicated by horns being blown, trucks careering through the city, and, in a very symbolic act, Prince Sihanouk shaving his head.

23. In early 1988 I encountered one of the first American tour groups to go to Angkor since the 1960s when I was in Phnom Penh. The group had travelled as part of a tour organized by Lindblad. Subsequently, Lindblad was prosecuted by the American government for violating the 'trading with the enemy' act and was forced into bankruptcy as a consequence. In May 1989 when I was in Cambodia, arrangements for visiting Angkor had improved and the group of scholars I was with was able to make a trip to the monuments. In 1990, despite the continued stalemate in the negotiations over a political settlement and continued warring between the State of Cambodia and the forces of the Khmer Rouge, Prince Sihanouk, and the Khmer Peoples National Liberation Front, the number of tourists to Angkor increased significantly. In part this occurred because the Cambodian government allowed some tour companies in Thailand

to organize tours which included direct flights from Bangkok to Phnom Penh (although not from Bangkok to Siem Reap).

24. Writing in 1981 Paul Quinn-Judge (1981:B19) quoted a member of the conservation staff at Angkor as saying:

> The last 10-11 years have been the worst ever.... First Lon Nol's South Vietnamese 'allies' stole as many statues as they could lay their hands on. Then the Khmer Rouge — we think, nobody knows about those days — carted more to the Thai border to raise foreign currency. Then, in the months after the destruction of Pol Pot, refugees fleeing to Thailand took some with them. And they're still disappearing, even today ....

Quinn-Judge adds: 'For anyone heading to Thailand a statue head from Angkor is like a cumbersome but valuable traveler's check. At the border they can be sold to an antique dealer's middle-man — one Bangkok dealer said he was receiving a "regular supply"'. For other reports on the state of Angkor since 1979, see Garrett (1982), White and Garrett (1982) and Richardson (1984).

REFERENCES

Anderson, Benedict R. O'G. 1983. *Imagined Communities: Reflections on the Origin and Spread of Nationalism.* London, Verso.

Aymonier, Etienne. 1897. *Voyage dans le Laos.* Volume 2. Paris, Ernest Leroux.

--------. 1900-03. *Le Cambodge.* 3 vols. I. *Le royaume actuel; II. Les provinces siamoises; III. Le group d'Angkor et l'histoire.* Paris, Ernest Leroux.

Briggs, Lawrence Palmer. 1951. *The Ancient Khmer Empire.* Philadelphia, The American Philosophical Society.

Chandler, David. 1983. *A History of Cambodia.* Boulder, Colorado, Westview Press.

Coedès George. 1930. 'Nouvelles données chronologiques et généalogiques sur la dynastie de Mahidrarapura', *Bulletin de l'École Française d'Extrême-Orient,* 29.

--------. 1963. *Angkor: An Introduction.* Translated and edited by Emily Floyd Gardiner. Hong Kongm, Oxford University Press.

Damong Rajanubhab, Prince. 1971. *Nirat Nakhon Wat [Journey to Angkor].* Bangkok, Phrae Phitthaya.

Dhaninivat Kromamun Bidyalabh Bridhyakorn, H.H. Prince. 1963. *The Royal Palaces.* Bangkok, The Fine Arts Department, Thai Culture, New Series, No. 23.

Fine Arts Department (Krom Sinlapakon). 1960. *Khrongkan lae raingan kansamruat lae khuttaeng boranwatthu nai phak tawan-okchiang nua ph.s. 2502 [Plan and Report of The Survey and Excavations of Ancient Monuments in North-Eastern Thailand 1959].* Bangkok.

--------. 1967. *Khrongkan lae raingan kansamruat lae khuttaeng boranwatthu nai phak tawan-okchiang nua phak 2 pho so 2503-2504 [Plan and Report of The Survey and Excavations of Ancient Monuments in North-Eastern Thailand. Part Two; 1960-1961].* Bangkok.

--------. 1988. *Prasat Phanom Rung [Phanom Rung Shrine].* Bangkok.

Garrett, Wilber E. 1982. 'The Temples of Angkor: Will They Survive?' *National Geographic,* 161.4:548-551.

Handler, Richard. 1985. 'On Having a Culture: Nationalism and the Preservation of Quebec's *Patrimoine*', pp. 192-217 in *Objects and Others: Essays on Museums and Material Culture,* ed. George W. Stocking, Jr. Madison, University of Wisconsin Press, History of Anthropology, 3.

Hanks, Lucien M. 1967. 'Bang Chan and Bangkok: Five Perspectives on the Relation of Local to National History', *Journal of Southeast Asian History,* 8.2, 250-56.

Keyes, Charles F. 1975. 'Buddhist Pilgrimage Centers and the Twelve Year Cycle: Northern Thai Moral Orders in Space and Time', *History of Religions,* 15.1, 17-89.

--------. 1990. 'Cambodia and the Legacy of Angkor', *Cultural Survival Quarterly,* 14.3, 60-63.

Kulke, Hermann. 1978. *The Devaraja Cult.* Translated from the German by I.W. Mabbett. Ithaca, N.Y., Cornell University, Southeast Asia Program, Data Paper, No. 108. Originally published in German in 1974.

Lajonquière, Lunet de. 1907. *Inventaire descriptif des monuments du Cambodge.* Vol. 2, Paris, Imprimerie Nationale.

Levine, Charles. 1978. *Insight Guides: Thailand.* Singapore, APA Productions.

Mus, Paul. 1975. *India Seen from the East: Indian and Indigenous Cults in Champa.* I. W. Mabbett, trans. Monash, Monash University, Centre of Southeast Asian Studies, Monash Papers on Southeast Asia, No. 3. First published in French in 1933.

Myrdal, Jan, and Gun Kessle. 1970. *Angkor: An Essay on Art and Imperialism.* Tr. by Paul Britten Austin. New York, Vintage. *The Nation.* Bangkok.

No Na Paknam. 1986. 'Prasat Phanom Rung kap Phu Angkhan [Prasat Phanom Rung and Phu Angkhan]', *Muang Boran*, 12.2, 63-70.

Nuechterlein, Donald E. 1965. *Thailand and the Struggle for Southeast Asia.* Ithaca, Cornell University Press.

Osborne, Milton. 1969. *Rule and Response: The French Presence in Cochinchina and Cambodia.* Ithaca, Cornell University Press.

Paisal Sricharatchanya. 1988. 'An International Squabble over a Slab of Stone', *Far Eastern Economic Review*, 5 May.

Paitoon Mikusol. 1984. 'Social and Cultural History of Northeastern Thailand from 1868-1910: Case Study of the Huamuang Khamen Padong (Surin, Sangkha and Khukhan)'. Ph.D. Dissertation, University of Washington.

Prathip Wahin. n.d.. 'Prasat hin Phanom Rung [The Stone Sanctuary of Phnom Rung], mimeographed, n.p. Obtained from Buddhist temple-monastery near the Phnom Rung shrine.

Quinn-Judge, Paul. 1981. 'Angkor Wat: Cambodia's "Heart" Is Slowly Being Broken', *The Christian Science Monitor*, October 14.

Quinn-Judge, Sophie. 1985. 'Thai Khmer Temples Offer a Safe Alternative to Angkor Wat', *Far Eastern Economic Review*, 23 May.

Reynolds, Frank E. 1978. 'The Holy Emerald Jewel: Some Aspects of Buddhist Symbolism and Political Legitimation in Thailand and Laos', pp. 175-93 in *Religion and Legitimation of Power in Thailand, Laos, and Burma*, ed. Bardwell Smith. Chambersburg, Pa., Anima Books.

Richardson, Michael. 1984. 'Letter from Angkor Wat', *Far Eastern Economic Review*, 19 April.

Srisakra Vallibhotama. 1986. 'Rop phu phanom rung [The Area of Phanom Rung Mountain: Relationship between Art and Culture, and the Natural Environment]', *Muang Boran*, 12:2, 48-58.

Suriyavudh Suksvasti, M. R. 1985. 'Bot wicai lae witthayaniphon thi nasoncai: prasat khao phanom rung [New Researches and Theses: Prasat Khao Phanom Rung]', *Muang Boran*, 11.4, 102-110.

Toem Wiphakphacanakit. 1978. *Prawatsat isan [History of the Northeast]*. Bangkok, Social Science Association of Thailand Press.

Wales, H. G. Quaritch. 1931. *Siamese State Ceremonies: Their History and Function*. London, Bernard Quaritch.

Wenk, Klaus. 1968. *The Restoration of Thailand under Rama I, 1782-1809*. Tucson, University of Arizona Press, Association for Asian Studies, Monographs and Paper, No. XXIV.

White, Peter, and Wilbur E. Garrett. 1982. 'Ancient Glory in Stone', *National Geographic*, 161.4, 552-89.

Wyatt, David K. 1984. *Thailand: A Short History*. New Haven, Yale University Press.

Chapter 10

IDENTITY AND AUTHORITY IN THAILAND

Hans-Dieter Bechstedt

INTRODUCTION

During the last two decades the issue of identity as a problem of groups or larger social collectivities has become an increasingly prominent topic in political, academic and public discussions. National and cultural identity in particular are key concepts when problems of development and social change are discussed mainly with respect to Third World countries. For example, the preservation, strengthening and development of cultural identity or national identity have become important objectives of many UNESCO statements on cultural programs. The reason is, among other things, that the United Nations and its various suborganizations are accustomed to taking the nation-state as their point of departure.[1] As Chan Heng Chee and Evers (1978) suggest, the development of national identity is a phenomenon found predominantly amongst the Westernized elites who attempt to make use of a deliberate policy of national identity formation for the purpose of nation building. They suspect that 'the insistence of Western political scientists to emphasize the importance of these questions is probably largely fostered by their own background and method of interviewing members of Westernized elites' (1978:117).

Many authors in their various books and articles on Singapore, Malaysia and Indonesia have given ample evidence of the broad and often indiscriminate use of classifications such as national or cultural identity not only within elite cultural or political circles, but also as an apparently frequent topic of public debate and private conversation in those countries.[2] The importance attributed to the questions of national and cultural identity, however, seems to hold true not only for the countries mentioned, but also appears to be crucial in other parts of the so-called Third World and has even surfaced in some Western countries.[3]

Compared with most of their neighbours the Thai people seem to have a strong and clear picture of what is needed to be a Thai, a perception maintained in popular culture and religious activities and passed on through the values and standards of parental and formal education. This fact is usually attributed to Thailand's relative ethnic homogeneity and the country's 'escape' from colonial subjugation. It is further related to a high identification with a specific cultural and traditional heritage, which is supported and strengthened by the ruling elite, whether it be the monarchy, the military or the business sector. Although legally sovereign, Thailand was substantially affected by European colonial empires, primarily British and secondarily French, as a result of a number of unequal treaties with those two countries. Anderson (1978:210) has referred to it as a 'semi-colonial, indirect-ruled condition'. Nevertheless it was the Thai ruling class which was responsible for introducing various social and political changes in response to external pressures. Thus it successfully managed to maintain a great many of its traditional ideals. Chan Heng Chee and Evers (1978:118) even maintain that the particular combination of being ethnic Thai, Buddhist and governed by an unbroken line of Thai kings has made the question of a national identity largely irrelevant to Thai elites.

As a result of rapid economic development and the accelerating process of modernization during the last ten years, however, the search for a national identity seems now to have become a subject of public debate in Thailand. Meanwhile the discussion on identity has gone far beyond academic circles and has spread to government speeches, newspaper comments and debates within religious or developmental groups. The Thai government even found it necessary in about 1980 to set up a National Identity Board under the Prime Minister's Office. In its publications and propaganda work of recent years it has added 'democracy' as the fourth pillar of Thai identity beside 'monarchy', 'Buddhism' and 'nation'.

Who are the Thais? What establishes Thai national and Thai cultural identity? These are questions in current debates. The answers may differ widely, depending on whether the respondent is a Thai politician, a Buddhist monk or a non-governmental rural development worker. While a representative of the business sector would refer to 'future-oriented identity', with values such as pragmatism, efficiency, and rationalism, a NGO-development worker may be more in favour of a 'regressive identity', looking for the preservation or even revival of cultural-political traditions of the past.[4] Yet, in most of these debates concepts like national or cultural identity, just to name the most important ones, are freely used as handy labels of convenience without too much concern about conceptual significances and differences between these categories. Moreover, in everyday life one can observe an indiscriminate use of the term 'identity', which implicitly is considered as a taken-for-granted category.

In the following discussion I will put less emphasis on an analysis of Thai collective identities such as national or cultural identity and focus instead on aspects of the formation of individual identity through the process of interaction. In this perspective, the concept of a 'collective identity' is to be considered as being in close relation to that of an 'individual identity'. Referring to Durkheim's concept of 'conscience collective', this collective consciousness is the sum total of the collective representations of a group, the aggregate of all values, norms, knowledge, attitudes and ideas which a group has in common and which should be integrated into a coherent world-view. This collective consciousness influences, if not determines, how people think about things, and provides a frame for the individual's social construction of reality. Thus, collective identity (the group's assumed collective self-conception) and individual identity (the psychological integration of the individual's personality) are dialectically related. In the words of the German sociologist Habermas (1976:93):

> The symbolic unity of a person, which is created and maintained by self-identification, is founded on the affiliation to the symbolic reality of a group, on the possibility to determine one's position in the world of this group. An identity of the group, which transcends and encompasses the individual life-histories, therefore is a prerequisite for the identity of the individual.

I will further argue that the often monolithic, positive-valued and ideologically biased usage of the concept 'identity' should be replaced by the concept of role and role expectations, at least when talking about the relationship between the individual and culture, nation, or any other such collectivity. Collective identity of the group is then translated into role demands of the group at the level of the individual.

With respect to Thailand I will present some results of empirical research on the perception of authority relations (Bechstedt 1987), i.e. on a circumscribed set of role expectations between persons with different social status, which are assumed to play a prominent role in Thai rural as well as urban social life and thus constitute an important part of peoples' individual as well as cultural identity. In doing so I will refer to the well-known social-psychological study of Phillips (1965) and critically re-examine some of his main assumptions about Thai peasant personality. Though he himself desists from using the term identity while focusing on an identification of various basic personality traits, those characteristics of the individual can nevertheless be interpreted as elements of a personal identity.

AUTHORITY AND IDENTITY FORMATION

Most social scientists in their studies on Thai society agree that the Thai social system is that of a highly hierarchically structured society, in which each member ranks the other in terms of superiority and inferiority and conforms to the numerous, culturally provided practices of etiquette. Across all social classes, the ideal seems to be upheld that life will be smooth and predictable if everybody knows his or her place and acts accordingly. However, Thailand's rapid economic development during recent years has, to a certain degree, begun to undermine the previously rigid and inflexible ascription of status. This development has generated an increasing demand for medical, legal, educational, technical, and other practitioners and has opened up new opportunities for certain strata of the urban population to acquire higher education. Together with the marked expansion of occupations in trade, banking, and manufacturing these changes have contributed to the growth of a new middle class in Thailand.

Twins are born one after the other, and will address each other as *phii* and *noong*, older brother/sister and younger brother/sister, respectively. As the formal genealogical structure of Thai kin terms demonstrates, there are no equals at all. Pupils in a group on the way to school are expected to walk according to their age; likewise, during their morning procession for alms the single file of monks is headed by the most senior one. At a wedding, a funeral, or an official party, all guests set great store on addressing each other according to rank and status. All Thai people, whatever the situation, are fully aware of their own as well as everyone else's position in the social hierarchy, and will reinforce this by appropriate manners and speech. Thus, many Western and Thai social scientists of different schools and orientations have agreed to adopt a patron-client framework or a related concept as a general guideline for the analysis of Thai society. As Evers (1980:1) observes, it is '... fast replacing the earlier "loose-structure" concept as an all pervading concept to analyze Thai society.'[5]

It was the first step of my research project on 'Change and Persistence in Thai Rural Society' in 1985/86 to find out how authority notions (beside those referring to anxiety and aggression) and their related social and cultural values are passed on by parental teaching which is assumed to contribute to the formation of the attitudes and personal ethos of subsequent generations. The study was conducted among rice-growing villagers of Thailand's upper central plains (Nakhorn Sawan and Phichit Province) as well as among construction workers at a huge Bangkok first-class hotel construction site. During that first stage I focused on the processes of primary socialization, conceived as the social making of the human being, which is embedded in a dialectic relationship with the social environment. It is the period in which, according to Habermas, the young person starts to develop his/her 'role identity', and at the same time to form his 'ego-identity' behind the predominant role expectations and the behavioral norms of the social environment.

The ego-identity of the adult person proves its ability by its creation of new identities and by its integration of overcome (past) ones in order to organize itself and its interactions into an unparalleled life history. Such an ego-identity allows those automations and at the same time those individualizations, which have their roots in the structure of the ego already on the level of role identity. The identity of the ego expresses the paradoxical relationship that the ego as a person is equal to all other persons, but as an individual is different from all other individuals. (Habermas 1976:95, my translation)

This proposition holds that through the processes of socialization the child will learn its sex identification and will acquire its moral standards and its achievement motive. The child's verbal and cognitive development is presumed to be largely determined by the stimulations he/she experiences in family life.

Thus, a total of 63 female informants (42 peasant women and 21 female workers) were questioned about their prospects of raising children, about sex preference and if they favour any of their children, about breast-feeding, weaning and toilet training. Particular emphasis was put on the mother's treatment of her children's aggressive behaviour and her disciplinary methods. This was because the style of restrictiveness versus permissiveness was supposed to have great impact on the development of the child's behavioral dispositions in terms of aggression, dependency, anxiety, submissiveness, compliance, and so forth. Finally, parental expectations, wishes and hopes for the future of the children were scrutinized, since these are held to be of consequence for the internalization of parental norms and standards.

To summarize, the mothers' expectations with respect to their children, that is, their image of an ideal child, can be reconstructed as follows. The ideal child is expected to be obedient, docile and submissive towards its parents, showing signs of loyalty and compliance at an early age. He/she should behave well, which first of all means paying respect to elders and speaking politely. Loving their parents, if mentioned at all, is not understood as an end in itself, but as an expression of the child's moral obligation in view of all that the parents have done for him/her.

While at preschool age the ideal son is not much bound by responsibilities. But as soon as he enters school, he is expected to be a diligent student, thus laying the foundation for an advanced education. This is perceived by most women as the necessary precondition for a salaried job in a nonagricultural occupation in one of the cities. If the financial situation of the parents does not allow the son to continue his education, he is expected to become a reliable and diligent peasant or worker. He should desist from typical male proclivity to irresponsibility and put on the yellow robe instead and enter the monkhood before getting married. Having established his own family and moved to the house of his bride and her family, he should not forget his parents. He should go to see them regularly, help them with their work or send them money, and even after his parents' death, he should regularly visit the temple and make merit for them.

The ideal daughter on the other hand, unlike her brother, has to assist her mother with household duties and with taking care of the younger siblings. At about the age of twelve, a well-mannered young lady should not wander around alone, or converse with any young man that she may happen to meet. She will be urged by her parents to play with other children of the same sex. By behaving in such a way, there will not be any reason for gossip, and the adolescent daughter can present herself as a desirable marriage partner. As soon as she has chosen someone, she and her husband are expected to reside in or at least near the parental home for a while and thus contribute to their parents' welfare. The youngest daughter is expected to inherit the parental house and to take care of her parents until they die.

Other results can be summarized as follows. Parents consider their children as an investment for their future. Children are raised in a spirit of moral obligation giving the impression that their upbringing creates a kind of debt which the children have to repay by taking care of their parents when they are old. The notion of the child-parent relationship in terms of reciprocity emphasizes a desire for protection and dependency. The child has to reciprocate for the parental care, protection, indulgence and dependence by showing his respect, obedience, conformity and a proper sense of obligation.

These observations fit well with the Thai Buddhist weltanschauung which describes a reliable order of mortality and goodness symbolized among other things by the home, elders, and especially by the mother. According to that ideal it is she who gives and takes care, feeds and loves her children, sacrifices herself for her dependents, and represents a refuge, a haven of safety, and a source of moral identity to her offspring. Because of this strong emphasis on the goodness of the mother, the child is obligated never to forget to return that goodness and benevolence, to show respect and obedience, and to feel morally indebted throughout his life. Thus, esteem, conformity and a sense of obligation towards elders and especially the mother are a strong theme in Thai culture (Mulder 1985:33, 63-64, 90-91).

On the basis of other data from the questionnaire as well as from my own observations, however, the child-parent relationship is not always as peaceful and tranquil as the ideal may suggest. Parents' expectations of their children are often mixed with uncertainties, doubts and fears of unrequited hopes. Parents worry that their children will neglect them when they are old and unable to work anymore. They fear for their children's future, as only a few of them are able to provide their offspring with land and property indispensable for a young couple when setting up a household. They are afraid that their children will turn to irresponsible behaviour, to drinking and gambling, causing quarrels and confrontations, and thus make the parents lose face.

Nevertheless, respectful submission to the authority of elders, such as parents or other family members, teachers, the Buddha and other religious symbols, the king and the Thai government - all considered to be essential to Thai identity or 'Thainess' — is first instilled into the child by parental teaching and later reinforced by the process of the child's secondary socialization, namely, school education. Such behaviour is reflected in the child's attitude of deference, submissiveness and passivity towards an adult. According to Liebig-Hundius, Thai children are relatively well-behaved, obedient and docile, when they are about to enter school:

They are well prepared to fulfil the expectations of society and of general good behaviour. They are accustomed to show obedience and familiarity with imitative learning. They have a positive attitude towards authority from which they expect patient instruction and guidance, but they are sensitive to direct coercion. They are not aggressive, but willing to respect the demands of others, and thus put up with retrenchments. They are used to a cheerful and harmonious social life, inclined to games and fun within their circle of intimate friends, but react in a shy and nervous way in new situations. It is easy to make them feel insecure, and they tend to run away when faced with problems. They show deference, reservation and shyness when facing authority.[6]

Religious instruction is one of the primary educational goals of elementary school education. At school the child will learn about the life of the Buddha, and will be instructed in some of his famous texts about ethics, morality and proper behaviour.[7] In addition to parents, the child will learn to show respect for superiors such as teachers and for the Buddha. He/she will frequently be reminded of the fact that he is deeply in debt to his parents and teachers who have provided him with vital information and essential knowledge, thus strengthening the child's feeling of moral obligation.

Furthermore, the child is taught to esteem the king and the Thai government as institutions that protect and maintain the Buddhist principles and its morality. According to B. Terwiel, in school teaching 'nationalism and Buddhism are closely interlinked' (1975:63). The basic elements of the specific Thai national identity, announced and sanctioned from above as a state ideology, and consisting of the king, the nation and Buddhism (today 'democracy' is added, however its content is to be understood), will find its most clearly visible expression during the morning flag-raising ceremony, when all children stand neatly dressed in their uniforms in orderly lines in front of the school building, the national anthem is sung and some Pali words are recited. Recognition of authority, tendency to conformity, and acceptance of social etiquette and polite manners are further stimulated by public appearances, processions and school celebrations.

From the beginning of its introduction by King Chulalongkorn at the end of the last century, the public educational system was considered by the ruling class as an instrument for promoting national integration and for propagating the subject's morality and virtues. As Liebig-Hundius suggests, with respect to the subordination of educational goals to the needs of government policy, nothing has changed to the present day. Methods and content of teaching as well as the teacher-pupil relationship still follow traditional patterns, emphasizing submission to the teacher's authority, discipline and other 'vassal' virtues (Liebig-Hundius 1984:67).

In conclusion, conformity and compliance with formal etiquette requirements of social life, respect and obedience to authority of elders and trust in their wisdom, protection, mutual dependence and reciprocity, moral indebtedness and a sense of obligation — all these seem to be significant aspects of Thai culture. These values represent exactly what Goffman has called the 'normative expectations of a society', which form the 'social identity'[8] of the individual.

VALUES AND RULES OF AN INFERIOR-SUPERIOR RELATIONSHIP

Given a highly hierarchically structured social system and the predominance of the abovementioned social values with their implied standards for child education, with regard to the personality structure of an individual we expect to find a profound predisposition to submit to authority.[9] As Phillips has put it, the Thai attitude towards authority 'represents what is perhaps the most explicitly expressed and highly ramified area of their social psychological life' (Phillips 1965:143).

In fact, a sense of subordination and superordination is already in evidence in the Thai language, but this does not seem to be distinctively Thai as we find similar expressions in the Burmese and Javanese languages. The Thai linguistic structure is such that it is impossible to address a person without referring to social status. Yet, notions of authority and the corresponding gestures and practices of etiquette are apparently more elaborate within the highly hierarchical systems of the civil and military bureaucracy and among the urban-based white-collar workers than among villagers or construction workers of rural background.

Phillips's comment that the 'entire structure of the family is predicated on a system of superordination and subordination' does not come as a surprise and is almost a universal truth. What is impressive, though, is the peculiar linguistic structure of the Thai language which contains a remarkably elaborate system of hierarchically ordered kinship terms, although in the course of daily interactions they are often used without explicit reference to their implication as kin categories.[10] Looking at the genealogical structure of Thai kin terms, we get a picture of 'maximum differentiation among kin with whom one is likely to have the most frequent and personally significant contact.... It is worth emphasizing here that this is a system in which, conceptually speaking, there are no equals' (Phillips 1965:12).

In the second part of my empirical research on the psychological manifestations of hierarchical interpersonal relations, among others,[11] I partly made use of the 'Social Completion Test' (SCT), as it was developed and applied by Phillips during his study of Thai peasant personality in the village of Bang Chan in the Central Plain in the early 1960s (Phillips 1965:12). My sample of the SCT comprises 108 adults, 69 peasants from two different villages and 39 workers from a Bangkok construction site. Phillips's study, though written more than twenty years ago, nevertheless is until now the only thorough, comprehensive, and empirical social-psychological study of life in a Thai rural community. The few subsequent studies rarely fail to refer to his work.[12]

The second part of my thesis then is first of all a discussion and critical reassessment of his work. It was done with the intention of making some critical comments on his applied theory as well as to prove the internal validity of his data after more than twenty years and within an environment which manifests geographical as well a social variations. For that reason, in several aspects alterations had to be made in the use of his testing material. So, for example, the samples (108 subjects) were clustered according to the dichotomies of peasants versus construction workers, peasants who own land versus those who do not, and male versus female. Furthermore I was less interested in the identification of authority as 'unimodel area (of) Thai psychological life' (Phillips 1965:156). I interpret my data, therefore, according to the following criteria. First, what particular situations are interpreted by the Thai peasants and construction workers in the area of authority relations, and what are their different strategies to deal with these relations? Second, of what quality are the emotions involved in their psychological connotations? Finally, what is the socio-economic framework in which the authority relations are embedded? The results of that second part of my research can be summarized as follows.

1. When asked how they would react if directed by a village headman or foreman to do something, most Thai peasants and construction workers imply that they would comply with the order without 'ifs' or 'buts', thus testifying convincingly to the assumed disposition on their part to accept and act upon the order of an authority figure. However, I disagree with Phillips's suggestion that the villagers invariably accept the prerogatives of any authority. The peasants' and workers' conformity to the demands of an authority figure according to my data obviously has limits and ends when their own personal interests are affected beyond a certain extent, or if the request is considered improper and inappropriate according to their ethical standards. Thai villagers will react to a superior with deference and submission as long as the latter meets his or her obligations towards his or her inferiors.

I do not look at Thai peasants or construction workers as people with a psychology structure involving firm and stable authority fixations. I rather perceive them as dramatis personae (actors) in a cultural role-play. These cultural roles are connected with social expectations and anticipated behaviour as well as with related norms and values. If one side does not act according to those expectations, the other side may not feel obliged to adhere to those norms and values.

Phillips's psychological concept assumes a congruency between the stimulus, i.e. the cultural system and its norms and values on the one hand, and the responses or reactions, i.e. the 'unimodal' basic personality traits, attitudes and behaviour respectively on the other. Such a model tends to neglect differences between individuals as well as within the structure of the individual personality. Furthermore, having constructed so-called 'neutral' stimuli or 'cultural-free' test items, he equates the responses of his informants with their attitudes and their assumed behaviour.[13] I suggest that any cultural system creates specific dispositions owing to the different perceptions and interpretations of a situation, depending on differences between individuals with regard to education, social strata, sex, etc.

I assume further that any cultural system creates specific dispositions within one and the same individual owing to the particular character of authority, and I doubt that there is an essentially neutral authority condition or a general dispositional or behavioral pattern concerning authority in itself. Attitudes to authority and the affectations involved with these structures are as varied as are the situations of authority. The relationships between a young male peasant and his father or his father-in-law, between himself and a monk, a teacher, a village headman or a government official have few common features apart from a general feeling of respect and esteem. While the relationship to this father is inescapable and may be an emotional mixture of awe, fright and love, the more pragmatic affiliation with a government officer may turn out to be of no benefit and therefore dispensable, whereas his bonds with the monk might be coloured by sentiments of religious veneration and moral obligation.

2. Again contrary to Phillips, sentiments of an inferior in relation to a superior are not only governed by feelings of esteem, respect, pleasure, honour, admiration and gratitude, but also by their emotional counterparts such as discomfort, awe, embarrassment and fright.[14] These conflicting sentiments are a reflection of the ambiguity of these kinds of superior-inferior relationships and remind us of the fact that if stripped of their emotional components they will reveal their true essence: asymmetrical power relations based upon unequal access to power.

In general, a superior is met with gestures of respect and deference. Thai villagers and construction workers, men and women alike, are very apprehensive of those conventional formalities that are culturally prescribed and socially demanded. Yet behind such a facade, there exist sentiments of displeasure, fear, and shyness, on the one side, but also happiness, gladness, pride and admiration on the other. Which of these negative or positive emotions become paramount depends largely on the concrete experiences of the peasants and workers with respect to the fulfilment or disappointment of their expectations concerning a superior, here a village head or foreman. The comparison of the villagers' attitude toward the village head in two different villages has given evidence of the broad variation of such sentiments, ranging from fear, high respect, and pride to ignorance, disrespect and even disparagement.[15]

Despite the fact that they may produce unpleasant feelings, ties to a superior are desired as an alliance with a patron which may bring about advantages in the eyes of the less privileged. Living in an environment with no promising alternatives, a dependency relation to a powerful superior under those conditions may be consistent with the economic rationale of the peasant. The ambivalence of such a relationship reflects his or her fear not to meet the requirements of his obligations towards that superior.

3. When placed in a position of power, most peasants and workers again are most concerned with the question of how to perform and behave well according to the conventional norms of such a position. Acceptance of a power role according to their view always implies proper, fair and honest conduct when facing subordinates. Their relatively great attention to negative attributes gives some reason for the assumption that, quite frequently, relationships between superiors and inferiors, cultural ideals notwithstanding, bring about frictions and tensions.

Few informants indicate that they will use a position of power in order to support their family, group of friends, or for the benefit of the community. In consideration of the fact that, for several years, activists of a non-governmental group have been operating in the two villages, these results are surprising. The activists of that organization promote particularly the aspects of unity and the cooperation of the community in order to strengthen the bargaining power of the peasant against rural capitalists like merchants, traders and money lenders. They have initiated a number of joint development projects and set up a farmers committee. All the members of that committee were respondents to my questionnaire. A position of power is first of all viewed in its emotional essence and in its significance for the ego, and much less in terms of its functional or instrumental implications.

Unlike Phillips, however, I do not see the peasant suffering from what he calls 'achievement failure'. Instead, Thai peasants are occupied by thoughts of how to enhance their income (and repay their debts) by shifting to another crop, the application of new technologies, small-scale entrepreneurial activities, and so forth. Thai peasants during the last decades as well as a great number of urban people from the so-called informal sector have not shown any resistance to innovations but have manifested flexibility and creativity in finding new strategies for survival.

4. A superior's treatment of a subordinate which is characterized by sympathy, affection and understanding, by fairness, honesty and good advice, is favoured by a majority of peasants as well as construction workers. On the other hand, betrayal and deceit, abuse of power, causing trouble and distress, disrespect and distrust, indifference and insincerity with imprudent speech are most feared. For all respondents, whether they are landowning peasants, tenants, agricultural or urban wage labourers, men or women, a good boss is judged less by his professional qualifications; only rarely is he evaluated in terms of generosity or flexibility. Rather, non-material traits, i.e. personal qualities such as sympathy and affection, are valued highest. And it is the fulfilling of emotional rather than material needs which is appreciated most. As a result, indicated by the findings already cited, a superior-inferior relationship is first of all considered a personal relationship. Because courtesy, proper speech and good manners are considered to be an indication of sympathy and personal proximity, it is on the presentational and face-to-face components of the relationship that the emphasis is placed.[16]

CONCLUSIONS

While presenting some results of previous empirical research on the perception of authority relations, I have tried to give evidence for my suggestion that specific patterns of mutual role expectations between a superior and an inferior play a dominant role in Thai rural as well as urban life, and thus constitute an important part of individual and cultural identity. The various aspects of a person's identity are developed, as we have seen, through the processes of interpersonal exchange, mainly during primary and secondary socialization, by which are created a set of values and norms as guidelines for one's own behaviour and that of others. In earlier work it was my intention to show how this informal body of rules and values — particularly those relevant to an inferior-superior relationship — is established in the psychology of a person and is passed on from one generation to the next via socialization (Bechstedt 1987: chapter 2).

The specific Thai peasants' notion of authority, apart from other concepts like moral obligation, reciprocity, dependency, gratitude etc., seems to be an important element of their 'world view' and thus obviously gives shape to their perception of power, social groups and political organizations. Moreover, these perceptions appear to be related to what is repeatedly reported as the peasants' preference for unequal alliances like patron-client relations as opposed to other choices like village-centred, horizontal, class-based associations. It could be demonstrated that describing authority solely in terms of character traits originating from the psychic structure of Thai individuals fails to interpret authority as a social relationship that evolved historically with all its specific characteristics and limitations. Such a perspective necessarily requires references to the social structural conditions in which interpersonal exchanges happen. It thus reveals the extent to which an identification with authority, here for example the authority of social institutions like the state, the monarchy and the Buddhist Sangha, creates a national identity and serves as a source of sanction and legitimation of the existing power structure in society.

Likewise, I would submit that such a view is less static and serves to suggest a possible disharmony between actual behaviour, on the one hand, and, on the other, a mental attitude derived, among other things, from the heritage of traditional social values and cultural prescriptions. It also provides a clue to the continuous strength of what some authors call the hierarchical 'sakdina ideology' (Chai-anan 1976; Chatthip 1980; Girling 1981; Boonsanong Punyodyana 1969). This ideology has shaped and its remnants still continue to shape the Thai peasants' value system, their 'world view' and their social attitudes down to the present. However, the hierarchical system of the past and its related social institutions have changed. New classes and 'strategic groups' have appeared (Evers 1982). Today, it is not the control of manpower but money and access to profits, shares and stocks that distinguishes those who are in power from those who are not. Nevertheless, in general, the Thai peasants' perception of society (and perhaps that of other social strata as well) appears to be strongly influenced by a set of 'unwritten rules of behaviour', i.e. an elaborate role-play between superior and inferior, which, according to Terwiel, shows many parallels to that of old Siamese history.

... formal structures, such as the systems of ranking and legal categorization of slaves and rights over their labour, have changed to such a degree that hardly any trace of the Ayutthayan organization can be found in present-day Thai society. In contrast, quite a different picture emerges from the study of the practice of etiquette and the informal, non-legalized, relationships which exist within the family and in society at large. (Terwiel 1984:34)

Several questions arise concerning the persistence of cultural values and ideologies in the context of fast-changing social institutions and organizations and a rapid modernization of society along Western concepts and rationality. Will the changes ultimately lead to disintegration and role diffusion, or to a newly defined, integrated self-concept? Will this new self-concept find its expression in a new spiritual and religious movement? Will the changes lead to an increase in social tensions and a general moral decline, as some suggest, or to a new social synthesis? Answers to questions such as these have to be left to further empirical explorations.[17]

ENDNOTES

1. The importance of this objective has been reiterated by the 21st General Conference in 1980 and in the Declaration of Mexico City on Cultural Policy in 1982. The recommendation to 'foster cultural identity' is set forth in the report of the UNESCO-sponsored International Commission for the Study of Communication Problems, also known as the McBride Report (cf. Heidt 1985).

2. For Southeast Asia in general, Chan Heng Chee and Evers 1978, Hassan 1978, Tamney 1973; for Indonesia, Legge 1964; for Singapore, Chiew Seen-Kong 1976, MacDougall 1976, Heidt 1985.

3. See for example F. Braudel 1987, Weidenfeld 1983, and especially the present-day debate among German sociologists about the hitherto assumed 'post-national identity' of the German people, an identity beyond territorial borders and ethnic boundaries and founded primarily on an identification with the political institutions of a pluralist, democratic community now facing a resurrection of nationalist sentiments owing to recent political changes in Eastern Europe (cf. Habermas 1990).

4. Chan Heng Chee and Evers in their analysis of national identity among the Westernized political elite of Southeast Asian countries have broken down the concept as follows: first, a 'regressive identity', most common in those countries which can look back to a long and proud cultural and political tradition; second, a 'progressive identity', where 'the past is seen as detrimental to progress, lack of development is ascribed to remnants of the feudal or colonial past and a new society, a new state and a new national identity is aspired to'; and third, a 'non-ideological identity', an identity through an 'ideology of pragmatism' (1978:118-119).

5. For a critical review of the analysis of Thai social structure in terms of a patron-client concept see Bechstedt 1990. As I argue, the patron-client model, carefully deduced and defined as against personal bonds on the one end, and purely coercive, contractual ties on the other end of an assumed continuum, may provide an appropriate tool for the analysis of the social-psychological components of superior-inferior relations. As an informal, dyadic relationship, based upon reciprocal, but nevertheless non complementary obligations, it is a model which might also yield a better understanding of the structure of Thai peasant social consciousness. As an exploitative relationship, ultimately based upon power,

but still keeping its features of a personal relationship, it should not be confused with class analysis. Some scholarly works on Thailand, mostly by those who are in favour of Embree's model of a 'loose structured social system' (Embree 1969), view Thai social structure either by applying the clientelist framework in a rather oversimplified and static manner (Hanks 1975), depicting Thailand as a highly harmonious and conflictless society (Phillips 1965), overemphasize the model's psychological equivalents (Piker 1964:310) and/or extend the framework for an explanation of the society as a whole (the social order as a system of combined hierarchies of patron-client relationships, as in Akin 1980). The concept per se, however, does not support a complacent view about traditional Thai society's uniqueness, as Kemp (1984) and Reynolds (1987) suggest, insofar as it cannot substitute, but rather complements a political and economic analysis of society in terms of classes or strategic groups and their relationship to the dominant mode of production. Beneath that macro-level of analysis, however, the patron-client model may help, for example, to identify traditional attitudes which operate as a barrier/promoter to the formation of class-based, egalitarian interest groups, like farmer associations, or village committees.

6. Liebig-Hundius 1984:60 (my translation). In a carefully planned and executed study, based on a large number of primary and secondary materials, the author deals with the question of how the Western principles of 'equality', 'participation', 'rationality' and 'moral autonomy' are perceived by Thai teachers and what role the educational experiences of prospective teachers play in establishing 'new' attitudes, and to what degree and in what ways these attitudes are influenced by the state's educational institutions.

7. However, as N. Mulder (1985:143) has noticed, the texts of the officially approved manuals on Buddhism appear to be mainly concerned with the perpetuation of social values, good citizenship, and respect for the core elements of the Thai order and its way of life. According to him they reflect the traditional Thai value system rather than an interest in presenting an understanding of the Buddhist message.

8. According to Goffman (1961) 'personal identity' refers to the singularity of the individual, who keeps his specific characteristics, his particular biography, and all his distinguished features, which allows us to distinguish one individual from another. It must be distinguished from what he calls 'social identity' which signifies the attribution or ascription of certain distinctive features, and which bear the character of normative expectations. The individual is required to subordinate himself to common expectations, to be like everybody else. With regard to personal identity, on the other hand, the individual is expected to be different from others, not to be like everybody else. These contradictory expectations require a balance, otherwise there is the threat of non-identity in a double sense. In the first case, the total absorption of the individual by alienated

and depersonalized role interrelations; in the second case, stigmatization owing to behaviour which deviates from the norm. Thus, following Goffman, 'ego-identity' as a subjective reaction, implying acceptance as well as resistance vis-a-vis the externally exposed expectations, must develop through the individual's continual attempts to mediate and reconcile both aforesaid forms of identity.

9. Social-psychological studies of the Frankfurt School on authoritarian rule have demonstrated the manifold ways in which the hierarchical conditions of a society are reflected in social values, actual behaviour and the psychic life of the individual (cf. for example Marcuse 1969, Adorno 1950, Horkheimer 1968, Fromm 1970).

10. Kemp (1984:60) argues that this disregard of the exact links of kinship in every-day communications is serving the goal of reducing the competitive and calculating dimension of the social hierarchy.

11. A third part of my project was devoted to the examination of such values as moral obligation, friendship, conflict avoidance, smooth interaction, and of psychological variables such as anxiety and aggression. In the fourth and final part of my thesis I tried to find out how far an expressed general attitude corresponds to actual behaviour, using subsequently, beside the data from participant observation, an open-ended questionnaire about concrete problems of everyday-life in particular with respect to local social hierarchies and actual power relations. Again, contrary to Phillips, in my mind the verbal response of any informant, but especially in the Thai context, carries the bearing of socially desired and culturally idealized behaviour according to anticipated role expectations. At best it reflects the cognitive and affective components of a social attitude or a mental disposition and it is not tantamount to actual behaviour.

12. See for example the studies of Piker 1964 (already aware of Phillips' book though released one year later), Mentzer 1973 and Suntaree 1985, among others. While Piker (1964:118-119) in his work about the socialization process in a Thai village concludes that '...the villager manifests a passive, almost fatalistic lethargy', and owing to his dependency conception is compelled to 'irrational activities', Mentzer (1973) in his study of the affect dimensions of Thai peasant personality similarly puts the emphasis on such stereotypes as a high need for dependency, lack of achievement orientation, and an all pervasive anxiety. Suntaree (1985), who in her study of the Thai world view likewise relies on crude, evolutionist concepts based on Western rationality, consequently ends up attesting that Thai people lack an achievement motive, revert to stoic fatalism, individualism and are obsessed by joyful *sanuk* behaviour. All these conceptions remind me strongly of those ethnocentric and ahistorical development theories of the late 50s and the 60s, when development backwardness of the so-called

Third World countries was explained by supposedly 'primitive mentality' or by the so-called 'magical prelogical mentality' of their people.

13. As an indication of the villagers' unanimous submission to people in authority, Phillips reports the following observation. 'During elections, villagers say that they are going to vote for the prime minister because "he is our Master. He has been very good to us. He is like our father, and we are like his children."' With regards to the peasants' electoral attitudes, for some of them paternalistic considerations may play a role, while for others the candidate's pledge to build a new road to the district market or to reduce the rice premium may be the decisive factor. Moreover, coercion or simply bribery may also influence the peasants' attitudes. In the course of my field research from 1984 to 1985, several by-elections were held in areas nearby, as well as an election of the city council in Bangkok. Talking with villagers about politicians, which I frequently did, I rarely noticed anything that could be interpreted as an expression of deference or compliance with authority. On the contrary, in the eyes of most peasants, the politicians in distant cities have lost much of their credit and reputation owing to a number of unfulfilled expectations and disappointed hopes. Above anything else it was this 'stimulus' of getting 50 or 100 *baht* that mobilized the villagers at the polls.

14. As Marcuse (1969:55) has characterized it: 'In any authority relation freedom and non-freedom, autonomy and heteronomy are associated with each other and combined in one person, in the authority object'.

15. In the case of Udom Pattana, a partly rice-, partly maize-growing village in Nakhorn Sawan province, the village head and largest land-owner had succeeded owing to his wealth, his political influence, his despotic leadership as well as his granting of favour and support to his dependents to ensure the loyalty of the villagers, while in Taak Daed, a rice-growing village in neighbouring Phichit province, the village head for want of resources, followers and dependents, could not manage to establish his influence and power, and hence was openly rejected by most of the villagers.

16. These findings match well with the observations of Mulder (1985:64-65), who believes that presentation is of great importance for Thai social and psychological life, leading to fulfilment of expectations, to social acceptance and recognition. Following Mulder, Thai society literally tends to accept persons at their face value, and rates highly the visible presentation to which deep feelings, and upon reflection, deep meaning are attached. Differences between peasants and construction workers, between tenants and agricultural wage labourers, and a comparison between the sexes within the framework of the present paper cannot be discussed due to lack of space.

17. J.L.S. Girling (1981:30-31) with regard to the Thai bureaucracy observes a
    conspicuous tension as a result of traditional values that still persist and pervade
    the attitudes and activities of its members, although the conditions that gave
    rise to them have long since passed. He sees that the traditional consensus
    based on paternalism, on former authority to the king, the princes and the nobility
    has been disrupted by contemporary social and economic changes, and above
    all by the development and growth of the manufacturing, commercial and service
    sector.

REFERENCES

Adorno, T.W. 1950. *The Authoritarian Personality*. New York.

Akin Rabibhadana. 1980. 'Patron-Client Relationship and the Self-Help Organizations of the Poor'. Paper presented to the Thai-European Seminar on 'Social Change in Contemporary Thailand', 28-30 May 1980. University of Amsterdam.

Anderson, Benedict R.O'G. 1978. 'Studies of the Thai State: The State of Thai Studies' in *The Study of Thailand: Analyses of Knowledge, Approaches, and Prospects in Anthropology, Art History, Economics, History and Political Science*, ed. Eliezer B. Ayal. Athens, Ohio, Center for International Studies.

Bechstedt, H.-D. 1987. 'Change and Persistence in Thai Rural Society: An Empirical Study of Hierarchical Interpersonal Relations and Their Psychological Manifestation'. Ph.D. Thesis, University of Bielefeld.

Bechstedt, H.-D. 1990. 'The Paradigm of the Patron-Client Model in Thai Rural Society'. Paper presented to the International Conference on Thai Studies, 11-13 May 1990, Kunming, China.

Bechstedt, H.-D. 1991. *The Paradigm of the Patron-Client Model in Thai Rural Society*. University of Bielefeld, forthcoming.

Boonsanong Punyodyana. 1969. 'Social Structure, Social system, and Two Levels of Analysis: A Thai View' in *Loosely Structured Social Systems: Thailand in Contemporary Perspective*, ed. H.-D. Evers. New Haven, Yale University, Southeast Asia Studies. Cultural Report Series no. 17.

Braudel, F. 1987. *L'identité de la France*. Paris, Arthand. 3 vol.

Chai-anan Samutravanich. 1976. *Sakdina and the Development of Thai Society*. Bangkok. (in Thai).

Chan Heng Chee and Hans-Dieter Evers. 1978. 'National Identity and Nation-building in Southeast Asia' in *Studies in ASEAN Sociology: Urban Society and Social Change*, ed. Peter S. J. Chen and H.-D. Evers. Singapore.

Chatthip Nartsupha, ed. 1980. *The Development of Capitalism in Thailand*. Bangkok. (in Thai).

Chiew Seen-Kong. 1976. Singaporean National Identity: An Alternative View', *Review of Southeast Asian Studies*, 1-4, pp. 1-10.

Embree, J.F. 1969. 'Thailand, a Loosely Structured Social System' in Hans-Dieter Evers, ed., *Loosely Structured Social Systems: Thailand in Comparative Perspective*. New Haven, Yale University, Southeast Asia Studies. Cultural Report Series no. 17.

Evers, H.-D. 1980. 'Patronage, Class and Culture: Notes on Central Issues in Current Research on Contemporary Thailand'. Paper presented at the Thai-European Seminar on Social Change in Contemporary Thailand. University of Amsterdam, 18-30 May 1980.

Evers, H.-D. 1982. *Sequential Patterns of Strategic Group Formation and Political Change in Southeast Asia*. University of Bielefeld, Sociology of Development Center. Working Paper no. 8.

Fromm, E. 1970 (1936). *Studien ueber Autoritaet und Familie.* Frankfurt.

Girling, J.L.S. 1981. *Thailand: Society and Politics.* Ithaca and London, Cornell University Press.

Goffman, E. 1961. 'Role Distance' in E. Goffman, *Encounters: Two studies in the Sociology of the Interaction.* Indianapolis.

Habermas, J. 1976. 'Koennen komplexe Gesellschaften eine vernuenftige Identitaet ausbilden?' in J. Habermas, *Zur Rekonstruktion des Historischen Materialismus.* Frankfurt, Suhrkamp.

Habermas, J. 1990. Der DM-Nationalismus. In: *Die Zeit*, No.15, 30 March 1990.

Hanks, L.M. 1975. 'The Thai Social Order as Entourage and Circle' in G.W. Skinner and A.T. Kirsch, eds. *Change and Persistence in Thai Society.* Cornell University Press.

Hassan, R. 1978. 'National and Ethnic Identities in Southeast Asia' in *Internationales Asianforum*, 1/2, pp. 155-164.

Heidt, E. 1985. *The Issue of National and Cultural Identities: Some Conceptual Considerations.* University of Bielefeld, Working Paper No.61.

Horkheimer, M. 1968 (1936). 'Autorietaet und Familie' in *Kritische TheoriePi.* Frankfurt. Bd. 1.

Jackson, P.A. 1989. *Buddhism, Legitimation, and Conflict: The Political Functions of Urban Thai Buddhism.* Singapore, Institute of Southeast Asian Studies.

Kemp, J.H. 1984. 'The Manipulation of Personal Relations: From Kinship to Patron-Clientage' in H. Brummelhuis and J.H. Kemp, eds., *Strategies and Structures in Thai Society.* Amsterdam.

Legge, J.D. 1964. *Indonesia.* Englewood Cliffs, New Jersey, Prentice Hall.

Liebig-Hundius, I. 1984. Thailands Lehrer zwischen 'Tradition' und 'Fortschritt'. *Eine empirische Untersuchungpolitisch-sozialer und paedagogischer Einstellungen thailaendischer Lehrerstudenten des Jahres 1974.* Wiesbaden

MacDougall, J.A. 1976. 'Birth of a Nation: National Identification in Singapore', *Asian Survey,* 16, pp. 510-524.

Marcuse, H. 1969 (1936). *Ideen zu einer kritischen Theorie der Gesellschaft.* Frankfurt.

Mentzer, E.H. 1973. 'Affect Dimensions of Thai Peasant Personality, as Assessed by the Rorschach, and Their Functional Relations to Aspects of Village Social Structure and Cultural System'. Ph.D. thesis, University of Washington.

Mulder, N. 1985. *Everyday Life in Thailand: An Interpretation.* Bangkok, Duang Kamol.

Phillips, H.P. 1965. *Thai Peasant Personality: The Patterning of Interpersonal Behaviour in the Village of Bang Chan.* Berkeley and Los Angeles.

Piker, S. 1964. 'Character and Socialization in a Thai Peasant Community'. Ph.D. thesis, University of Washington.

Reynolds, C.J. 1987. *Thai Radical Discourse: The Real Face of Thai Feudalism Today*. Ithaca, Cornell University, Southeast Asia Program.

Suntaree Komin. 1985. 'The World View Through Thai Value Systems' in Amara Phongsapich et al., *Traditional and Changing Thai World View*. Bangkok. Chulalongkorn University, Social Research Institute.

Tamney, J.B. 1973. 'The Scarcity of Identity: The Relation Between Religious Identity and National Identity' in Hans-Dieter Evers, ed., *Modernization in Southeast Asia*. Singapore.

Terwiel, B.J. 1975. *Monks and Magic: An Analysis of Religious Ceremonies in Central Thailand*. Lund.

Terwiel, B.J. 1984. 'Formal Structures and Informal Rules: An Historical Perspective on Hierarchy, Bondage and the Patron-Client Relationship' in H. Brummelhuis, and J.H. Kemp, ed., *Strategies and Structures in Thai Society*. Amsterdam.

Weidenfeld, W. 1983. *Die Identitaet der Deutschen*, Muenchen, Carl Hanser.

Chapter 11

WHAT IS *THE* THAI VILLAGE?

Philip Hirsch

[I]n an increasingly urbanized social and political environment, images of the past, in this instance of the village and its supposed organization, are part of a contemporary discourse about Thai identity and the directions in which Thai society should proceed. (Kemp 1988:1)

It is difficult to consider Thai identity without specific attention to rural identity, both the self-identification of rural Thais and the imposed identity of urban and foreign lookers-on. There is a popular sense that what is genuinely Thai (*thai thae thae*) emanates from rural life, and this means village life. In film, advertising and popular imagery, villagers (*chaobaan*) are often portrayed as the quintessential Thais, whose culture and ways of life are thought of as having deviated least as a result of external influence. Villages are where society's roots are embedded (Seri 1986). Associated with this notion are sets of ideas about community — what it is, was, or should be. The village community as locus of identity is associated with a diversity of views on what the village actually is.

The question of what a Thai village is (or is not) can be approached from at least two perspectives. One is to consider whether there is in fact such a thing as a village in the sense of an identifiable rural community, and if so to consider what the character of that entity is. Another position, one given more credence in the following discussion, is to consider the village not in terms of its essence but as a discursive category.

Examining the *notion* of village (rather than the village itself) as territorial unit, as imposed structure, as administrative instrument, or as tool of standardisation, obviates the cul-de-sac or circular enquiry of whether or not there is such a thing as a village. Instead, attention is directed to the way in which the discourse of village reflects changing relations between the Thai state and rural populations, between rural classes, and between different groups of developers working in the area of rural development. This approach leads to a view of the Thai village as an arena of struggle between national and local identity for control over resources and over concepts of development.

DE-ESSENTIALISING THE THAI VILLAGE

When in 1984 I first arrived to do fieldwork in and on *my* village in a recently settled district of Uthaithani, I spent the first few days doing and asking many things that now seem strange. One recurrent question was, 'Where is the *village*?'. I did not quite know what it would look like when I found it, but nevertheless I had a vaguely uneasy feeling that the isolated house I was staying in, surrounded as we were by open fields peppered with blackened tree stumps, was somehow peripheral to this thing I had come to study. I could see at a distance several clusters of similar houses, or rather the fruit trees that surrounded them, and wondered which one contained the core I was seeking.

Of course the question in my mind was subtly different from the one I was asking out loud. I was asking, 'Where is the *village*'; in my mind was, 'Where is *the* village', that standardised construct that had taken form in my mind as a product of my own cultural background, published studies of peasant society (e.g. Redfield 1956) and other Thai villages (notably Potter 1976), and previous visits to parts of Thailand where it appeared that the village had a less ambiguous reality.

I soon found out that my abode was as much, or as little, a part of Bung Khiew as any other house. Like many other areas of settlement on the fringes of the Central Plains, houses here were scattered and farmers usually lived close to the fields that they worked. The 'community' of Bung Khiew, as I understood it then, had few of the markers of village that I had expected. Temple, school, and significant clusters of houses were all outside the ill-defined area Bung Khiew seemed to occupy. The inhabitants of Bung Khiew made merit at one of two different temples and sent their children to two different schools. One temple and one school were in Ban Dong, the administrative village of which Bung Khiew was (but is no longer) a part.

This baffling early fieldwork experience could have immediately raised a number of questions. The obvious one would have been to ask what it was I was looking for in my search for *the* village. My research topic was (fortunately, I think) far enough away from this and similar questions that they have only been raised in retrospect, partly as a result of a workshop held in Amsterdam in April 1988 on the theme, 'The Village Revisited: Community and Locality in Southeast Asia' (*Sojourn* 1989, Special Issue). The agenda of the workshop revolved around the debunking of myths concerning the village community in Southeast Asia, and there were a number of contributions on Thailand (Hirsch 1991a).

Two ways of looking at the problem emerged out of the workshop. One is to question the notion of village community by querying its very existence. Jeremy Kemp (1987) describes the 'seductive mirage' that the village community represents for those who attempt to understand the organisation of rural society in Southeast Asia. He shows how little Hua Kok in Pitsanulok fits the model of Redfieldian community in the sense of a discrete entity of corresponding social and physical boundaries. He goes on to suggest that the notion of discrete rural community in effect negates the reality of links with the wider system, particularly the state.

This line of investigation also concerns the extent to which ecology, regional culture, and history have resulted in units of social organisation that we can identify as village communities in rural Thailand. Yet in questioning the existence of the village community, in seeing it as contingent, are we not leading ourselves toward an essentialist impasse? In measuring the existence or otherwise of village community by correspondence between physical and social boundaries, there seem to be two ways to proceed. One is the cul-de-sac of discovering that, indeed, there is no such correspondence. Where to then? The other is the circular path of answering our own questions by using our own definitional criteria and deciding whether Bung Khiew is a village community in terms of these criteria.

I suggest that a more worthwhile project is to de-essentialise our notion of village, and to recognise that the village exists as discourse. We should not be limited by a realist notion of village as a social-cum-physical essence. Rather, we should be looking at what the village means, how it is used and manipulated, and how the construct impinges on rural society and rural identity.

VILLAGE AS DISCOURSE

The discourse of village is produced at a number of levels. For purposes of administration, official discourse divides the rural population and territory into about 60,000 discrete units, or *muubaan*, that may or may not conform with local social boundaries (cf Keyes 1979). Associated with these units are a number of other structures of leadership and organisation that increasingly represent the power of the state in rural Thailand. The discourse of village is also part of the populist portrayal of traditional rural social organisation reflected in the writings of a number of prominent non-governmental development workers (e.g. Apichaat Thongyuu, Seri Phongphit, Prawate Wasi, Bamrung Bunpanya). Many academic writings maintain the discourse of village as an essential aspect of rural social organisation, either implicitly by adopting the community study mode of research (Kingshill 1960; Kaufman 1960; Potter 1976), or explicitly by interpretation of rural society as first and foremost village-based (Chatthip 1984). Most importantly, rural Thais themselves have a discourse of village that overlaps, but does not necessarily coincide, with these alternative discourses. The name of a community, structures of kinship and non-formal leadership all mark out local identification with a particular *muubaan*, albeit one that often has ambiguous boundaries. Utong (1991) provides a detailed study of the meaning of the village to those who live there.

In the same way that mapping and boundaries form part of the discourse of the modern nation-state (Thongchai 1988), the delimitation of villages by territorial boundaries is part of a discourse of power exerted by central authority over rural populations. The village as a territorial unit is an important part of state-led rural development strategy, particularly since the Fifth National Economic and Social Development Plan. The imperfect fit between *muubaan* boundaries and indigenous social community has frequently been noted (Keyes 1979; Kemp 1988), but this imperfection has usually been interpreted in terms of inefficiency of administration rather than as an aspect of shifting power relations that are part of state incorporation of rural political process. Bounding of rural populations, and the implicit control that comes with it, is an essential part of the state discourse of village. Bounding is effected both by the establishment of formal boundaries around villages, within which state-initiated structures are established, and within the village — for example in programs of fence construction to delimit individual households (Hirsch 1991b).

Another aspect of village as discourse is the village as a level or stratum of Thai society. Middle class Bangkokians and local officials alike talk of *chaobaan* (villagers) to differentiate them from urbanites, intellectuals, those with power. Yet this identification often implicitly negates another sort of differentiation, connoting traditional village society as relatively homogeneous and classless.

VILLAGE AS IMPOSED STRUCTURE

The village as a structure imposed by the state can be demonstrated in a number of ways. Use of the village as an administrative instrument is an important part of district-level government. The state increasingly acts in, not just on, the village, and the discourse of village is most immediately significant at this level. Leadership orientation is fundamental to this cooptive state strategy. Standardisation is in many ways the crux of state discourse regarding *the* Thai village. This is effected in a number of ways, including nationwide programs such as the Phaendin Tham Phaendin Thong (lit. Land of [Buddhist] Virtue, Land of Gold) scheme, through physical re-organisation and bounding of villages by fencing, and by use of disciplinary instruments such as competitions. These overlapping programs are described in more detail below, but it is relevant at this point to note that much of the criticism of such state initiatives (for example in academic and non-government organization circles) as petty, peripheral to villagers' needs, or ineffective, tend to miss the role they play in imposing ideas about the village, thus serving as an instrument of state power. Military schemes also use the discourse of village in a number of programs emanating from the 66/23 policy, which from 1980 set about the task of 'pacifying' the Thai countryside by political as well as military means, largely through a variety of initiatives that came under the rubric of rural development (Hirsch 1987).

The village as an administrative instrument is manifest first and foremost by the hierarchical cellular structure of local administration. Provinces are divided into districts, districts into *tambon* (sub-districts), and *tambon* into *muubaan* or villages. Historically, the state administration has been extended to newly settled areas by a type of 'successive cell division' (Uhlig 1984), by which *muubaan* become *tambon*, *tambon* become districts, each of which is then divided up into new *muubaan* and *tambon* respectively. As the bottom rung, the *muubaan* is supposed to represent the natural community. It is the level at which censuses are taken, orders are conveyed from government officials to the population at large via monthly meetings, development groups are set up, and funds are allocated. An ideal *muubaan* will have its own school, temple, and more recently newspaper reading room, loudspeaker tower, public hall, and other amenities that are markers of development.

The village as an administrative instrument is closely tied to the changing functions of local leadership. Twenty years ago, Michael Moerman noted the 'synaptic' role of the village head, who was in the ambivalent position of community representative to the district administration and official representative in the community (Moerman 1969). In the intervening years, village heads, and even more so *kamnan* (*tambon* heads), have become more important as mouth, eyes, and ears of the state in the village. This is not to suggest that village heads are unambiguous representatives of state interests at the expense of village representation. Rather, the increased role of the state in administrative and political process at the local level makes the position of official leaders an essential medium of incorporation by the state.

Nowhere is the role of the state in mediating local process more apparent than in state-led rural development programs. Rural development programs are often framed in terms of enhancing citizen participation in wider social, economic, and political processes, as part of a democratisation process in which previously isolated populations are to benefit by incorporation into the larger system. Yet by the same token the programs impose standardised forms on the village itself, representing what Sulak Sivaraksa in his keynote address characterises as *meuang* imposed on *baan*. By this he implies a hegemony of urban, Westernised, centralised value systems over rural, Thai and local systems of culture and social organisation. The village in the state and the state in the village are two sides of the same coin (Hirsch 1989). Moreover, rural development programs rely heavily on the discourse of village, a discourse that is essentially a totalising one.

The totalising discourse of village in state-led rural development can be seen most clearly in the standardisation encouraged by various programs. *The* Thai village emerges as a particular physical, social, and administrative ideal toward which such programs aspire. The ideal is a subtle blend of, among others, populist and traditionalist ideas, administrative convenience and control, urban and modern values, and democratic forms. By way of illustration, I will briefly outline a number of overlapping programs that have been put into place in recent years.

The Phaendin Tham Phaendin Thong program epitomises the use of populist ideology combined with administrative purpose in the state's defining and redefining of the village. The program is based on ideological training sessions that emphasise unity, individual virtue through abstinence from *abayamuk*, the Buddhist vices of drink, gambling, and adultery. Model Phaendin Tham Phaendin Thong villages to be emulated are often villages where these vices used to be rampant and associated with violence, but conversion of the *nakleng* (strongman) village head or *kamnan* to Phaendin Tham Phaendin Thong results in a new era of peace and harmony. The program originated with a District Officer in Loei province in 1984 and was adopted as a national program to be implemented at district level. Importantly, however, training programs and other activities are set up at the village level, with village heads and committees playing a key role.

Many communities in rural Thailand, particularly on the edges of the Central Plains, are scattered so as to give farmers ready access to their fields. A target of a number of rural development programs is to encourage nucleated settlement, the aim of which is to provide centralised facilities such as electricity, roads, and sometimes piped water. However, the other side of this is 'ease of administration' (*kaan pokkhrong ngaai*) facilitated by nucleated settlement. But frequently villagers resist moving away from homesteads, particularly where the size of the settlement is so large as to make daily travel to the outlying fields an inconvenience. It is interesting that in Uthaithani and elsewhere in Central Thailand, nearby Lao villages are sometimes held up as models of what a village should be like. The Lao are said to be more unified (*saamakhii kan dii*) and together (*phrom*) than local Thais, partly owing to the nucleated form of Lao communities. This suggests that *the* Thai village is a standardising discourse as much as a centralising one. In a similar vein, Tony Diller in this volume identifies an important distinction between central and standard Thai language, the latter of which is also a normative construct.

Associated with Phaendin Tham Phaendin Thong and with other district activities in the village is another level of bounding, that of fencing. Villagers throughout Thailand are encouraged to 'develop' their village by building fences around their homesteads. Rusticity is combined with neatness, and wagon wheels, gateways with pictures of the King and Queen, signs with the names of village committee members, and fences at the front boundary of houses with road frontage all mark the standardising project of state-led rural development. The correct physical layout and appearance of *the* Thai village is a sub-discourse in itself, whose implications are not limited to the pettiness of village beautification. They are an expression of externally conceived notions of rurality, of an attempt to impose a rural identity that at once incorporates Thainess and positions the village within a larger entity. Ironically, certain of the markers — such as white fences and wagon wheels — are reminiscent of 4-H clubs in the mid-western United States, quite probably reflecting the North American training of many Thai officials.

A secondary agenda, particularly of facets such as fencing and name signs, is at another level of bounding and hence of control a sort of Foucauldian normalising gaze. Village neatness also translates into greater transparency for outsiders, who can more readily identify individual households - and their comings and goings - and establish reward systems for those individuals or villages willing to conform.

An important part of state-led rural development programs, and vital to putting them into place, are village competitions (*kaanprakuad muubaan*). To extend the Foucault metaphor, competitions can be seen as disciplinary mechanisms in support of the official discourse of village. Each year, villages are entered in provincial, regional, and national development competitions, with state officials as instigators, arbiters, and often the main beneficiaries in terms of acquiring merit points (*khwaamdii khwaamchoob*) for success. Levels of development are measured by progress in the above programs, as well as by the initiation of development activities. For all of these, the village head and village committee are fundamental, and the *muubaan* has defined for it a common purpose supposedly based on harmony and self-advancement. The use of competitions in this way is not limited to Thailand and has not gone without critical comment, but once again it is surprising that most criticism is directed at the superficiality of this sort of development instead of the rather effective role that competitions play in furthering a particular discourse of village.

Finally, if the above can be seen as hegemonic instruments in support of a particular discourse of village, there is a rather more overt use of power applied in several military mobilisation programs in rural areas. Part of the Army's 66/23 policy after 1980 was to use political pacification measures in sensitive rural areas. Schemes such as National Defense Volunteers, National Reservists, and the 'Dream of Peace' movement combine welfare aspects of development with increasing central control through the use of local eyes and ears (Hirsch 1987; Suchit 1988). The scheme most closely identified with village organisation is the self-defense development village scheme (*or phor por*), which involves a special village committee, a clearly delimited village boundary, and facilities such as guard posts and barriers at the road entries to the main area of settlement.

VILLAGE AS ARENA OF STRUGGLE

What does all this have to do with identity? As I suggested at the start, rural identity is a fundamental, even though not always explicit, aspect of Thai identity, and the village is a basic construct of rural social organisation. More to the point, *the* village not only means different things to different people, but as a discourse it is used for quite specific purposes. The state does not have a monopoly on the discourse of what a village is or should be. Debates over local and national identity, control over resources, and concepts of development all make use of the discourse of village, and the village thus becomes an arena for each of these struggles.

Evidence of the contested nature of the village can be sought in local reaction, response, and resistance to some of the programs outlined above. In some cases, particularly where a village has been successful in winning a competition at a regional or national level, there may indeed be a sense of pride and village 'togetherness' instilled as a result. However, there are numerous cases of scepticism and criticism before, during, and after such programs. In the case of villagisation (i.e. encouraging or forcing villagers to move from their outlying homesteads into a nucleated settlement), such as in Ban Mai in Uthaithani (Hirsch 1989), villagers may simply refuse, or else build a token shack on the allocated house plot but maintain the original residence with its convenience of being close to the fields and, significantly, far from the pestering (*jukjikjai*) of the community. Similarly, Bung Khiew villagers refused to build fences unless the District Office provided the resources. Elsewhere, villagers involved in land disputes with the District Office have refrained from erecting signs with nameplates, claiming that '*we* all know each other, and the signs would only make it easier for *them* to pick us off easily', as a village leader in Pakham, Buriram, involved in a dispute over eucalyptus planting on village lands put it. Another countervailing response to the official discourse of village is in the bypassing of official leaders and the importance of informal or natural leaders (*phuunam thammachaat*). Rarely do these involve direct confrontation of the official discourse of village; rather they are what Scott (1986) calls everyday forms of resistance, and they are thus quiet expressions of an identity alternate to that imposed by the state.

It should be stressed that villagers are not rejecting the discourse of village *per se*, but rather a discourse of the village as an imposed construct. Utong (1991) has considered the village from the point of view of those who live there and finds that Nong Kham (in Kamphaengsaen District of Nakhon Pathom) is very much a reality for its inhabitants, who are less than appreciative of state efforts to redefine the village by means of programs such as those described above.

A second aspect of the village as contested space concerns divisions within local communities. The idea of a harmonious rural community has always been something of a myth, contradicted by the cleavages based on kin, faction, and unequal access to resources. One aspect of the state agenda is to impart a sense of unity (*saamakhii*) to rural populations. This has two dimensions, national and local. National unity is often stressed in training programs in terms of healing internal divisions in order to counter external threats, and it can be seen as part of the 66/23 agenda. It is manifested at the local level through a discourse of unified community that is expressed most strongly in training for National Reservists and Village Scouts (Muecke 1980).

Yet this theme of unity runs counter to growing class divisions in many rural areas and resultant competition over resources. In more prosperous areas this process is well advanced, but in recent years peripheral areas have also seen increased competition over land, both between local people and between villagers and state authorities. Approximately one third of all farmland in Thailand is forest reserve land, providing the livelihood for at least 6 million rural Thais (Feder et al. 1988). Eviction of farmers from these lands to make way for eucalypt plantations, reservoirs, and other projects has become one of the most pressing issues affecting rural Thailand (Hirsch and Lohmann 1989). Resettlement villages established for displaced people are promoted to those affected as a chance to become legitimate citizens instead of *khon theuan* (lit. illicit persons), as well as to receive the benefits of electricity, roads, fenced houseplots, and other services. The loss of land that such schemes usually means for forest reserve dwellers makes them a bitter point of contention.

Meanwhile the village as spatial expression of a harmonious community of interest is undermined by changing production relations internal to village society. Many *thaokae* ([ethnic Chinese] merchants, moneylenders) are now ethnic Thais, sometimes kin of poorer villagers upon whom the latter rely for credit. Official position such as village head has been used on numerous occasions for personal enrichment, for example by illicit use of development funds.

Finally, the village as a contested discourse is evident in the approach to development taken by academics and non-governmental development workers. Chayan Vaddhanaphuti identifies what he calls five traditions of village study in Thailand: loose structure (such as the studies on Bang Chan); critique of loose structure (e.g. Potter's Chiengmai Village); the economic and social history approach (David Johnston, Chatthip); political economy (Andrew Turton, Chayan himself, Anan Kanchanaphan); and the development workers' village study model (Chayan 1991). These traditions not only utilise different models of village structure (or lack of it); they also reflect different theoretical and ideological perspectives on rural Thai society and economy.

Village culture independent of the state — Sulak's *baan* vs *meuang* — is a prominent theme of writers and practitioners such as Apichaat Thongyuu, Prawet Wasi, Seri Phongphit and Bamrung Bunpanya. This discourse of village stresses the integrity of village culture, kinship and other social bonds, common spirits, traditional wisdom, and, in Apichaat's words, a world view in which the village is the macro-entity, while society outside the village is the micro-entity (Apichaat 1984). This is an applied model in the sense that it underlies the concept of self-reliance in many small scale development programs, particularly in the Northeast and the North (Seri and Hewison 1990; Gohlert 1990).

CONCLUSION

In looking for Thai identity in rural identity, and in looking for this in turn in the village, we often search for remnants; hence the 'back to the roots' approach to village culture (Seri 1986). But are we not often imposing an identity rather than seeking one out? Surely rural identity or village identity is defined as such only in relation to the wider system. To talk of a *Thai* village identity is already to acknowledge the village as part, usually a subordinate part, of that system. To talk of *the* Thai village is to acknowledge the success of a particular discourse of power. The development concept has not so much destroyed villages, as suggested by Sulak, as it has re-created and re-defined them.

REFERENCES

Apichaat Thongyuu. 1984. *Watthanatham kab ngaan phatthanaa* [*Culture and Development Work*]. Bangkok, Saangsan Press.

Chatthip Nartsupha. 1984. *Sethakit muubaan thai nai adiit* [*The Thai Village Economy in the Past*]. Bangkok, Sangsan Press.

Chayan Vaddhanaphuti. 1991. 'Traditions Of Village Study In Thailand', in Philip Hirsch, ed., *The Village In Perspective: Community and Locality in Rural Thailand*. Chiengmai, Social Science Research Institute.

Feder, Gershon, Tongroj Onchan, and Yongyuth Chalamwong. 1988. 'Land Policies and Farm Performance in Thailand's Forest Reserve Areas', *Economic Development and Cultural Change*, 36, 483-501.

Gohlert, Ernst W. 1990. *Power and Culture: The Struggle against Poverty in Thailand*. Bangkok, White Lotus.

Hirsch, Philip. 1987. 'Socialisation of the Military or Militarisation of the Society?', *Far Eastern Economic Review*, 11 September 1987.

Hirsch, Philip. 1989. 'The State in the Village: Interpreting Rural Development in Thailand', *Development and Change*, 20.1, 35-56.

Hirsch, Philip, ed. 1991a. *The Village In Perspective: Community and Locality in Rural Thailand.* Chiengmai, Social Science Research Institute.

Hirsch, Philip. 1991b. 'Bounded Villages And The State On The Thai Periphery', in Philip Hirsch, ed., *The Village In Perspective: Community and Locality in Rural Thailand.* Chiengmai, Social Science Research Institute.

Hirsch, Philip and Larry Lohmann. 1989. 'The Contemporary Politics of Environment in Thailand', *Asian Survey*, 29.4, 439-51.

Kaufman, Howard. 1960. *Bangkhuad: A Community Study in Thailand.* Locust Valley, N.Y., J.J. Augustin.

Kemp, Jeremy. 1987. *Seductive Mirage: The Search for the Village Community in Southeast Asia.* Centre for Asian Studies, Amsterdam.

Kemp Jeremy. 1988. *Community and State in Modern Thailand.* Sociology of Development Centre, University of Bielefeld. Working Paper No. 100.

Keyes, Charles. 1979. 'Local Leadership in Rural Thailand', in Clark D. Neher, ed., *Modern Thai Politics.* Cambridge, Mass., Schenkman.

Kingshill, Konrad. 1960. *Ku Daeng - The Red Tomb.* Chiang Mai, The Prince Royal's College.

Moerman, Michael. 1969. 'A Thai Village Headman as a Synaptic Leader', *Journal of Asian Studies*, 28.3, 535-49.

Muecke, Marjorie. 1980. 'The Village Scouts of Thailand', *Asian Survey*, 20.4, 407-27.

Potter, Jack M. 1976. *Thai Peasant Social Structure*. Chicago, University of Chicago Press.

Redfield, Robert. 1956. *Peasant Society and Culture*. Chicago, University of Chicago Press.

Scott, James. 1986. 'Everyday Forms of Peasant Resistance', *Journal of Peasant Studies*, 13.2, 5-35

Seri Phongphit. 1986. *Back to the Roots: Village and Self-reliance in a Thai Context*. Bangkok, RUDOC.

Seri Phongphit and Kevin Hewison. 1990. *Thai Village Life: Culture and Transition in the Northeast*. Bangkok, Mooban Press.

Suchit Bunbongkan. 1987. *The Military in Thai Politics 1981-86*. Singapore, Institute of Southeast Asian Studies.

Thongchai Winichakul. 1988. 'Siam Mapped: A History of the Geo-body of Siam'. Ph.D. dissertation, Sydney University. University of Hawaii Press, forthcoming.

Uhlig, Harald, ed. 1984. *Spontaneous and Planned Settlement in Southeast Asia.* Hamburg, Institute of Asian Affairs.

Utong Prasasvinitchai. 1991. 'The Thai Village from the Villagers' Perspective', in Philip Hirsch, ed., *The Village In Perspective: Community and Locality in Rural Thailand.* Chiengmai, Social Science Research Institute.

Chapter 12

RUMOURS, FOUL CALUMNIES AND THE SAFETY OF THE STATE:

MASS MEDIA AND NATIONAL IDENTITY IN THAILAND

Annette Hamilton

My title is taken from a translation by Prince Prem Chaya of Pra Ruang's speech, from a play by King Vajiravudh, Rama VI. The translation is dated 1943, and was published in *Siamese Idyll* in 1946. The volume was re-issued by the National Identity Board in 1986. Pra Ruang is the legitimate King of old Sukhothai; he addresses all those who have come to greet him as their lawful ruler. The speech exhorts those assembled to beware of creating rivalry in the kingdom, of treating with enemies from motives of greed, of spreading or listening to rumours. The passage concludes: 'Let other tongues laud and respect the name/of Thai, till it resounds throughout the world!/ Love race and creed, as in the days of yore/and Thai land's name shall live for evermore'.[1]

National identity is a central modernist concept. As has now been extensively argued (e.g. Anderson 1983 and, with a different implication, Gellner 1983) it is a construct, rather than a description of a thing-in-itself. Yet the extent to which the notion has been incorporated uncritically into contemporary political and cultural discourse requires some consideration. Its use can be seen as a discursive ploy. Once such a 'thing' is postulated, the debate comes to be focussed on what it 'is', thereby obscuring the fractures and differentiations of subject-hood in any complex social setting. Its use becomes universalised, embedded uncritically in a Europeanist discourse concerning the state (see Chatterjee 1986).

Everyday language, especially in the media, identifies nation-states as individual actors on the model of human beings. Indeed, this usage has become so commonplace that its peculiarity has become invisible. 'America' decides to do something, 'Germany' disagrees, 'Greece' shows itself flexible, 'Russia' avoids the issue, and so on, as if these were entitites endowed with intelligence, character and interests of their own, separate from their component populations. The depiction of nation-states as human-like, willing, and autonomous makes it all the more important for their populations to identify with them correctly, uniformly and precisely, in order to experience vicariously the action on a global scale to which their citizenship compels them. The identification of the capital city with the state carries this imaginary identification even further: 'Canberra indicated today', 'Bangkok rejected'.[2]

Analysis of national identity has been inextricably linked with the issue of nationalism and dominated by the perspectives of political science. While this approach is important, it tends to obscure the central cultural framework within which all discourses of identity, national or otherwise, inevitably develop and circulate. Identity is, in part, a question of individual consciousness and hence depends on the narratives and practices through which individuals experience themselves and 'others' in their specific cultural and social milieux.

Undoubtedly many human beings have feelings of passionate attachment to place, usually the place they know best and have grown up in. This may well provide the basis on which the extension of attachment to the nation can occur. Ultimately any sense of national identity must rest on the perceptions of difference and otherness which arise from the communicative relations and social intersection between identifiable groupings. It is difficult to imagine that national identity could become an issue in the absence of other nations (or ethnes) against which to construct a notion of national self. Equally important, however, is an awareness of historical time within which the nation can be imagined as an entity with stability and continuity. While all social groups will be aware of 'others' if these others possess different characteristics (especially language, religious beliefs, and cultural practices), the conditions of modernity have made such an awareness a global phenomenon with powerful political consequences. One way of understanding this phenomenon is through a concept such as 'the national imaginary', the circulation of images and ideas about a national self and national others, most powerfully brought about through the effects of mass media (Hamilton 1990a).

The emergence and consolidation of a concept of national identity in Siam/Thailand[3] has largely been examined through a political-social framework. The specific forms of nationalist ideology have largely been attributed to the fact that the constitution of the nation did not derive from nationalist anticolonialism, but rather emerged through internal struggles dominated by alternately competing and collaborative relations between varying factions of the monarchy, the aristocracy, the bureaucracy, the military and an emergent middle-class (Anderson 1978).

I will suggest, however, that transformations in consciousness, first among the elite but soon among the rising bourgeoisie and now among 'ordinary people', can be attributed as much to cultural and aesthetic factors as to the consequences of political struggle or official nationalism. The early penetration of print media, the impact of Japanese and Western film, and the immense prestige attached to international experiences, provided the conditions in which a radical transformation of imagination could take place. At first concentrated among the elite, the early penetration of mass media to a broader sector of the population brought about the conditions in which new forms of a national imaginary could develop and circulate.

The central importance of mass media to the Thai power elites has been marked for a century by the enthusiastic promotion of new communication technologies and their extension throughout the countryside. The mass media, it seems, provide an opportunity to extend official ideology rapidly and effectively in a context where the unity of the nation can otherwise only be maintained through coercive administrative and economic measures backed by the use of force.[4] The role of the mass media in the construction of an authorised national identity stems from the need to unify ideologically a population which little more than a century ago was only 'integrated' into the state (if such it could be called) through the economic extractions of tax farmers and the tattoo-marks on the right or left wrist which indicated to whom the individual 'belonged'.[5] From the perspective of a system of internal colonialism,[6] 'the masses' occupy the same relationship to the elites as did colonial peoples to their colonisers. The problems of hegemony have been further complicated by the presence of non-Thai minorities, such as Muslims in the south, so-called hill-tribes along the north and western borders, and Chinese who became increasingly visible through the channels of commerce during the late nineteenth and early twentieth centuries, many of whose descendants have come to dominate commercial life and parts of the bureaucratic arms of the state.

Yet the possibility of subversion through the media is also apparent, and hence constant efforts at control through a variety of official and unofficial pressures, including rigid censorship and informal sanctions, have accompanied the extension of media services. Ideological domination through the media depends on the ability to maintain surveillance and control over its activities and products. But modern mass media have the potential to escape from the clutches of the state, while the readings of an audience may not conform to the intention of the broadcasters and image-managers. The efficacy of state control over media may provide its own negations; the circulation of discourse may escape from the channels intended to control it. And, where the populace is well-aware that the mass media and its messages are censored and controlled, this only provides an even more fertile ground for the proliferation of rumours, gossip, and the circulation of information, criticism and sometimes wild imaginings. In Thailand what is *not* said, the resounding silences, can open up fissures through which an unofficial discourse is constructed and rapidly circulated. The competing circuits of power at every level of society ensures that even the forbidden may be available, and that which cannot be said may be expressed in other ways.

PRINT MEDIA, FICTION, AND OTHERS

The enormous social and cultural impact of print-media in Thailand would require a far more detailed analysis than is possible here. The extension of literacy from the late nineteenth century, together with the increasing availability of new and popular forms of narrative based on 'foreign' models and incorporating 'foreign' themes, paved the way for the circulation of new images of self and other and laid the foundations for the cultural expressions of national identity promulgated under King Rama VI, many of which were subsequently incorporated into the image-repertoire of 'modern Thailand'.

Throughout the nineteenth century contact with the West became increasingly forceful, causing destabilization and fear in many quarters. The Bowring Treaty forced changes on the administration and finances of the kingdom. Christian missionaries made their way into the court itself, promulgating alien concepts of everyday behaviour and of the cosmic order. Treaties of extraterritoriality and the actual loss of territory to France and Great Britain seemed deeply compromising to Siamese independence. These and other twists of fate required a transformation in the way the elites were obliged to see themselves and understand the broader world to which they were now inextricably connected. Central to this process was the ambivalent response to Western models in dress, manner, and cultural form. The emulation of the West, and most importantly the emphasis placed on Western education, can be understood as providing a means whereby the elite could appropriate at least the outward signs of Western advancement and present themselves in its images.

At the same time more subtle effects were occurring through technological changes in communication which brought into focus a new kind of mental experience. The introduction of fiction through popular narratives and later film inevitably remoulded the imagined relation between self, society, and the world of others. The presence of narrative forms mediated by the marketplace has been identified by Lasch as a critical moment in the development of modernity.

Reality itself is no longer real in the sense of arising from a people's shared understandings, from a shared past, and from shared values. More and more, our impressions of the world derive not from the observations we make both as individuals and as members of a wider community but from elaborate systems of communication, which spew out information, much of it unbelievable, about events of which we seldom have any direct knowledge. (Christopher Lasch, *The Minimal Self*, quoted in Davis 1987:5)

As will become apparent below, this process is far from complete in Thailand even today. Yet the impression of the world available to the Siamese people was opened up to images especially through the early introduction of Western forms of fiction, which supplemented and extended the awareness of difference already circulating through other forms of writing.

The first Thai-script printing press, introduced by the missionary Dr. Dan Beach Bradley in 1836, was used to publish the first newspaper, the *Bangkok Recorder*, in 1844. Reynolds (1973:65-68) has discussed some of the early publishing ventures, including journals, periodicals, historical writings, Buddhist sermons and government announcements. Both King Mongkut (1851- 1868) and King Chulalongkorn (1868-1910) were deeply committed to new developments in communication technology, as were other members of the royal family. As events of the nineteenth century unfolded, the question of what was Siam (and what was not-Siam) became increasingly significant, both in relation to the outside world and in settling the proper position of immigrants such as the Chinese and the other minorities within the kingdom.

In print-media, the negotiation of these questions took place primarily through three channels: the publication of works from (or recuperations of) the Siamese past, in the form of many historical chronicles, tales and other writings; the publication of writings about 'others' by Siamese writers; and the translation and publication of writings from outside.

In the first category, apart from chronicles, were classics of Thai romantic poetry composed by members of the courts of Kings Rama II and III, as well as Sunthon Phu's *Phra Apai Mani*. Many of these works were pubished serially and sold at one *saleung* per chapter (Mattani 1988:10). Examples of the second include an immensely popular chronicle of the Mon people, *Rachathirat*, published in 1880, and two works by King Rama V, *Lilit Nithra Chakhrit*, an adaptation of the 'Thousand and One Nights' which introduced the exotic land of Arabia, and *Ngo Pa*, a poetic tragedy concerning a love triangle among the Aboriginal Ngo people of the south. The intent of the latter work was to show how even 'uncivilized' people are capable of love and sacrifice. This work suggested that 'others' within the Kingdom were worthy of respect, and indeed the King is said to have brought one such person into the court, placing the insider 'other' in the heart of the kingdom.[7]

In the last category were works of two kinds. Stories and tales of Chinese origin were early established in popular taste. *Sam Kok* (*The Three Kingdoms*), a translation of a Chinese historical tale, appeared in print in 1865. Its immense popularity prompted the publication of many other Chinese narratives; at least thirty-three Chinese tales appeared between 1870 and 1922 (Wibha 1975:19), establishing the enduring popularity of Chinese stories still notable today in the plethora of Chinese historical and romantic productions on film and television.

More alien, however, was the flood of translations and adaptations of Western popular writings such as those of Sir Arthur Conan Doyle, Sir H. Rider Haggard, Guy de Maupassant and Alexander Dumas. Local writers emulated such stories, and this initiated a controversy about the influence of Western writing through the concept of *nangseu an len*, 'reading for pleasure'. A short story, *Sanuk Neuk*, published in 1886 in *Wachirayan Wiset*, a bi-weekly journal, caused distress in religious circles by its representation of four monks of Wat Bowonniwet. The abbot was outraged at the depiction of the monks and the content of their conversations, and the king himself was obliged to explain the difference between 'truth' and 'fiction' (Anderson 1985:13; Mattani 1988:21).

Singularly little theoretical attention has been focussed on the effects of fiction even in a Western historical framework (but see Chambers 1984:218-221). Davis (1987) has considered the social impact of fiction in eighteen century Europe and argued that prose forms such as the novel began to provide a mediation between self and world which earlier had been provided by religion: '...the distinction between fact and fiction, self and other, inner and outer began to collapse in an entirely new way and with significant consequences' (Davis 1987:5). Mattani has discussed the problems of realistic portrayal in Thai fiction, against the older forms in which 'traditional poets ... could camouflage social reality and criticism under the cloak of imaginary fantasies' (1988:58). 'Realism' is seen as 'too close to reality', while Thai readers to the present time 'identify the characters and events in novels with real persons and their true stories'. It seems likely that there is a double reality effect in the Thai response to fiction. Traditionally the means of 'telling the truth' was to narrate through conventional fabulous forms, where stock characters depicted events which could be used to understand 'the real' of contemporary life. Where a story is presented 'realistically' the result is an identification of the fictional protagonists with real people and events.

The same situation is quite apparent today in contemporary Thai film and television. Stories which can be read as political are presented through a fantasy historical past, while viewers identify film and television narratives as depictions of real events and identify the stars with the characters they play. 'Fiction' and 'reality' run into each other in the popular imagination (Hamilton 1990c).

A second aspect of the reception of fiction concerns the moral or ethical framework within which popular interpretations are offered. One of the earliest Western fictions was a translation of Marie Corelli's *The Vendetta*, serialised in the magazine *Lak Witthaya* in 1902. In response, Luang Wiratpariwat wrote *The Non-Vengeance*, presenting a 'better' ending which provided forgiveness rather than revenge (Mattani 1988:22; Wibha 1975:64). There is a powerful expectation that all stories must end on a moral or uplifting note, providing hope for the future. Karmic consequences must be depicted in such a way as to reassure the audience that evil is punished while good understanding and reconciliation are always possible. Thai productions based on Western fictional models of the social realist form were and still are rejected by the popular audience, both in writing and in film (Hamilton 1990c). 'Realist fiction' in popular Thai culture seems a contradiction in terms.

Nevertheless, the introduction of Western popular fiction, and its almost instant reduplication by Thai writers had a significant effect on the development of the national imaginary, particularly in relation to the West, or, more accurately, the world of the *farang*.

Yet the popular response to narrative has retained more traditional understandings, in particular, the belief that narratives have social and moral effects, and that contentious or divisive truths are best told through fables and allegories.

The spead of popular literature in the late nineteenth and early twentieth centuries no doubt instilled a greater interest in reading generally, and another new figure appeared on the scene in the form of the journalist. Generally of middle-class rather than elite background, journalists frequently provided a voice of criticism and dissent in monthly journals such as *Tulawiphak Photanakit* and *Siriphotchanaphak*. One, Thianwan, proposed reforms such as the abolition of slavery and the modernization of transport and communications. He was considered insane and sentenced without trial to sixteen years imprisonment (Wibha 1975:26). Reynolds (1973) has discussed another of these figures, K.S.R. Kulap, who wrote satires on the elite and their Western mannerisms and who received seven days labour in the royal stables for suggesting the incompetence of a king.

While new forms and expressions in print introduced new genres and images to the reading public, performance arts, which had always been a major component of communicative culture, also underwent significant changes. The *lakhon phuut*, a dramatic form using speech rather than formal poesy, was introduced, while even in the more traditional forms new elements in music, plot, dance and sets appeared. Contemporary Western stories, such as an adaptation of *Madame Butterfly* set in Chiangmai, appeared. A very popular new form was the *lakhon phan thang*, ('thousand-style drama') in which characters appeared in exotic foreign costumes, especially Burmese, Chinese, Lao and Western, while the tunes sung represented the respective nationalities (Mattani 1988:23).

While print media and these forms of dance-drama were relatively confined to the official and aristocratic classes, cinema emerged in the Bangkok environment with what was almost certainly a powerful impact on a broader section of the population.[8] On 9 June 1897 it was advertised in the Bangkok Times that Mr. S. G. Maschovsky and his troupe would show a Parisian cinematograph at Mom Chao Alungkarn Theatre the following day. Some accounts suggest that in 1896 a Japanese film preceded this event. Certainly by 1904 Japanese-made films were being shown to great public interest in Bangkok (Wibha 1975:67). The first cinema was built by a Japanese investor in 1905 (Sethaporn et al. 1985:52). I have found little evidence concerning the showing of films during the period from 1905-1916, but presumably they must have continued to some extent. Prince Kamphaengphet put together a film-making team during this time and made numerous short films for the court and aristocracy.

Thus, by the accession of Rama VI in 1910, mass media had penetrated the aristocracy and official classes, primarily in the form of Thai writings including chronicles, traditional narratives, and translations from the Chinese, as well as the first foreign films. An awareness of Siam as possessing a long and significant history was promulgated through the writings of royalty, while the representation of others appeared in print and in the performing arts. A broader awareness of the world of others, both outside (*farang* societies abroad) and inside the kingdom (the large number of *farang* residents[9]), as well as the Chinese, the Mon, and other minorities was now inescapable. King Vajiravudh had already been an active participant in the artistic and literary activities of the court before his accession and these activities intensified after he occupied the throne.[10]

King Vajiravudh was the first bicultural monarch. Educated in England from 1893-1902, he received military training at Sandhurst Military Academy and read history and law at Oxford (Vella 1978:2-3). He succeeded to the throne in 1910. The development of official nationalism has been largely associated with his reign (Anderson 1983; Kullada 1987); however it is clear that the foundations of this nationalism were already established

(Murashima 1988) and the early twentieth century was a period when rapid social transformations were taking place at many levels. New ideas and images were circulating in ever broader circles, and problems stemming from the 'outside' world were now supplemented by difficulties emerging from the economic and political changes within. While it would be wrong to attribute the rise of nationalistic ideology solely to the influence of King Vajiravudh, it is difficult to ignore his role in the *cultural* propagation of nationalistic sentiment.

King Vajiravudh is frequently derided by Thai and Western scholars as a dilettante and playboy who refused to tackle the real problems of the kingdom and instead invested most of his time and energy in trivial artistic pursuits. The court became focussed on the composition and performance of literary works, and classical and modern drama, with an assemblage of gifted dancers, musicians, writers and poets assembled around the king (Vella 1978). Many received rewards in titles, property and money, which caused considerable disaffection among others of the elite who disapproved of his behaviour. Among the most influential of the excluded were members of the military, who were particularly incensed by his role in establishing the Wild Tigers Corps, no doubt a threat to the Defence Department. Problems of finance and administration also plagued his reign and set him at odds with the bureaucracy, which since the turn of the century had increasingly challenged the power of the monarch (see Kullada 1987:107).

The rising new class was composed largely of those who had received Western education and training. These bureaucratic arrivistes had no necessary loyalty to the traditional ruling class, although they imitated its Westernised lifestyle (Kullada 1987:108). However it is likely that they were among the most enthusiastic readers in the kingdom and the most receptive to new ideas circulating through the media. This may well explain why the king dedicated so much time to writing and the circulation of literary and dramatic works, and to the fostering and preservation of cultural materials. He himself translated and adapted many English and French plays with moral, social and patriotic themes, especially those with themes of nationhood and national unity. He translated Shakespeare and adapted Sanskrit drama from English translations. He utilised these classical myths and legends as part of the structure of nationalism (Mattani 1988:29). Historiography and research into the past flourished (Pin Malakul 1975). The king also used popular Western forms in his writings. For example, *Huachai Chai Noom* (*The Heart of a Young Man*), serialised in *Dusit Samit* in 1921 under his pen name Rama Jitti, dealt with the personal dilemmas arising from the encounter with the West. The story is told in a sequence of eighteen letters about the problems of a young Thai educated abroad who experiences difficulties and social absurdities on returning to Thailand. Among the most strongly criticised are traditional marriage arrangements and the exploitation of women, including the prevalence of polygyny. The hero of the story makes the mistake of marrying a Westernised Thai wife, but she follows Western customs and is unfaithful to him (Wibha 1975:77). This work exemplifies the ambivalence of the Siamese elite towards Western life and customs. Another important work was his last, a play in five acts in Thai verse representing a mixture of Western love melodrama and classical-style mythic traditions (Dhani 1975:157-163).

The popularity of such writings was now being challenged by the further development of the cinema. Commercial film import companies were established in 1916 and 1919, and during the early 1920s cinemas spread to the major provincial towns (Wibha 1975:67). In 1922 *The Three Musketeers* was shown as a serial requiring forty-eight reels of film. A film magazine, *Phapayon Siam*, appeared, publishing a wide variety of film stories in booklet form and subsequently a number of other popular film narratives (e.g. *The Count of Monte Christo*) appeared in the same way. Because Thai versions of these stories proved so popular, cinema houses themselves began to commission young Thai writers to translate the scripts, which led them to write new forms of fictional stories. This seems to have been instrumental in the first publication of prose fiction in paperback, the most popular of which was melodramatic love stories (Wibha 1975:68). The presence of these forms provided the background against which the King's own translations and promulgation of 'worthy' Western literature may be understood.

The first Thai feature film, *Naang Sao Suvan* (*Heavenly Maiden*) was produced in 1922 with an all-Thai cast, but by an American producer, Mr. Henry A. MacRae, on behalf of Universal Pictures. Other ventures followed, but the first totally Thai production did not appear until July 1927.

Thus the new media flourished and spread new ideas and ways of thinking throughout the kingdom. King Vajiravudh's efforts to create a national consciousness clearly arose from the desire to absorb the surface signifiers of the West and yet retain some authentic or essential Siamese-ness at the same time. It is difficult to specify precisely which elements were most important to the king and which were most influenced by his nationalist ideology. At one level there was an economic aspect, especially directed against the rising affluence and domination of the Chinese (Skinner 1957). Also, the apprehension of loss of authentic cultural forms seems to have been profoundly significant. Equally, however, the question of identity touches on inner consciousness, and a refusal, in common with more directly colonised elites elsewhere, to accept the superiority of Others, principally Westerners. These questions require much closer investigation incorporating an intrapsychic rather than solely political-social-economic framework, following the work of the subaltern studies theorists (Chatterjee, 1986; Spivak 1987, 1990). King Vajiravudh's solution was manifestly unsuccessful, but it is impossible to consider contemporary issues related to 'Thai identity' except through the shadow cast by the forms of cultural, as well as political, nationalism promulgated by this monarch.

The basic platforms of national unity laid down at that time have remained influential through the many ups and downs of Thai history. The significance of the mass media in promoting national identity was lost on nobody, least of all after the coup of 1932. While it is quite impossible here to trace the precise mechanisms by which the successive governments have attempted to control the mass media's influence and turn it to officially-sanctioned goals, there is no doubting the importance which all governments have placed on the media. Whereas during earlier periods the media introduced and circulated new images of Siam in relation to the world outside, the media after 1932 came increasingly to focus on images within, especially the suppression of otherness which might threaten the stability and security of the state.

IMAGES OF THE NATION AND THE CONTEMPORARY MEDIA

The contemporary mass media in Thailand continue to reflect a tension between an official version of national identity and a second, hidden dimension which circulates through multiple channels and has the effect of undermining the representations of the first. Problems concerning the interpretation of 'the real' surface here; what is 'truth' and what is 'fiction' are by no means clearly separated, even when watching the news.

The two most important means by which the state attempts to exert control over media are first, control over permission to broadcast or print, and second, control over product and content through a labyrinthine system of censorship. For instance, the Cinema Act (1971 and amendments) provides guidelines set out by the Ministry of the Interior, banning films which portray such things as an unfavourable attitude toward the national religion, the history of notorious criminals, and 'films on politics which may discredit the present government or stir up violence' as well as 'plots insulting or leading to an unfavourable attitude toward the Royalty'. In addition army regulations ban films showing demonstrations or protest marches and films which portray government officials or personnel as animals. The Ministry of Education lays down additional rules directed at the protection of minors and students (Sethaporn et al. 1985:52 ff).

In the broadcast media a dual system has evolved with both state-run and commercial bodies entrusted with all broadcasting. However, even commercial services obtain their licences to operate from state bodies and are able to continue only after meeting stringent broadcasting conditions. These relationships are far from stable. The commercial and enterprise aspects of broadcasting and the state's need to control it often come into conflict. Thus, in radio a high level of apparent deregulation occurred in the 1960s; in response, Radio Regulation 1968 was promulgated, which resulted in commercial radio outside the capital being monopolised by the military network. Now all stations were charged with the duty of upholding national interest, opposing socialism and communism, promoting Thai traditions and social values (Ubonrat 1989:42). Broadcasting Regulation 1974 sets out a common set of goals for all broadcast media in Thailand. These include the promotion of the constitutional monarchy, the promotion of national interests in politics, military and economy, the promotion of national consciousness and responsibility of the citizen towards the nation, the religion and the monarchy, the suppression of opposing ideologies, the dissemination of news from the government to the citizens in order to establish a correct understanding, and the preservation of tradition and culture.

Both television and radio are required by law to provide certain programs which aim to strengthen national identity and unity. These may be called the official programs, most importantly news, military commentaries, and Sunday sermons relayed from the military and the Deparment of Public Relations. In addition all radio stations must broadcast the national anthem each morning from 8.00 to 8.03 and each evening from 6.00 -6.03 (excep

Sundays). In provincial towns and many villages a system of public loudspeakers ensures that all official programs are unavoidable by the people. As the national anthem begins at 8.00 a.m. and 6.00 p.m. all persons are required to stand still, leave off whatever they are doing, and observe respectfully the period of the anthem's broadcast. At the end of each broadcast uniformed staff of public bodies such as the post office raise and lower the national flag. Similarly, cinema audiences must stand at attention for the broadcast of the national anthem before each feature, while carefully chosen images of king and country appear on the screen. During 1988-89 these images incorporated a wide variety of situations in which various members of the royal family were shown among plain folk, at the sites of Royal Land Reform Villages, for instance, among Muslims in the South, inspecting agricultural programs and the like. These simple routines ensure the bodily as well as psychological recognition of the power of the nation.

In addition, all radio stations must broadcast three periods of official news, Monday to Saturday (7.00-8.00, 12.30-1.00, 7.00-7.30 and 8.00-8.30) along with two military commentary programs each day, Monday-Saturday. Entitled *Siam Manusati* (The Conscience of Siam) and *Pua Pandin Thai* (For the Land of the Thai), these current affairs programs are produced respectively by the Army Security Unit (Psychological Operations Centre) and the Army Programme Production Centre (Ubonrat 1989: 69-70).

After nation-wide television coverage was achieved in 1979 (although the first television stations in Thailand began broadcasting in 1952) television news became significantly more important and influential than radio news (although the popular news programs, which are current affairs programs rather than official bulletins, continue to be widely listened to on radio, Ubonrat 1989:78). The control of news is one of the most contentious issues in Thailand. The news is the most widely watched television program, according to many surveys; this no doubt has something to do with the fact that no other programs are allowed to air during the period from

7.30-8.30 p.m.   While there is some variety in the presentation methods and construction of television news, basically all news programs follow a format which presents an innocuous public interest program immediately before the news (for example, rural innovations and farm prices, road safety, educational programs), then follows with important national and international news stories up to 8.00.   From 8.00-8.15 or so is taken up with 'Royal News', which includes details of the activities of the royal family as well as the prime minister and sometimes other important figures such as the Army Chief of Staff.   Then a variety of local stories may be broadcast, sometimes with a rural focus.   There will be weather reports, sometimes market reports, and some stations then broadcast a further half hour of news.

The structure of the TV news broadcast is based on Western models, although it often features three presenters (one male and two female) rather than the usual single male (Australia) or one older male and one younger female (U.S.A.).   The first image of most news broadcasts presents an outline map of Thailand, and many programs also feature clever computer graphics presenting images of the country with the pattern of television links between capital and regional centres brightly illuminated.   The outline of the geo-body, of what constitutes the nation, is thus reiterated and reproduced in consciousness every day (cf. Thongchai 1987).

Television news utilises selected news items beamed in/by satellite and tries to give a broad world coverage in the international segments.   While viewers are interested in this, particularly in major world events, tragedies such as accidents, droughts and earthquakes, and anything to do with famous international celebrities, it is the local and royal news segments which, in many homes and even more in public places, is watched with careful impassivity.   It is here that the assumptions of state control over the audience may be challenged and where 'reader reception' becomes the primary issue.   Precisely because everybody knows the news is not really what is happening, (something which all viewers believe but cannot state in public) watching the domestic news becomes a major act of cultural interpretation. Stories as portrayed on 'the news' provide the substance for interpersonal conversations between intimates, who may re-interpret or deconstruct 'what is happening' through commonly-held beliefs about the nature of power and the hidden narratives which are used as explanatory frameworks.

These hidden narratives provide a framework in which current events can be interpreted. Among the most significant are those concerning the destiny of the Chakri dynasty and the dynamics of interpersonal relations among members of the royal family (both past and present); accounts of the manipulation of cosmic forces by prominent politicians and power-brokers to ensure their success; scenarios concerning other nations and their secret intentions towards Thailand (especially Vietnam and Japan). There is nothing particularly unique about these kinds of stories except that in Western nations they can be, and are, freely published and circulated. In Thailand the rules governing publication prevent any discussion whatever concerning the monarchy and forbid the publication of material which might lead to conflict between Thailand and other nations. Narratives touching on cosmic and magical powers are also repressed, being considered irrational, while narratives asserting corruption, greed, violence, gangsterism and stand-over tactics by police and politicians can be hinted at only indirectly.

A very good example of a hidden narrative occurred during the time of the disastrous floods in the south of the country late in 1988. News and Royal News programs frequently depict social prestations, for example important people making donations in white envelopes to various charities or other appeals. When the seriousness of the floods in the south became known, appeals were started up all over the country and nightly news showed all manner of important people making large donations. The initial media depiction of the event was of a terrible national tragedy brought about by the forces of nature, to which the responsible members of society responded by generous donations. It was not long, however, before stories began to be told of whole villages of people abandoned for days without any official visits, let alone relief or other assistance. The information which was circulating through the non-official media (mainly word of mouth, through the experiences of the many volunteers who rushed to assist and found in many places utter disorganisation and no coordination of relief attempts) began to focus on the question of where the substantial sums of money were going, since they manifestly were not being distributed to the most needy.

At this point the 'it is said' became dominant: the attribution of an account to an unknown other, which receives far greater credence than the official version on the mass media. It began to be said, for example, that high officials in the affected provinces had taken most of the aid for themselves; that village headmen had received relief supplies but given all of them to their own kinsmen; that most of the goods (such as sacks of rice) which had been donated by concerned citizens had simply been sold off to merchants, with officials in the collection centres pocketing the profit.

Against an official image of the compassionate and concerned leaders of the state, mobilised to the assistance of the citizens in a time of crisis, emerged a counter-discourse, largely oral, concerning the venality and ruthlessness of unnamed high officials and power-holders, who took the opportunity to line their own pockets unscrupulously at the expense of the suffering farmers and fisherfolk of the southern provinces. Whether or not these accusations and suspicions were true, partially true, or entirely false could never be known, because such accusations could never be made in public (least of all in the mass media) and hence could never be publicly tested.

Whereas the image of the state presented by the media is one of benificence and compassion, another discourse circulates which asserts the universality of corruption, ruthlessness and power at the expense of another imagined community, the ordinary people who always end up suffering and can never seek justice. The humour with which these understandings are shared, however, implies that this 'we' can endure anything, and rise above it; the inevitable patterns of life express themselves again and again, the powerful 'eat' the poor and weak, but the poor and weak endure.

One interesting outcome of the media coverage of the floods in the south concerned the issue of environmental management. From early in the events, it began to be hinted that behind the disaster lay the activities of illegal loggers who had stripped the forests bare. Many of these illegally cut timbers were stored high in the mountains awaiting the arrival of trucks to take them away to the timber-mills. In the deluge, they cascaded down the mountains onto the villages below and caused the most serious damage through destruction of property and death.

Without of course naming names, the news broadcasts soon began to suggest that the real blame should be attributed to these individuals. This brought about a dramatic focus of attention in the country onto the issue of illegal logging and environmental destruction, and created a new space within which the government was obliged to take some kind of action. New regulations were promulgated, and it seemed that the government had quickly responded to an issue of public concern. The fact that negotiations began almost at once to obtain timber from nearby Myanmar and Laos did not, however, come into the picture. The image of the Thai nation as a unique entity has been so thoroughly embedded in popular consciousness that the broader regional realities, trans-national issues in environment, for instance, have no purchase.

Nevertheless environmental issues have since that time come to the fore in providing a base from which opposition and dissent in the kingdom can be expressed. While this is also part of a world movement (which itself is promulgated and circulated through the media) the situation in Thailand differs in that no other issue has been able to bring together the same variety of individuals (students, intellectuals, writers, poets, members of the elite) since the events of 1973. The massive media coverage of the floods in the south, and subsequent attention to other environmental issues both nationally and internationally, without doubt provided a major means through which these oppositional forces have been able to consolidate a collective consciousness. The presentation of environmental issues through the mass media (and English-language newspapers are also important here) has allowed a new identity for the third element in the national imaginary, the 'educated people', who are generally portrayed (or at least portray themselves) as sensitive and intelligent people with the welfare of the nation's poor and powerless as a primary concern.

RELIGIOUS EXPRESSION AND NATIONAL IDENTITY

One of the most important symbols around which a continuing sense of national identity is structured is that of the Buddhist religion. The presence of non-Buddhists, whether hill-tribe animists, Christians, or Muslims, is generally rendered absent from the media altogether. The only exception to this of recent times has been the depiction of the monarch visiting Islamic communities in the south, especially in the context of reconciliation with bandits and communists. In these depictions, featured especially on the royal news, the monarch is shown with Muslims who, in spite of their religious identity, demonstrate physically and in their expressions the correct demeanour and attitudes of respect which mark the proper relation between monarch and citizens. Thus the 'difference' can be acknowledged but at once negated through incorporation.

The importance of religious identity is reinforced by the compulsory religious broadcasts on Sundays. All factions of the *sangha* recognise an urgent need to preserve Buddhist ethics especially under the social impact of the late twentieth century. Even certain non-conformist monks, such as Buddhadhasa Bhikkhu, are given air-time to present their views. Nevertheless the presenters of the religious programs are selected from the higher levels of the religious community. And the basic structures of the sermons traverse profoundly familiar ground: the 'four virtues', which focus on individual self-restraint, and the 'five values', emphasising the importance of work, obedience and loyalty to the nation, the religion and the king. The texts of these sermons sometimes touch on matters such as the economy, but the message is that prosperity depends on the merit of the citizens and their commitment to duty and order. Crime and corruption are depicted as emerging from non-Buddhist principles, such as greed and selfishness. While the rich may be at fault, so too are the poor who are lazy and imprudent, and who indulge in wrong behaviour, especially drinking and sex. Contemporary Buddhist ideology stresses an image of degeneration as a fundamental aspect of the current cosmic condition of the world[11] and often seems hostile to the present social and economic system, while emphasizing that there is nothing the individual can, or should, do about it.

These presentations of Buddhist doctrine have a wider influence than the broadcast audience alone, since they must structure to some extent the sermons of monks in real life (as against on television or radio). Countless cheap pamphlets and booklets also flood the markets and bookstalls, containing the views of a variety of monks and other religious commentators.

The popularity of these works should be considered against the popular circulation of extremely counter-orthodox discourses in the realm of the religious and supernatural. The orthodox Buddhist doctrines, with their stress on correct behaviour, duty and morality, come up against the other dimension of Thai everyday life experienced by people particularly at the lower levels of society, where contacts with officials and powerholders of various kinds are often conspicuous by the absence of Buddhist virtues. The extent to which people are required to pay off police and officials as well as criminal elements constitutes an underside to the representation of a moral and virtuous social realm. In addition, of course, many varieties of popular religion and practice move far from the bland correctness of the orthodox Buddhist sermon. The proliferation of seers and magical practices, spirit mediums and sacred amulets, suggest another world of cosmic power far removed from the television sermon, and these too have their means of circulation through mass media, from the cheap magazines and comic books which include tales of ghosts, hell-beings, and mystical prophecies, to the monthly magazines detailing important amulets and their powers. Even marginalised Buddhist sects, banned from radio and television, are able to circulate their views by the use of audio-cassettes and even videos. (Ubonrat 1989:117). Thus a media realm for a subversive or non-orthodox religious and magical world view exists and flourishes side-by-side with the official versions which reiterate the conventional assumptions of what it means to be a good Thai citizen.

MEDIA AND PUBLIC OPINION

In contemporary democratic states one of the most important mechanisms of power is the management of images and the creation of channels through which power-holders can gauge their popularity. This practice, generally known as public relations, is in the hands of educated professionals whose task is to assess the image-response of the population, as well as its views on policies. A highly sophisticated system of information-gathering operates in the form of opinion polls, phone-in programs, target voter interviews and so on. The management of public policy issues, in the private sector as well as the public, is brokered through advertising campaigns and other influence-gauging means of creating channel of communication to and from the people. While many criticisms can be made of the validity and value of all this, it nonetheless provides at least some measure of connection from the people back to the power-holders.

In Thailand, however, there is no space for public opinion of this kind. Public opinion exists, if at all, only in the elite sectors. In fact, one suspects that the State is not particularly interested in the views of the general public. Democratic processes are little understood and infrequently practiced, and during the brief recent periods of democracy the mechanisms used to gain power were largely those of old forms of patronage, vote-buying and influence. This operates at all levels, from the national to the *tambon*, and the Thai people have had little experience of any effects of their views on the political process. Although there is some tolerance of direct protests, as in the farmers' group which gathers outside the district office, (which may well be reported on nightly television) the notion that the statistical quantity of opinion might have some special weight seems to be quite alien. The views of important and educated people are the only ones that count.

Another source for the circulation and management of opinion in Western democracies is the radio phone-in program, where listeners telephone their favourite presenter and put their views on current events. This is of course a development of letters-to-the-editor, but one infinitely more influential and far-reaching since there may be thousands listening simultaneously. In Thailand, phone-in programs are explicitly forbidden by the broadcasting regulations and are held to represent a possible threat to national security. The media are hardly used at all for election purposes, although lengthy extracts from certain individuals' speeches may appear on the evening news. The entire mechanism of polling and media advertising for political purposes seems to be avoided. When elections for the governorship of Bangkok were being held the party of Governor Chamlong advertised by putting up stencilled rice bags along the main arteries of the city.

Nevertheless, ideas about ordinary people abound in the media. The imaginary construction of the components of the nation is a product of simplistic ideas re-affirmed daily in the mass media, drawing on a fund of readily-identified images and narratives. In the case of Thailand, these components are strongly identified regionally. For instance, while *chaobaan* (villagers) are good, hardworking, obedient Thais who work uncomplainingly in the hot and muddy ricefields, they are always identified in media stories by their village, district and province of origin. Stereotypical images abound, both of *chaobaan* and of others who occupy a special place in the national imaginary. The northeasterners of Isaan (whom I have never seen identified in media programs as being of Lao ethnicity) are impoverished, un-beautiful, unintelligent and uneducated, but good workers. Chiangmai is the home of the most beautiful women in Thailand. The south is full of bandits and rebels (whose Islamic identity is occasionally mentioned, but only when it is in subordination to the king or the state); criminality flourishes here, and it is very dangerous. The hill-tribes are colourful and basically harmless and should assimilate as soon as possible and become more like *chaobaan* so as to preserve the forests. Certain provinces, such as Petchaburi, are particularly associated with criminal activity, the world of the *nagleeng* or gangster. Closest to home are the poor of Bangkok itself, the slum-dwellers on whose behalf charities, investigations, studies, re-housing projects and a myriad of other activities are reported daily to demonstrate the compassion of the state and its component elites for the suffering poor on their doorsteps.

There is no ideological space within which these stereotypical images can be challenged or deconstructed; on the contrary, the mass media incorporate these images and retail them back to the people.[12] However, the extreme separation of the elite and its bureaucratic agents from the life of the great number of people means that messages (images) provided through the media may be interpreted quite differently, or not interpreted at all. Nevertheless, the very presence of media and the images and ideas of otherness circulated through them necessarily evoke some kind of response.

Whereas the state is easily able to control access to the airwaves, certain other media create more difficulties. Although there is rigid censorship applied to imported film and although local film-makers cannot make films outside these rigid conventions, this does not prevent the importation of foreign ideas and narratives on film. While the censors are active in blacking-out pieces of bodies, the overall meaning of foreign films may be highly subversive of the consensus world view endorsed by the state. Yet the market ensures that such films penetrate into the most remote regions of the country.

In provincial towns and villages regular film-screenings take place at markets and on fair days and other national events, such as the king's birthday. Programs screened usually include one Chinese film (usually from Hong Kong), one Thai film, and one foreign film. The most popular foreign films include all those containing superheroes such as Sylvester Stallone and Arnold Schwarzenegger, war films such as *Platoon*, and horror films depicting supernatural or alien beings, such as *Aliens*. Late at night semi-pornographic films (Chinese or Western) may be shown. Among men the most popular films are the gangster films with orchestrated scenes of violence, massacre by machine-gun, torture and death. Thai film-makers have also released films with similar themes, and this genre is among the most popular at video outlets.[13] Pornographic videos have also entered the country and can be obtained under-the-counter at many video stores, in spite of the rigid crackdown instituted in 1988 (Hamilton 1990b).

These films confirm and circulate the images of violence, corruption, crime and gangsterism which form a sub-text to the image of everyday life in Thailand, an image which is severely repressed in official circles but constitutes part of the everyday conversation and understandings of people all over the country.

Police who demand pay-offs after every traffic accident, no matter how minor; officials who allow people in high places access to forest reserves for commercial purposes; local power-figures without whose support no venture can be started or can continue; professional assassins who might be around the next corner; bogus monks and nuns who profit by fleecing the gullible; scandals such as those surrounding the royal decorations and the Chit Fund — all of these events, some of which receive a minor airing particularly in newspapers and magazines, others of which circulate as part of the truth of local existence, provide the converse side to the image of Thai life and the nation promulgated by the official media.

Especially remarkable is the prevalence of popular magazines such as *191*, devoted to the graphic and actual depiction of death by violence. Available on every provincial town newstand, these magazines show in full colour the decapitated body found in the rice-field; the decomposing corpse of the murdered prostitute, the woman who has had her breasts cut off, each breast neatly lined up next to her body, the victim of a gangster feud. The custom of the police in reconstructing the crime with the accused and a journalist/cameraman results in the less lurid of such cases being shown on nightly television news. Magazines such as *191* provide the full picture, along with texts purporting to be interviews with the various individuals involved, sometimes including the murderer.

The fascination of people with these images, I suggest, grows in part from the repression of the negative so central to the official control of the media, and to the existence of circuits of power and influence, known to everyone but also hidden from public scrutiny in the context of a highly controlled information environment. The Thai nation, officially depicted as a site of unity, infused with Buddhist values, upheld by a proud military tradition, and under the beneficent influence of a monarchy ever-responsive and compassionate to the needs of the people, is countered by an anarchistic, disordered world, full of unscrupulous power-holders and unpredictable spiritual forces.

The seemingly constant construction of Thai nationhood, and the sense of identity which the citizen should experience, seems in some ways to have produced a situation where a ritualistic affirmation of these values exists side by side with their contestation. Ubonrat (1989), for example, has analysed the way in which popular music of the *luktoong* genre, while reflecting a rural/peasant perspective and a questioning of urban/bourgeois values, also includes tracks which give assent to the dominant imagery. Two verses of the song *Sayam Muang Yim* (*Siam, the Land of Smiles*) suffice as an example:

> Be proud that you are a Thai
> Uncolonised and generous
> Siam is the Land of Smiles
> We should be proud.
> ....
>
> We Thais love our nation and religion
> Adore the virtuous King
> Respect our rights, forever welcome
> With a Siamese smile.
> (Quoted in Ubonrat 1989:184)

Yet, in another sense, the dominant imagery provides a powerful focus for identity as a member of a community which is united in its separateness and difference from the sources of anarchy and disruption. This is affirmed over and over in popular culture as the world of the ordinary person, doing his or her best against the array of dangers ever present in the world. Whether smalltown petty capitalists, market vendors, rural producers, the urban worker, or the archetypal commentator of modernity, the big city taxi driver, this sense of a virtuous and ultimately victorious Thai identity, opposed as it is to the evils in the broader society, is confirmed and recirculated through conversation, popular songs, sayings, in popular theatre (e.g. *likay*), and in peoples' commentaries on the media, whether it is the television news or a gangster film through which they may be reading local politics or even national-level events.

Thus the rigid control over what can be broadcast and represented provides a fertile ground through which the repressed and forbidden can enter public consciousness, often in distorted and lurid forms. This is the spawning ground of the rumours and foul calumnies which so worried King Vajiravudh, and for a kind of contagious madness which springs up and circulates, such as the case of the queen's dream which foretold impending disaster for all persons whose names contained a particular letter of the alphabet and which brought normal life to a standstill one weekend in 1988 after it was mentioned on television news. Official silence, and the state of indirectness which stems from the avoidance of issues, is, I believe, fundamental to the construction and flow of popular images and information throughout the country, and to the highly ambiguous and fluid interpretation of 'the truth' which so characterises popular discourse.

The construction of national identity through the circulation of images has proceeded both within and against the mass media. From the middle of the nineteenth century, when the first printed narratives in Thai script appeared, to the end of the twentieth, when every conceivable variety of media (satellites, cable television, cellular telephones, as well as the broadcast media, films, audiocassettes and videos) has saturated virtually the entire country, the media have been responsible for a double effect. Foreign ideas, ways of thought, images and understandings demand some account of what it is to be Thai. The introduction and circulation of Western realist fiction destabilised the traditional narrative conventions through which the real could be encountered and the truth could be told. Successive Thai governments have used mass media to construct a model of the nation which suppresses difference and conflict and homogenises the component population through a set of images which indeed comes to possess a 'reality effect' at least for the dominant sectors of the society.

The images endorsed by the mass media seek to create a set of acceptable self/state relations, as viewed by elites. The lived experience of the everyday world, however, provides multiple channels through which alternative interpretations may emerge. Owing to further rapid developments in media technologies, especially DSB (direct satellite broadcasting), as well as the circulation of videos and the importation of film and popular culture materials from West and East alike, the long history of the media as a favoured means of state-sanctioned ideological hegemony may well be coming to a close. Whether this will simply be replaced by the hegemony of late capitalist global images, consumption and the commodity is the crucial question as the twenty-first century approaches.

ENDNOTES

1. *Siamese Idyll*, Chatra Books, Bangkok 1946. A number of other poems, including 'The Fall of Ayuthaya April 1767' and 'Litai the Good' were written in 1932-33 around the time of the end of the absolute monarchy and celebrate the institutions of monarchy and the virtues of kings. These are exemplars of the way in which current political and social events may be made the subject of otherwise forbidden comment by being presented through historical narratives.

2. A recent book by a political scientist (Bloom 1990) discusses the uncritical acceptance by those working in the field of international relations of this mode of thought. The author suggests that this usage obscures many issues, but he accepts that individuals *do* share in a 'national identity' and then seeks to understand the psychological mechanisms involved. The possibility that 'national identity' may not be a single position shared by all citizens within a state does not seem to have occurred to him.

3. In this paper I have used Siam to refer to the country in periods when it was so called, and Thailand after the name was changed. With regard to spelling, I have followed most of the spellings in the works cited, except where one spelling form is dominant in the literature, e.g. Vajiravudh, or where the spelling in the original is so unsuitable as to be misleading, e.g. Ram Chitta for Rama Jitti.

4. The problems of integration of the tributary states and the exactions on the peasantry form a leit-motif to the early problems of the state (see e.g. Ramsay 1979; Anderson 1978:203). The assumption is usually made that these difficulties arose from the lack of effective centralised control and the isolation of distant areas. It would be interesting to know more about the world-view and experiences of the various rebellions which occurred in the late nineteenth and early twentieth centuries. In the Holy Man rebellions, at least some of the leaders were monks who had spent considerable time in Bangkok, and hence their views must have been substantially affected by the new awarenesses in the capital.

5. Among the many studies of the pre-modern social formation Hong Lysa's is preeminent (Hong Lysa 1984). The utter subjection of people to their rulers and superiors is difficult to map onto Western concepts of the state, which is no doubt why Anderson argues that there was no 'state' in Thailand in pre-modern times. The relative autonomy of the provinces provided added complexities to national integration (Bunnag 1977).

6. In a work in preparation I am considering the way in which the model of 'internal colonialism' might illuminate the Siamese case. This model has been used to account for the conditions of ethnic or indigenous minorities encapsulated by modern nation-states (e.g. Australian Aborigines, Native Americans) but it may have much utility for Thailand, especially when seen in the light of Max Weber's original use of the term in the Eastern European situation where the problem was to resettle and stabilise loyal populations on lands distant from central power.

7. Craig Reynolds (personal communication) brought this to my attention, for which I thank him. The significance of this action, however, should not be over-estimated. Colonial rulers, from the time of the early Spanish conquests in the Americas up to the court of Queen Victoria, frequently took Aborigines or 'natives' to the centres of power. In part this seems to have been pure spectacle and curiosity; in part, too, it provided the basis on which the encounter with colonized 'others' could be made visible in the metropolitan centres.

8. It is difficult to locate much information about the earliest reception of cinema in Bangkok and in the country more generally. I am deeply indebted to the enthusiastic support of Dr. Songyot Waewhongse of Silipakorn University (Nakhon Pathom Campus) who shares my interest in Thai cinema and has assisted in locating a number of accounts of the development of cinema. Much of the information in this section comes from a paper by Dome Sukrongse in *Silpa-Wattanatam*, unfortunately undated.

9. During my research on the social history of Hua Hin I was fortunate enough to meet Mrs. Lee Rhodes of the River Kwai Family Camp, Kanchanaburi. She and her family had been residents of Bangkok from before 1920, and she provided a vivid picture of the life of expatriates and the local elites in the polo-clubs of Bangkok. During World War II she took her horses to Hua Hin and began the tradition of riding on the beach. She has lived in Thailand all her life. Material from her account will be published in a forthcoming work 'Local Memories, Local Histories'.

10. For example, in 1908 he founded a school for *khon* in the palace, focussing on traditional forms of dance-drama, because he feared the classical traditions of the form were dying out. See Greene 1971:130.

11. I have had it explained to me by a number of people, including a monk, that our present age, mid-way in the 5000 year cycle between the life of the last Buddha and of Maitreya, the Buddha to come, is especially marked by its

corruption and distance from the moral foundations of a virtuous existence. Some accounts suggest this is the mid-point of the cycle and things will get better from now on; others say that things will continue to deteriorate for another 2500 years until a monk will be signified only by the wearing of one square inch of yellow robe. Under these cosmic circumstances there is really nothing anyone can do other than look after his or her own interests and attempt to ensure the most beneficent rebirth possible, which becomes increasingly important as things on a planetary scale become worse and worse. As Craig Reynolds points out (personal communication) there is nothing in the Pali Canon or the commentaries about 2500 years; this is an invention of modern Buddhist consciousness.

12. The power of these images comes in part from their very everydayness. A study of the changes in the image repertoire in film would be especially valuable, although difficult now due to the destruction and loss of so much early Thai film material (Songyot Waewhongse, personal communication).

13. See Anderson 1990 for a discussion of the political significance of one such film.

REFERENCES

Anderson, Benedict R. 1978. 'Studies of the Thai State: the State of Thai Studies'. In Eliezer B. Ayal, ed., *The Study of Thailand: Analyses of Knowledge, Approaches and Prospects in Anthropology, Art History, Economics, History and Political Science.* Athens, Ohio, Ohio University Center for International Studies.

--------, 1983. *Imagined Communities.* London: Verso.

--------, 1985. 'Introduction' in Benedict R. O'G. Anderson and Ruchira Mendiones, ed. and trans., *In the Mirror: Literature and Politics in Siam in the American Era.* Bangkok, Editions Duang Kamol.

--------, 1990. 'Murder and Progress in Modern Siam', *New Left Review,* 181 (October), 33-48.

Bloom, William. 1990. *Personal Identity, National Identity, and International Relations.* New York, Port Chester and Melbourne, Cambridge University Press.

Bunnag, Tej. 1977. *The Provincial Administration of Siam.* Kuala Lumpur, Oxford University Press.

Chambers, Ross. 1984. *Story and Situation: Narrative Seduction and the Power of Fiction.* Manchester, Manchester University Press and Minneapolis, University of Minnesota Press.

Chatterjee, Partha. 1986. *Nationalist Thought and the Colonial World: A Derivative Discourse.* London, Zed Books for the United Nations University.

Davis, Lennard J. 1987. *Resisting Novels: Ideology and Fiction.* New York and London, Methuen.

Dhani Nivat, Prince. 1975. 'King Rama VI's Last Work', in Mattani Rutnin, ed., *The Siamese Theater, A Collection of Reprints from Journal of the Siam Society.* Bangkok.

Gellner, Ernest. 1983. *Nation and Nationalism.* Oxford, Basil Blackwell.

Greene, Stephen. 1971. 'Thai Government and Administration in the Reign of Rama VI (1910-1925)'. PhD thesis, University of London.

Hamilton Annette. 1990a. 'Fear and Desire: Aborigines, Asians and the National Imaginary', in *Australian Perceptions of Asia. Australian Cultural History, No. 9.*

--------, 1990b. 'Video Crackdown, or, the Sacrificial Pirate'. Asian Cinema Studies Conference, Melbourne, La Trobe University, July 1990.

--------, 1990c. 'Family Dramas: Film and Modernity in Thailand'. Asian Cinema Studies Conference, Melbourne, La Trobe University, July 1990.

Hong Lysa. 1984. *Thailand in the Nineteenth Century: Evolution of the Economy and Society.* Singapore, Institute of Southeast Asian Studies.

Kullada Kesboonchoo. 1987. 'Official nationalism under King Vajiravudh', in *Proceedings of the International Conference on Thai Studies.* Canberra, Australian National University. Vol.3, Part 1, 107-120.

Mattani Mojdara Rutnin. 1988. *Modern Thai Literature: The Process of Modernization and the Transformation of Values.* Bangkok, Thammasat University Press.

Murashima, Eiji. 1988. 'The origin of Modern Official State Ideology in Thailand'. *Journal of Southeast Asian Studies*, 19.1, 80-96.

Pin Malakul, M.L. 1975. 'Dramatic achievement of King Rama VI'. *Journal of the Siam Society*, 63.2 July, 264-271.

Ramsay, Ansil. 1979. 'Modernization and reactionary rebellions in Northern Siam', *Journal of Asian Studies*, 38.2 (February), 283-297.

Reynolds, Craig. 1973. 'The Case of K.S.R. Kulap: A Challenge to Royal Historical Writing in Late Nineteenth Century Thailand', *Journal of the Siam Society*, 61.2 (July), 63-90.

Sethaporn Cusripituck, Silpachai Bijayendryodhin, Theerawuti Kongpricha. 1985. *Communication Policies in Thailand: a Study Report.* Report submitted to UNESCO. Bangkok.

Skinner, George W. 1957. *Chinese Society in Thailand: an Analytical History.* Ithaca, New York, Cornell University Press.

Spivak, Gayatri Chakravorty. 1987. *In Other Worlds: Essays in Cultural Politics.* New York, Methuen.

Spivak, Gayatri Chakravorty. 1990. *The Postcolonial Critic: Interviews, Strategies, Dialogues.* Sarah Harasym, ed. New York, Routledge.

Thongchai Winichakul. 1987. 'Siam Mapped: A History of the Geo-body of Siam'. *Proceedings of the International Conference on Thai Studies.* Canberra, Australian National University. Vol. 1, 155-164.

Ubonrat Siriyuvasak. 1989. 'Radio in a Transitional Society: the Case of Modern Thailand'. PhD thesis, University of Leicester.

Vella, Walter. 1978. *Chaiyo! King Vajiravudh and the Development of Thai Nationalism.* Honolulu, University Press of Hawaii.

Wibha, Senanan, 1975. *The Genesis of the Novel in Thailand.* Bangkok, Thai Wattana Panich.

PHILIP HIRSCH teaches in the Department of Geography, University of Sydney. In 1990 Oxford University Press published his *Development Dilemmas in Rural Thailand*. In 1991 he began a new research project on the impact of resource development in Laos and Vietnam.

PETER A. JACKSON directs the Thai National Curriculum Project, in the Australian Capital Territory's Department of Education, Canberra. His doctoral dissertation on the Buddhist thinker Buddhadasa was published by the Siam Society in 1988, and a study of urban Thai Buddhism, *Buddhism Legitimation, and Conflict*, followed in 1989.

CHARLES F. KEYES teaches in the Department of Anthropology, University of Washington, Seattle. An author of numerous books and articles, his *Thailand: Buddhist Kingdom as Modern Nation-State* (Boulder 1987) is a widely read introduction to the country. He recently completed fieldwork in northern Southeast Asia for a research project on ethnicity.

CRAIG J. REYNOLDS is in the Research School of Pacific Studies at the Australian National University, working on an intellectual history of modern Thailand. A Thai translation of his *Thai Radical Discourse* (Ithaca 1987) was published in 1991 by the Santi Pracha Dhamma Institute as *Khwamkhit waek naew khong thai*.

CHAI-ANAN SAMUDAVANIJA a member of the Faculty of Political Science at Chulalongkorn University, has published widely in Thai and English on Thai political culture, political history, and politics. His most recent book in Thai is *Physics and Politics: Towards a Comprehensive Theory of Politics* (Bangkok 1990), and he is completing another book, tentatively entitled *Evolution of the State vs. Political Power.*

SULAK SIVARAKSA is a prolific essayist and skillful orator. He is a director of the Santi Pracha Dhamma Institute which furthers the goals of peaceful coexistence and strengthening Buddhist values in the modern world. A revised edition of his *Siam in Crisis* appeared in 1990.

B. J. TERWIEL now teaches at Munich University. In connection with a long-standing project on Tai peoples outside of Thailand, he is currently translating Ahom and Shan texts on astrology. He is also participating in a multi-disciplinary study of newly-discovered manuscripts relating to Kaempfer's early eighteenth-century account of Siam and Japan.

GEHAN WIJEYEWARDENE is in the Department of Anthropology, the Research School of Pacific Studies, Australian National University (ANU). He edited and contributed to *Ethnic Groups Across National Boundaries in Mainland Southeast Asia* (Singapore 1990). He also edits the *Thai-Yunnan Newsletter* and recently organized The Richard Davis Card Index and Thai-Yunnan Project Bibliography and Database for computer access at the ANU.

NOTES ON CONTRIBUTORS

HANS-DIETER BECHSTEDT is currently attached to the Faculty of Political Science at Chulalongkorn University in Bangkok. His research on interpersonality relations in Thai society has resulted in a revisionist interpretation of Thai culture and personality studies and the patron-client model (University of Bielefeld, forthcoming).

NERIDA M. COOK teaches in the Department of Anthropology and Sociology at Monash University. After writing an M. A. thesis on pious laywomen in Thailand (*mae chi*), she recently completed her doctorate on Thai astrology at the Australian National University (1989).

ANTHONY V. DILLER teaches Thai in the Faculty of Asian Studies, Australian National University. He has written many articles on Thai sociolinguistics, and with Preecha Juntanamalaga he is completing a reference grammar of Thai. He drew on his expertise in comparative methodology to intervene in the debate on the authenticity of the first Thai inscription (*Journal of the Siam Society* 1988).

ANNETTE HAMILTON a member of the anthropology section of the School of Behavioural Sciences at Macquarie University, has been doing research since 1989 on culture, development, and the media in Thailand. A major manuscript on modernity and tourism in Thailand is nearing publication. Her 'Fear and Desire: Aborigines, Asians and the National Imaginary' was published in *Australian Cultural History* in 1990.

INDEX

Alsdorf, James, 270
Anderson, Benedict R.O'G., 294
Angkor, 262-7, 281
  heritage value, 264-6, 280
  reigning dynasties, 273-4
  Siamese occupation, 275-7
Angkorean empire
  influence of political relations
    on heritage interest in,
    280-2
  restoration of period shrines,
    280-1
  Thai successorship claims, 267
Anuman Rajadhon, Phya, 20, 44,
  51-2, 105, 108
Apichaat Thongyuu, 336
Association Act, 70
Astrological Association of
  Thailand, 236
astrology, 233-53
  criticisms of national use of,
    251-2
  function of individual
    consultations, 236-41
  function of political astrology,
    246-7, 251-3
  horoscope of Bangkok, 23,
    243-4
  national horoscope, 23, 234,
    244-7, 250
  and national identity, 242-51,
    252
  patterns of use amongst social
    groups, 237
  political predictions, 247, 250
  reevaluations based on 1932
    Revolution, 249
  and the theory of karma, 240-1

authority relations, 4, 296-312
  Buddhist teachings, 301
  differences between urban and
    rural groups, 304
  in the family, 299-301, 304
  with monarchy and
    government, 302, 303
  peasants' attitudes towards,
    305-12
  value of personal qualities,
    310
Aymonier, Etienne, 276
Ayudhya kingdom, 63, 70,
  264-5, 266
Ayutthaya period, 202, 210, 219,
  246
  political structures, 212-13

baan, 54, 57, 330
  See also villages
Bamrung Bunpanya, 336
Ban Hin Taek, 176, 178-9
Ban Mai, 334
Ban Rom Klao conflict, 174
Bandung Conference, 54
Bang Chan, 305
Bangkok horoscope, 23, 243-4
Barker, James, 166
Batson, B.A., 135
Battambang, 173, 263
Bechstedt, Hans-Dieter, 4, 237
Bidyalongkorn, Prince, 52-3
Blundell, E.A., 169
borders See territory
Boworadet, Prince, 136, 141
Bowring Treaty, 245
Brahmanism, 212-14, 219, 264-5
broadcasting media, 356-9